THE
RYDER CUP

THE
RYDER CUP

A History of Golf's
Greatest Match

Peter Pugh and Henry Lord

with Bruce Critchley

CORINTHIAN BOOKS

Published in the UK in 2010 by Corinthian Books, an imprint of
Icon Books Ltd, Omnibus Business Centre,
39–41 North Road, London N7 9DP
email: info@iconbooks.co.uk
www.iconbooks.co.uk

Sold in the UK, Europe, South Africa and Asia
by Faber & Faber Ltd, Bloomsbury House,
74–77 Great Russell Street,
London WC1B 3DA or their agents

Distributed in the UK, Europe, South Africa and Asia
by TBS Ltd, TBS Distribution Centre, Colchester Road,
Frating Green, Colchester CO7 7DW

Published in Australia in 2010
by Allen & Unwin Pty Ltd,
PO Box 8500, 83 Alexander Street,
Crows Nest, NSW 2065

Distributed in Canada by Penguin Books Canada,
90 Eglinton Avenue East, Suite 700,
Toronto, Ontario M4P 2Y3
ISBN: 978-190685-016-6

Typeset in New Baskerville by Marie Doherty

Printed and bound by
CPI Mackays, Chatham, Kent, ME5 8TD

Contents

About the authors

PETER PUGH was educated at Oundle and Cambridge, where he was a member of the golf team. He has written many books on golf and golf clubs as well as about 50 company histories, including *The Magic of a Name*, a three-volume history of Rolls-Royce.

HENRY LORD has written three highly successful books on golf, co-authoring *Creating Classics: The Golf Courses of Harry Colt, Masters of Design: Great Courses of Colt, MacKenzie, Alison & Morrison*, and *St Andrews: The Home of Golf*, all published by Icon Books. A lifelong lover of the game and its history, he has had wide experience in both playing and writing about golf.

BRUCE CRITCHLEY played for Great Britain & Ireland against the USA in the Walker Cup and has commentated on top golf tournaments for over 25 years, first on the BBC and recently as the leading golf commentator on Sky, for whom he will be covering the 2010 Ryder Cup.

List of illustrations

1. The Great Britain Ryder Cup team in 1929

2. Fred Daly, the Open Champion (left) and Charlie Ward discuss the larger American ball that they used in the match between Great Britain and the Oxford and Cambridge Golfing Society before the 1947 Ryder Cup so that they could get used to it

3. The Great Britain team at Waterloo station before leaving for the 1947 match

4. Sam Snead drives at the 5th at Ganton watched by Charlie Ward in the 1949 match

5. Great Britain's Bernard Hunt driving in the 1953 match at Wentworth.

6. Great Britain's Eric Brown drives from the 3rd tee on his way to victory at Lindrick in 1957

7. Captain Dai Rees held aloft by Bernard Hunt and Ken Bousfield following the British victory at Lindrick in 1957, the first British victory for 24 years

8. Peter Alliss and Christy O'Connor in the 1965 Ryder Cup match at Royal Birkdale

9. The 1969 match at Royal Birkdale finished in an exciting draw as Jack Nicklaus conceded a two-and-a-half-foot putt to Tony Jacklin on the final green

Acknowledgements

The authors would like to thank Bruce Critchley, who wrote *The Captain's Challenge*, published by Icon Books. This book was tremendously helpful in terms of the history of the Ryder Cup from the captains' point of view. They would also like to thank John Lord for reading the manuscript and contributing helpful suggestions, as well as the editorial team at Icon Books, Duncan Heath and Sarah Higgins.

Foreword

In some ways it is surprising that the Ryder Cup survived through to the wonderful series of matches that has lit up golf during the last 30 years. The previous five decades were so one-sided that it would have been quite understandable if one team or the other had decided the game just wasn't worth playing. For the British and Irish, however demoralising another thumping defeat may have been, a Ryder Cup badge was in itself a mark of career achievement; to talk of a professional as a Ryder Cup player meant more than saying he won this match or that.

For the Americans the same was true; they enjoyed the glamour of representing their country, of parading under the flag, and in an era of little international travel to play golf – after all, most of what was best in professional golf was to be found in the United States – the occasional overseas trip was quite good fun. Most, too, came away from the event with glossy records, personal victories easily outweighing the occasional loss or halved game. But to them the Ryder Cup, because they almost always won it so easily, was more of a 'made for TV' event or exhibition match than serious golf. Indeed, it was only when American television started to lose interest, and so not show the biennial contest, that the players, Jack Nicklaus in particular, began suggesting that the British team needed bolstering if the match was to continue.

Nicklaus, in putting forward the idea of 'our' side being
made up of the rest of the world, expressed almost surprise
that the British seemed to want a really serious 'red in tooth
and claw' contest, seeing little wrong in the bland, gentle
get-togethers that had epitomised the Ryder Cup for most
of the Golden Bear's competitive years. He never understood that regularly getting hammered was not nearly as
much fun as meeting up every two years for some friendly
golf and winning all the time. Indeed the Americans seem
to have replaced their idea of the ideal Ryder Cups of the
pre-1970s era with the Presidents Cup, which they win all
the time without anybody breaking into a sweat. They may
find the International Team suddenly losing interest in continuing with the match.

But these last 30 years! What a change and what a shock
to the Americans that golf, when close and partisan, can
be a pulsating and terrifying experience. It has taken the
USA most of that time to accept that victory really does matter, that winning requires huge personal commitment and
exposure of nerve, and that there is no such thing as a good
show and a top ten finish; it is win or lose, glory or public
scorn, and no fat cheque at the end to soften the blow of
not quite finishing top.

Europe has, of course, been the beneficiary. It has taken
the spoils and for much of that time has done so with the
lesser group of players. Captaincy, as shown in particular
by Tony Jacklin, but copied time and again by his successors, has played a vital part in these successes. He, and they,
have delivered that most wonderful of achievements: victory against the odds. Those odds are no longer stacked
against the Europeans; indeed, the idea of Europe being
the underdogs would seem to be a thing of the past, at least
for a generation.

Perhaps the most enjoyable aspect of the recent titanic tussles has been that after three consecutive losses, the United States team felt they needed to win just one match to keep playing; that their top players might start to find excuses for not turning out; that their supporters would lose interest in a contest they no longer seemed able to win. Last time around they did win and strangely, for the very first time, Europe undoubtedly had the better collection of players; Nick Faldo demonstrating how important a thirteenth player the Captain can be, being completely out-thought by his opposite number Paul Azinger. One thing is certain; there is no question of the Ryder Cup stopping now!

Bruce Critchley

Chapter 1
Reasonably Even

A stuttering start
Gleneagles 1921 and Wentworth 1926

Adequate money must be found
Worcester, Massachusetts 1927

'Smell the flowers'
Walter Hagen

Must be native-born
Moortown 1929

Henry Cotton left out
Scioto, Columbus 1931

The tough Taylor
Southport and Ainsdale 1933

The Americans are better
Ridgewood, New Jersey 1935

'Win on home soil'
Southport and Ainsdale 1937

A stuttering start

The original idea for a match between the professional golfers of Great Britain and the United States probably came from the Ohio businessman Sylvanus P. Jermain. He enthused the great Walter Hagen while James Harnett, circulation manager of *Golf Illustrated*, gave his backing too. They, along with the United States Professional Golfers' Association (PGA), encountered some problems raising the money and there was also some argument about who would be eligible to play. Was it to be only professionals born in the USA, or could European-born players be picked too? Eventually, with each player given $1,000 to cover his expenses, a team was sent to play the match on the newly opened King's Course at Gleneagles in June 1921.

The match was played alongside the *Glasgow Herald* 1,000 Guineas Tournament and, by comparison, attracted little public enthusiasm; once the crowds had seen George Duncan pick up the £160 (about £10,000 in today's money) prize, they went home and failed to return for the Great Britain vs. USA match. For the record, the home side won by nine points to three with three matches halved. No one seemed to think there should be a follow-up match.

6 June 1921 Gleneagles, Perthshire, Scotland *Captains:* J.H. Taylor (Great Britain and Ireland), E. French (USA)			
Great Britain and Ireland		**United States**	
Foursomes			
G. Duncan & A. Mitchell (halved)	½	W. Hagen & J. Hutchison (halved)	½
E. Ray & H. Vardon (5 & 4)	1	E. French & T. Kerrigan	0
J. Braid & J.H. Taylor (halved)	½	C. Hackney & F. McLeod (halved)	½
A.G. Havers & J. Ockenden (6 & 5)	1	W. Reid & G. McLean	0
J. Sherlock & Josh Taylor (1 hole)	1	C. Hoffner & W. Mehlhorn	0

(continued)

6 June 1921 (continued)			
Gleneagles, Perthshire, Scotland			
Captains: J.H. Taylor (Great Britain and Ireland), E. French (USA)			
Great Britain and Ireland		**United States**	
Singles			
G. Duncan (2 & 1)	1	J. Hutchison	0
A. Mitchell (halved)	½	W. Hagen (halved)	½
E. Ray	0	E. French (2 & 1)	1
J.H. Taylor	0	F. McLeod (1 hole)	1
H. Vardon (3 & 1)	1	T. Kerrigan	0
J. Braid (5 & 4)	1	C. Hackney	0
A.G Havers	0	W. Reid (2 &1)	1
J. Ockendon (5 & 4)	1	G. McLean	0
J. Sherlock (3 & 2)	1	C. Hoffner	0
Josh Taylor (3 & 2)	1	W. Mehlhorn	0
Great Britain and Ireland 10½; USA 4½			

Enter Samuel Ryder and his younger brother, James. In St Albans, Hertfordshire, the brothers had built up a successful business selling packets of seed for a penny each through the post. A workaholic but also a good local community man as well as a devoted Christian, Sam Ryder was advised by his church minister to play golf for exercise and relaxation. He began to play at the age of 50 and, in true thorough Ryder style, paid the local club professional in 1901 to come to his house six days a week to give him lessons. Within a year he was good enough to join the local club, Verulam, and within another year was elected Captain.

In the early 1920s Ryder's business, the Heath and Heather Company, sponsored professional tournaments; in one, held at the Verulam, he paid every player a £5 appearance fee. That is about £300 in today's money but even so, it seems paltry by today's standards. At the time, though, it was so novel that everyone was staggered. The winner would receive £50, which was only £5 less than the winner of the Open received. It was all good enough to attract the top players including Harry Vardon, James Braid, George Duncan, Sandy Herd and the eventual winner, Arthur

Havers. Also competing was Abe Mitchell, the professional at North Foreland in Kent.

Ryder and Mitchell became friends and Ryder contracted Mitchell at a then-generous fee of £500 a year (about £30,000 in today's money) to become his personal tutor. Mitchell increased Ryder's interest in the professional game and when the opportunity for a Great Britain match against the USA arose again, Ryder wanted to be involved.

In early 1926 the British sent an invitation to their American counterparts to take part in a match at Wentworth before their attempted qualification for the Open Championship at nearby Sunningdale. On 26 April the newspapers announced that:

Mr S. Ryder, of St Albans, has presented a trophy for annual competitions between teams of British and American professionals. The first match for the trophy is to take place at Wentworth on June 4th and 5th.

When the match took placed at Wentworth on 4 and 5 June 1926, the strong Great Britain team won easily. Even the masterly Walter Hagen was convincingly beaten 6 and 5 by George Duncan. Abe Mitchell beat Jim Barnes by 8 and 7. However, the match was not deemed to be an official match. *Golf Illustrated* explained it like this:

Owing to the uncertainty of the situation following the [General] Strike in which it was not known until a few days ago how many American professionals would be visiting Great Britain, Mr J. Ryder decided to withhold the cup, which he has offered for annual competition [note the 'annual'] between the professionals of Great Britain and America. Under the circumstances the Wentworth

Club provided the British players with gold medals to mark the inauguration of the great international match.

And indeed, as a result of the strike several Americans did not travel. Rather than cancel the match, Ryder invited a number of non-Americans to make up their team. As a result, the US PGA refused to sanction the match as the first 'official' Ryder Cup match.

4–5 June 1926			
Wentworth Golf Club, Surrey, England			
Captains: E. Ray (Great Britain and Ireland), W. Hagen (USA)			
Great Britain and Ireland		**United States**	
Foursomes			
A. Mitchell & G. Duncan (9 & 8)	1	W. Hagen & J. Barnes	0
A. Boomer & A. Compston (3 & 2)	1	T. Armour & J. Kirkwood	0
A.G. Havers & G. Gadd (3 & 2)	1	W. Mehlhorn & A. Watrous	0
E. Ray & F. Robson (3 & 2)	1	C. Walker & F. McLeod	0
E.R. Whitcombe & H. Jolly (3 & 2)	1	E. French & J. Stein	0
Singles			
A. Mitchell (8 & 7)	1	J. Barnes	0
G. Duncan (6 & 5)	1	W. Hagen	0
A. Boomer (2 & 1)	1	T. Armour	0
A. Compston	0	W. Mehlhorn (1 hole)	1
G. Gadd (8 & 7)	1	J. Kirkwood	0
E. Ray (6 & 5)	1	A. Watrous	0
F. Robson (5 & 4)	1	C. Walker	0
A.G. Havers (10 & 9)	1	F. McLeod	0
E.R. Whitcombe (halved)	½	E. French (halved)	½
H.J. Jolly (3 & 2)	1	J. Stein	0
Great Britain and Ireland 13½; USA 1½			

Adequate money must be found

Finally, all seemed set fair for a proper start when a match was arranged to take place at the Worcester Country Club in Massachusetts in June 1927. However, all was not yet sweetness and light.

It is difficult to believe now when golf clubs are very proud of their professional if he is a tournament player or, better still, he is selected for the Ryder Cup team, but in the 1920s British clubs were reluctant to let their professional have the time off to participate in the match, especially if it was held in the USA. Then there was the question of money. Even travelling second class by sea, the cost was more than the PGA could afford.

George Philpot, editor of *Golf Illustrated*, launched an appeal for £3,000 (about £180,000 in today's money). He wrote to every golf club and backed this up with a strong request for support in his magazine:

> I want the appeal to be successful because it will give British pros a chance to avenge the defeats, which have been administered by the American pros while visiting our shores in search of Open Championship honours. I know that, given a fair chance, our fellows can and will bring back the Cup from America. But they must have a fair chance, which means that adequate money must be found to finance the trip. Can the money be found? The answer rests with the British golfing public.

The appeal was spectacularly unsuccessful and Philpot wrote scathingly, also in his magazine:

> It is disappointing that the indifference or selfishness of the multitude of golfers should have been so marked that what they could have done with ease, has been imposed on a small number. Of the 1,750 clubs in the British Isles whose co-operation was invited, only 216 have accorded help. It is a deplorable reflection on the attitude of the average golfer towards the game.

In the end, with the donations from the clubs and from Canada, Australia, Nigeria and even the United States, plus £100 from Sam Ryder, they were still £500 short of the target. Philpot put in £500 (£30,000 in today's money) of his own and was appointed team manager.

Another serious problem arose when, just before the team were due to sail from Southampton, Abe Mitchell, the team captain and probably their best player, was struck down with appendicitis.

The next problem was the rough passage the team endured crossing the Atlantic. Finally, when they arrived, feeling very out-of-sorts, in New York, they were dismayed to find that Walter Hagen had organised a big reception for them. Arthur Havers, the 1923 Open champion, would say later:

> The whole thing about going to America was a culture shock for most of us. When we got to New York, the entire team and official were whisked through without bothering with customs and immigration formalities.
>
> There was a fleet of limousines waiting for us at the dockside, and, with police outriders flanking us with their sirens at full blast, we sped through New York. Traffic was halted to let us through; it was a whole new world for us. Everywhere we went we were overwhelmed with the hospitality and kindness of the Americans.
>
> Suddenly we were in a world of luxury and plenty, so different from home ... Even the clubhouses were luxurious with deep-pile carpets, not like the rundown and shabby clubhouses at home, which was all most of us really knew.

And the lavish entertainment continued. The British party were taken to the Westchester-Biltmore Country Club for a gala dinner and after a long night went to the Yankee Stadium to see Babe Ruth's New York Yankees play the Washington Senators. Hagen offered them another night on the town but they declined and staggered off to their hotel.

Eventually, the British team got down to practice but some, especially George Gadd, did not recover well from the rough sea passage and then, out of the blue, on the eve of the match, the Americans requested alterations to the playing format. They wanted four changes:

1. For the foursomes ('Scotch' foursomes as they called them) to be changed to fourballs
2. For any match level after 36 holes to be continued until there was a winner (It is important to remember that all matches, both foursomes and singles were over 36 holes.)
3. For two points instead of one to be awarded for a four-ball victory
4. For both teams to be allowed to substitute a player in singles on the second day.

George Philpot was outraged by these last-minute requests and conceded only the point about the substitutes.

As it turned out, the Americans need not have worried about the 'Scotch' foursomes, as they won them 3–1 and indeed crushed the British team throughout the match with the final score 9½–2½. The real difference between the two teams was their performance on the greens.

Bernard Darwin, the best writer on golf in the twentieth century, wrote in *The Times*:

The British team played well enough through the green, but on the putting greens there was a marked inferiority about the visiting team.

Ted Ray, who had been appointed Captain when Mitchell fell ill, told the *Daily Express*:

Our opponents beat us fairly and squarely and almost entirely through their astonishing work on the putting greens, up to which point the British players were equally good. We were very poor by comparison, although quite equal to the recognised two putts per green standard. I consider we can never hope to beat the Americans unless we learn to putt. This lesson should be taken to heart by British golfers.

3–4 June 1927			
Worcester Country Club, Worcester, Massachusetts, USA			
Captains: E. Ray (Great Britain and Ireland), W. Hagen (USA)			
Great Britain and Ireland		**United States**	
Foursomes			
E. Ray & F. Robson	0	W. Hagen & J. Golden (2 & 1)	1
G. Duncan & A. Compston	0	J. Farrell & J. Turnesa (8 & 6)	1
A.G. Havers & H.J. Jolly	0	G. Sarazen & A. Watrous (3 & 2)	1
A. Boomer & C.A. Whitcombe (7 & 5)	1	L. Diegel & W. Mehlhorn	0
Singles			
A. Compston	0	W. Mehlhorn (1 hole)	1
A. Boomer	0	J. Farrell (5 & 4)	1
H.J. Jolly	0	J. Golden (8 & 7)	1
E. Ray	0	L. Diegel (7 & 5)	1
C.A. Whitcombe (halved)	½	G. Sarazen (halved)	½
A.G. Havers	0	W. Hagen (2 & 1)	1
F. Robson	0	A. Watrous (3 & 2)	1
G. Duncan (1 hole)	1	J. Turnesa	0
Great Britain and Ireland 2½; USA 9½			

'Smell the flowers'

At this point, not only did the Americans have the better golfers but they were also leading the way in establishing the top golf professionals as significant, and potentially wealthy, members of society. No one epitomised this development more than Walter Hagen. Golf professionals in Britain were often not allowed to enter the clubhouse by the front door; indeed, at the Open Championship at Deal in 1920 Hagen hired a footman and a Rolls-Royce to serve as his dressing room because he was refused entrance to the clubhouse changing room. Having won the US Open in 1914 and 1919, Hagen soon realised he could make more money playing in exhibition matches than he could in tournaments and between 1914 and 1941 he played in no fewer than 4,000, earning around $1 million. However, he always maintained that money was not important to him, saying that he didn't want to be a millionaire; he just wanted to live like one. Another of his favourite sayings was:

> I never hurry. I never worry. Always stop to smell the flowers along the way. It's later than you think.

As well as making money in exhibitions he was also one of the first to make significant money endorsing golf equipment – in his case, Wilson Sports, who produced some of the first matched sets of irons and named them after him: 'Walter Hagen', or 'Haig Ultra'.

He was also well known for his dashing wardrobe of tailored clothes in bright colours and the result was the nickname 'Sir Walter'. Altogether he did much to raise the status – and the earnings – of golf professionals in the USA. Gene Sarazen would say of him:

> All the professionals ... should say a silent thanks to
> Walter Hagen each time they stretch a check between
> their fingers. It was Walter who made professional golf
> what it is.

The strange thing was that he hit a lot of erratic shots, but
his powers of recovery were second-to-none and his short
game was superior to anyone's. No one else did more to
prove the saying: 'Drive for show, putt for dough'. Hagen
never allowed pressure to get to him. On the eve of the
final match of the 1926 PGA Championship, when he was
out on the town, he was told that his opponent, Leo Diegel,
was already in bed. He replied: 'Yeah, but he ain't sleeping.'

This calm approach earned him eleven major titles,
more than anyone else except Jack Nicklaus and Tiger
Woods, and we should bear in mind that the Masters did
not exist when he was at his peak, between 1913 and 1930.

Must be native-born
There was some controversy before the second Ryder Cup
match which was to be played at Moortown Golf Club, near
Leeds, on 26 and 27 April 1929. Sam Ryder decreed that all
participants must be native-born citizens of the countries
they were representing.

This weakened the US team and Hagen announced
before the matches that 'foreign-born' players would be
picked for the US team. He made the point that they had
been allowed to fight in the war for their newly adopted
country, so surely they could be picked to play golf for it
too.

The British team was considerably stronger than the one
that had been thrashed two years earlier. Abe Mitchell was
back and there were three new up-and-coming professionals; Henry Cotton, Stewart Burns and Ernest Whitcombe.

Ray, Havers and Jolly were dropped and only Charlie Whitcombe, Fred Robson and Archie Compston survived from the earlier team. However, the British team were still dogged by a lack of money. The golfing public had still not cottoned on to the match as more than a glorified exhibition; a new *Golf Illustrated* appeal raised only the paltry sum of £806 (less than £50,000 in today's money).

Once the Americans arrived their main problem was not an enthusiastic reception, as had been the case with the British team in New York, but the foul British weather. The practice days at Moortown were wet and cold with a strong wind. Added to this, the Americans were not allowed to use the steel shafts that they had been using for the last three years. The Rules Committee at the Royal and Ancient Golf Club had refused to legalise them in Great Britain. The Americans had no choice but to revert to hickory shafts.

Fortunately for the Americans, the weather relented a bit on the opening day of the match. It was still very cold but the rain stopped and the strong wind gave way to a light breeze. For the first time the golfing public turned up in big numbers to watch the matches. The results of the four-somes were disappointing for Great Britain as they lost two matches and halved one (where they were one up with one to play). The only British winners were Abe Mitchell (Sam Ryder, in the crowd, will have been very pleased about that) and Fred Robson who, after being all square at lunch, beat Gene Sarazen and Ed Dudley 2 and 1.

For the singles on the second day, British captain George Duncan found himself playing none other than 'Sir' Walter Hagen. Duncan had beaten Hagen in the first unofficial match at Wentworth in 1926 and, whatever Hagen's achievements in stroke-play tournaments, felt he would continue to beat him in matchplay. For his part Hagen is supposed to have said to his team when he discovered he was playing Duncan: 'Well boys, there's a point for our team right there.'

But then, Hagen always liked making remarks like that (he is the golfer who is supposed to have said when he turned up for one of the Majors: 'Who's coming second?').

The story continues in that Duncan is said to have heard this remark and, thus goaded, played the golf of his life. He completed the first eighteen holes in 69 and eventually won by a staggering 10 and 8; this against a man who was a superb match player. (Nor was Hagen any slouch when it came to stroke-play, as he demonstrated when he won the Open Championship by six clear shots a few weeks later.)

Born in September 1883 in Methlick, Aberdeenshire, George Duncan was apprenticed as a carpenter. A great all-round sportsman, he turned down an offer to become a professional footballer with Aberdeen and became a professional golfer instead. He won the first post-First World War Open Championship at Royal Cinque Ports in 1920. He also came close to winning the 1922 Open after a magnificent round of 69, which at the time was only the third-ever round under 70 in the Open. In the final round he fluffed a chip from what became known as 'Duncan's Hollow' in front of the 18th green and lost to Walter Hagen by a stroke.

He gained some sort of revenge by beating Hagen 6 and 5 in the match at Wentworth in 1926 in what was (but, as we have seen, was not officially) the first Ryder Cup match and then again at Southport in 1929 following Hagen's goading remark about him securing a certain point for the Americans when he learnt he was playing Hagen.

Duly inspired, the British produced four more victories and a half and won the match 7–5.

The large crowd had become very enthusiastic in support of their team and Bernard Darwin felt compelled to write in *The Times*:

It was a crowd that did not, I imagine, know a great deal about golf. While realising that golf does not give so many opportunities of shouting as football, they were resolved to make the difference between the two games as small as possible. So they ran, cheered and once, I'm afraid to say, forgot themselves so far as to cheer when an American missed a short putt.

Darwin also wrote in *The Times*:

The Americans fought back with a cheerful gallantry that could not be surpassed; they never gave in and never grudged a victory, but, for once in a very long while, they were the underdogs, and they struggled in vain.

26–27 April 1929 Moortown Golf Club, Leeds, England *Captains:* G. Duncan (Great Britain and Ireland), W. Hagen (USA)			
Great Britain and Ireland		**United States**	
Foursomes			
C.A. Whitcombe & A. Compston (halved)	½	J. Farrell & J. Turnesa (halved)	½
A. Boomer & G. Duncan	0	L. Diegel & A. Espinosa (7 & 5)	1
A. Mitchell & F. Robson (2 & 1)	1	G. Sarazen & E. Dudley	0
E.R. Whitcombe & T.H. Cotton	0	J. Golden & W. Hagen (2 holes)	1
Singles			
C.A. Whitcombe (8 & 6)	1	J. Farrell	0
G. Duncan (10 & 8)	1	W. Hagen	0
A. Mitchell	0	L. Diegel (8 & 6)	1
A. Compston (6 & 4)	1	G. Sarazen	0
A. Boomer (4 & 3)	1	J. Turnesa	0
F. Robson	0	H. Smith (4 & 2)	1
T.H. Cotton (4 & 3)	1	A. Watrous	0
E.R. Whitcombe (halved)	½	A. Espinosa (halved)	½
Great Britain and Ireland 7; USA 5			

Henry Cotton left out

Controversy was – and still is – never far away in Ryder Cup matches and Great Britain shot themselves in the foot for the next match which was to be played at Scioto Country Club, Columbus, Ohio on 26 and 27 June 1931. They decided that all of their team had not only to be born in Britain, but also resident in Britain. This ruled out three of their best young players – Henry Cotton, Percy Alliss who was the professional at Wannsee Golf Club in Berlin, and Aubrey Boomer who was at St Cloud in Paris.

Cotton began an acrimonious discussion – the first of many – with the PGA about their insistence, agreed with the US PGA, that all the team return to Britain immediately after the match. Furthermore, the PGA wanted all money earned in exhibition matches to be shared equally among the team. Cotton disagreed with both rulings and wrote an article for Golf Illustrated in which he said:

> It was pointed out to me that if I enjoyed the benefit of a free passage, it was not fair for me to use that benefit for my personal gain by staying after the team had returned and playing as a free lance. It was this that caused me to intimate to the Professional Golfers' Association that I was quite prepared to pay my passage out and back. Here again the Association found my suggestion unacceptable.

Cotton went further and asked Alliss and Boomer to join him in a private tour to the USA. Alliss agreed, and he and Cotton planned to appear at Scioto during the match. In spite of this provocation the PGA were very keen for Cotton to play for the British team and said that, if he wrote a letter of apology, they would overlook his behaviour. Cotton refused and consequently the British team was weaker than it could have been.

Meanwhile in the USA, for the first time the US PGA organised a qualifying tournament. The committee had already picked Hagen, Sarazen, Farrell, Espinosa and Diegel but thirteen others had to play a gruelling 90 holes to try to secure one of the remaining four places.

When the day arrived, in marked contrast to the freezing temperatures of Moortown two years earlier the temperature was 100°F (almost 38°C). This would affect the British as badly as the cold weather at Moortown had the Americans. As it turned out, the British team was outplayed from start to finish. The foursomes were lost 3–1, with only Abe Mitchell and Fred Robson earning a point by beating Leo Diegel and Whiffy Cox 3 and 1. On the second day, the heat did not relent and Britain lost the singles 6–2 to give an overall result of USA 9, Great Britain 3.

Inevitably there was much criticism of the team and of the PGA for leaving out Cotton, Alliss and Aubrey Boomer, though some of the more thoughtful appreciated that the conditions had been almost impossible for the British team. One journalist wrote:

> It is unkind to hit a man when he is down ... Nevertheless, one must regret that Charles Whitcombe was so modest as to leave himself out of the Foursomes and so charitable as to play Duncan at all. Duncan has been a very great golfer, but he is not one now, and why should it be pretended that he is?

The PGA moved that never again should the match be played at the height of the American summer and, fortunately, the US PGA agreed. As we shall see, the 1933 match at Ringwood, New Jersey, was played in September.

26–27 June 1931			
Scioto Country Club, Columbus, Ohio, USA			
Captains: C.A. Whitcombe (Great Britain and Ireland), W. Hagen (USA)			
Great Britain and Ireland		**United States**	
Foursomes			
A. Compston & W.H Davies	0	G. Sarazen & J. Farrell (8 & 7)	1
G. Duncan & A.G. Havers	0	W. Hagen & D. Shute (10 & 9)	1
A. Mitchell & F. Robson (3 & 1)	1	L. Diegel & A. Espinosa	0
S. Easterbrook & E.R. Whitcombe	0	W. Burke & W. Cox (3 & 2)	1
Singles			
A. Compston	0	W. Burke (7 & 6)	1
F. Robson	0	G. Sarazen (7 & 6)	1
W.H. Davies (4 & 3)	1	J. Farrell	0
A. Mitchell	0	W. Cox (3 & 1)	1
C.A. Whitcombe	0	W. Hagen (4 & 3)	1
B. Hodson	0	D. Shute (8 & 6)	1
E.R. Whitcombe	0	A. Espinosa (2 & 1)	1
A.G. Havers (4 & 3)	1	C. Wood	0
Great Britain and Ireland 3; USA 9			

The tough Taylor

For the 1933 match to be held on 26 and 27 June 1933, at Southport and Ainsdale, the PGA was determined to make a fresh start after the debacle of 1931 and elected the first non-playing captain, five times Open winner John Henry Taylor. Taylor was a renowned disciplinarian (he had initially pursued a military career) and he first tackled the question of players such as Cotton, Alliss and Boomer and their overseas residency. Alliss had returned to Britain so he was available, but Cotton was at the Royal Waterloo Club in Belgium and Boomer was still in France.

Some wanted to amend Sam Ryder's trust deed but both Taylor and the PGA were adamant that the rules would not be changed to accommodate Cotton and Boomer. Noting how unfit the British team had been in 1931, Taylor recruited a physical fitness expert from the British Army, Lieutenant Alick Stark. He decreed early morning runs along Southport beach as well as rub-downs to loosen up the golfers' muscles. Taylor, at 62 years old, set a good example by running alongside the golfers.

For their part the Americans brought what Bernard Darwin noted in *The Times* was 'a very strong side, if anything stronger than that which our men so gloriously defeated on that freezing day at Moortown'.

As ever, there was some controversy when the laid-back Hagen (retained as the US captain) failed to turn up to exchange teams' orders at the first two times arranged with Taylor. The tough Taylor refused to be disorientated by this gamesmanship and sent a message to Hagen that if he failed to show at the third arranged tie the match was off. Hagen showed up and the match began.

For once the British performed well in the foursomes and led 2½–1½ at the end of the first day. Scenting victory, and probably learning that the popular Prince of Wales was a spectator, a 15,000-strong crowd turned up for the singles. Just as at Moortown, there was some less than sporting behaviour from sections of the crowd who cheered errant shots and missed putts by the Americans. George Sarazen would later complain that the atmosphere was more like that of a fairground than a golf course.

And Bernard Darwin of *The Times* wrote:

Golf was originally a game for the few, played on remote open spaces in decorous silence. But the world is too well used now to the popularity of games to be surprised that a great golf match should be treated almost like a great match in league football.

The gentleman on the megaphone harangued the crowd, introducing it to novel topics, the danger of tumbling on slippery grass and the presence of pickpockets. This last seemed prophetic for in the match between

Hagen and Lacey a perfectly innocent spectator picked
up Lacey's ball in the rough and had to be pursued and
brought back by an army of stewards armed with lances
bearing red and white flags.

The excitement certainly built. At lunch time, the singles
were all square and thus Britain was still one point ahead
overall. The Americans soon put the teams level when
Sarazen beat Alf Padgham 6 and 4 in the top match. This
was something of a surprise because it was reckoned that
Hagen had put Sarazen top as a sacrificial lamb. Most knew
that the urbane Hagen and the tough Sarazen, of Italian
extraction, did not see eye to eye. Hagen had in fact paired
himself with Sarazen in the foursomes in order to quash
rumours of a feud, but then lost no opportunity to blame
him when they secured only a half.

Further down, matches swung to and fro. The ageing
Abe Mitchell won but shortly afterwards Hagen and Wood
both won, and with four matches still to be decided, the
Americans were now one point ahead overall. First, Alliss
won, so the teams were all square with three matches to go.
Then Havers beat Diegel so the Brits were one ahead again.
But then Charlie Whitcombe lost, so back to all-square with
one match to go.

Syd Easterbrook and Densmore Shute came to the last
hole all-square. It could not be closer. Both were bunkered
off the tee. Easterbrook played safe out of the bunker while
Shute bravely went for the green and was bunkered again.
After their third shots both were on the green and both
about twelve feet from the pin. Apparently Hagen was going
to advise Shute to play safe because a half would mean the
USA, the current holder, would retain the Cup. However,
he was standing next to the Prince of Wales and thought
it would be discourteous to move, so stayed where he was.

Shute went for the hole, missed and finished about six feet past it. The nervous Easterbrook did not go for broke and finished about four feet short. Shute putted and missed. Easterbrook had his putt to win back the Cup. He holed it!

The British were ecstatic but the Prince of Wales was, of course suitably restrained in his comment as he presented the Cup to Taylor:

> Naturally I am unbiased in these matters, but I can only say that we over here are delighted to have beaten you over there.

The future magnificent golf commentator, Henry Longhurst, covering his first Ryder Cup, wrote:

> There were thousands of people who rushed about the course, herded, not always successfully, by volunteer stewards brandishing long bamboo poles with pennants at the end, which earned them the name 'Southport Lancers'. Many had come to see the golf, more perhaps to see the Prince of Wales, himself a keen golfer, who had come to give the Cup away.
>
> We saw him in the end presenting it to dear old J.H. Taylor, non-playing captain of the British team, almost beside himself with pride, and we saw Hagen with that impudent smile that captured so many male and female hearts saying, 'we had the Cup on our table coming over and we had reserved a place for it going back!' Above all, we saw what was one of the most desperate finishes to any international match played to this day.

Longhurst would write of Easterbrook's efforts on the last green:

So now Easterbrook was left with his 4-footer, with a nasty left-hand borrow at that, and the complete golfer's nightmare – 'This for the entire match'. Even at the age of 24 I remember thinking, 'Better him than me'. Easterbrook holed it like a man and the Cup was Britain's.

It was to be a long time before Longhurst or anyone else would be able to write that again.

26–27 June 1933			
Southport & Ainsdale Golf Club, Southport, England			
Captains: J.H. Taylor (Great Britain and Ireland), W. Hagen (USA)			
Great Britain and Ireland		**United States**	
Foursomes			
P. Alliss & C.A. Whitcombe (halved)	½	G. Sarazen & W. Hagen (halved)	½
A. Mitchell & A.G. Havers (3 & 2)	1	O. Dutra & D. Shute	0
W.H. Davies & S. Easterbrook (1 hole)	1	C. Wood & P. Runyan	0
A.H. Padgham & A. Perry	0	E. Dudley & W. Burke (1 hole)	1
Singles			
A.H. Padgham	0	G. Sarazen (6 & 4)	1
A. Mitchell (9 & 8)	1	O. Dutra	0
A.J. Lacey	0	W. Hagen (2 & 1)	1
W.H. Davies	0	C. Wood (4 & 3)	1
P. Alliss (2 & 1)	1	P. Runyan	0
A.G. Havers (4 & 3)	1	L. Diegel	0
S. Easterbrook (1 hole)	1	D. Shute	0
C.A. Whitcombe	0	H. Smith (2 & 1)	1
Great Britain and Ireland 6½; USA 5½			

The Americans are better

Thanks to this win, the British team assembled for the next match, to be played at Ridgewood, New Jersey, on 28 and 29 September 1935, full of optimism. Before they sailed, the team were given a good-luck dinner at the Grosvenor

Hotel in Park Lane. All three Whitcombe brothers from Burnham, Somerset – Ernest, Charles and Reg – were in the team but once again Henry Cotton and Aubrey Boomer were deemed ineligible because of their residence in continental Europe.

The new PGA Secretary, Commander R.T.C. Roe, confidently announced:

> Though my association with professional golfers in an official capacity is somewhat short, I feel that no team could go to America with a greater opportunity of success than Whitcombe and his boys.

He confidently insured the Cup for the return trip.

Walter Hagen was again captain of the United States team, which like the British team had plenty of experienced players as well as four rookies.

The optimism of the British team was reinforced by the rescheduling of the match from midsummer to September so that they did not have to endure the sweltering heat. However, this optimism was quickly dented on the first day of the match when they lost the foursomes 3–1, two of the matches by very large margins. Nor did things go better in the singles, with the Americans winning the first four and effectively settling the match. Ultimately the score was 9–3, another convincing win for the United States on their home soil.

Back in Britain there was plenty of criticism. *Golf Illustrated* which, as we have seen, had always supported the Ryder Cup, wrote:

> The best team we ever sent played about as badly as it knew how. Scores running into the high eighties tell their own tale, which must be one of summary defeat.

And *Tatler* wrote: 'Better not to go at all than be beaten like this every year.'

The American magazine *Time* wrote, under the headline 'Ryder Rout', that the British had been 'roundly whipped, in a tournament distinguished more by the US team's off-the-course uniforms than by the quality of anyone's game'.

28–29 September 1935			
Ridgewood Country Club, Ridgewood, New Jersey, USA			
Captains: C.A. Whitcombe (Great Britain and Ireland), W. Hagen (USA)			
Great Britain and Ireland		**United States**	
Foursomes			
A. Perry & J. Busson	0	G. Sarazen & W. Hagen (7 & 6)	1
A.H. Padgham & P. Alliss	0	H. Picard & J. Revolta (6 & 5)	1
W.J. Cox & E.W. Jarman	0	P. Runyan & H. Smith (9 & 8)	1
C.A. Whitcombe & E.R. Whitcombe (1 hole)	1	O. Dutra & K. Lafoon	0
Singles			
J. Busson	0	G. Sarazen (3 & 2)	1
R. Burton	0	P. Runyan (5 & 3)	1
R. Whitcombe	0	J. Revolta (2 & 1)	1
A.H. Padgham	0	O. Dutra (4 & 2)	1
P. Alliss (1 hole)	1	C. Wood	0
W.J. Cox (halved)	½	H. Smith (halved)	½
E.R. Whitcombe	0	H. Picard (3 & 2)	1
A. Perry (halved)	½	S. Parks (halved)	½
Great Britain and Ireland 3; USA 9			

'Win on home soil'

Two years later, it was back to Southport and Ainsdale, scene of the memorable British victory of 1933. The events of 1935 were forgotten and, buoyed by the return of the country's best golfer, Henry Cotton, now established at Ashridge Golf Club to the south of London, the hopes of the British team were high. He had not played since the 1929 match but in the interim had won the Open Championship twice, and his final round of 71 at Carnoustie in July 1937 in lashing rain was considered one of his finest. The fact that he finished ahead of five of the US Ryder Cup team also helped boost British confidence.

Cotton was born in Holmes Chapel in Cheshire in 1907 and his father could afford to send him to the boarding school, Alleyn's in Dulwich in south London. It was there he showed his individuality and determination when as a good cricketer he was selected for the 1st XI before he was a prefect. After he and the other non-prefects in the team had been forced to carry the gear of the six prefects back to the school by public transport, he wrote to the headmaster to complain. The headmaster ordered that he was to be caned but Cotton refused to accept his punishment. Banned from the cricket team, he took up golf and became a professional golfer at seventeen; he was almost certainly the only professional educated at a 'public' school.

He was known for working extremely hard at his game and would often practise until his hands bled. Professionals were treated as an inferior class by most golf club members and Cotton worked hard to change this attitude. He insisted on being made an honorary member of any club with which he was associated.

He was clearly Britain's best golfer in the 1930s and won the Open in 1934 and 1937. During the Second World War he served in the RAF and, when possible, played exhibition matches to raise money for the Red Cross. He was awarded an MBE for this work. He won the Open again in 1948 and captained the Ryder Cup team in 1947 and 1953.

He retired from competitive golf in the early 1950s and became a successful golf course architect designing, among other courses, Le Meridien in the Algarve. He also wrote many books on golf and established the Golf Foundation which helped thousands of boys and girls get started in golf.

Like Walter Hagen, Cotton enjoyed the good life of champagne, caviar, Rolls-Royces and bespoke tailored clothes. He was made an honorary member of the R&A and was created a knight just before he died, at the age of 80, in 1982.

Charles Whitcombe would be captain of the British team for the third time. Walter Hagen would again be captain of the US team, though this time in a non-playing capacity.

The foursomes were close but with Cotton and Padgham disappointing everyone by losing to Byron Nelson and Ed Dudley, the British ended the day 2½–1½ down to the Americans. The British would need a good start to the singles and they got it so that, after four matches and with four to go, the teams were tied at 4–4. Percy Alliss was having a very close game with Gene Sarazen who enjoyed a great piece of luck at the par-three 15th. He hit his tee shot over the back of the green and it landed in a woman's skirt. She jumped up, thereby pitching the ball back on to the green. Sarazen holed the putt for an outrageously lucky two, won the hole to go one up and held on to win. As it turned out, it was not critical as the Americans won all the remaining matches for an overall comfortable victory of 8–4.

The Americans were certainly pleased and President Roosevelt sent this message:

> To the greatest general in the world: Congratulations on leading the greatest golfers in the world to a wonderful victory which brings great honour to your Country, the PGA and your fellow professionals who are proud of you. Your achievement will go down in golfing history as the greatest of all time; we salute you, admire your courage and honour you as champions and heroes.

Captain Walter Hagen, perhaps overcome by this but more likely disconcerted by his notes blowing away just as he was about to make his victory speech, said: 'I am very proud to be the captain of the first American team to win on home soil.'

This was greeted by an astonished silence and, realising his error, he continued: 'You'll forgive me, I'm sure, for feeling so at home here in Britain.'

He had, after all, won the Open Championship four times.

And that was it for ten years as the Second World War took its toll on all sporting events. In 1939 both countries got as far as picking their teams for the match scheduled to be played at Ponte Vedra in Florida in November, but when British Prime Minister Neville Chamberlain uttered those doom-laden words on 3 September – 'I have to tell you now that no such message [from the Germans] has been received and that consequently, this country is at war with Germany' – Commander Roe cabled the US PGA to say that the match would have to be postponed. He did not say for how long, but no one was under the illusion that this war would be over by Christmas – which is what they had thought, wrongly of course, of the war that had broken out in August 1914.

29–30 June 1937 Southport & Ainsdale Golf Club, Southport, England *Captains:* C.A. Whitcombe (Great Britain and Ireland), W. Hagen (USA)			
Great Britain and Ireland		**United States**	
Foursomes			
A.H. Padgham & T.H. Cotton (4 & 2)	1	E. Dudley & B. Nelson	0
A.J. Lacey & W.J. Cox	0	R. Guldahl & T. Manero (2 & 1)	1
C.A. Whitcombe & D.J. Rees (halved)	½	G. Sarazen & D. Shute (halved)	½
P. Alliss & R. Burton (2 & 1)	1	H. Picard & J. Revolta	0

(continued)

29–30 June 1937 (continued)

Southport & Ainsdale Golf Club, Southport, England

Captains: C.A. Whitcombe (Great Britain and Ireland), W. Hagen (USA)

Great Britain and Ireland		United States	
Singles			
A.H. Padgham	0	R. Guldahl (8 & 7)	1
S.L. King (halved)	½	D. Shute (halved)	½
D.H. Rees (3 & 1)	1	B. Nelson	0
T.H. Cotton (5 & 3)	1	T. Manero	0
P. Alliss	0	G. Sarazen (1 hole)	1
R. Burton	0	S. Snead (5 & 4)	1
A. Perry	0	E. Dudley (2 & 1)	1
A.J. Lacey	0	H. Picard (2 & 1)	1
Great Britain and Ireland 5; USA 7			

Chapter 2

Americans almost completely dominant

Still the putting that counts
Portland, Oregon 1947

The 'Wee Ice Mon'
Ganton, Yorkshire 1949

Little hope of victory
Pinehurst, North Carolina 1951

'The melancholy fact was ...'
Wentworth, Surrey 1953

'Better than ever before'
Thunderbird, Palm Springs, California 1955

'You could have knocked us down with a feather'
Lindrick, Yorkshire 1957

Crushed again
Eldorado, Palm Springs, California 1959

Still the putting that counts

How was the Ryder Cup going to fare after the most cataclysmic war in the world's history? And where would the money come from to pay for the players' travel and accommodation expenses?

Fortunately, a man not dissimilar to Sam Ryder (who had died in 1936) appeared on the scene. This one was American and, like Ryder, he had come to golf fairly late in life. He also shared the same enthusiasm for the game and for mixing with the players. He wanted to treat all players, both the famous and the relatively unknown, as though they were guests in his own house. His name was Robert Hudson, he was based in Portland, Oregon, and he had made his money in food-processing, describing himself self-deprecatingly as a 'prune merchant'. He sponsored the 1946 PGA Championship where he heard about the financial difficulties of restarting the Ryder Cup matches, and he agreed to finance the cost of the whole match due to be played in November 1947. Stipulating only that the match be played in Portland, he paid for the British team to sail out on the *Queen Mary*.

Hudson was a flamboyant character in the mould of Walter Hagen and laid on a banquet for the players in New York to which he also invited film stars such as Dorothy Lamour. He gave the British team gifts of clothes and radios and then went with them on the train journey to Oregon in the north-west, a journey which took three and a half days.

The Americans had settled on a new selection process based on performances in key tournaments between January 1946 and 1947. There was some criticism of it but it is still the basis of the system used today, and in 1947 it produced a strong team under the captaincy of Ben Hogan. The British team, most of whom had served in the armed forces during the war and played relatively little golf, had only three players from the 1937 team; Henry Cotton, Dai Rees and Sam King. They were going to have a very tough time trying to beat an American team of whom most had been able to play throughout the war on a scaled-down tournament circuit. For example, Byron Nelson, excused from military service because of haemophilia, had won thirteen out of 23 tournaments in 1945 and eighteen out of 31 in 1946. (We should not gain the impression that every American golfer enjoyed a 'soft' war. One of the team, Lloyd Mangrum, was decorated for his part in the D-Day landings.)

The first problem at Portland was the weather. The area had suffered its heaviest rainfall for 65 years all through October and the course was almost water-logged. This was likely to suit the long-hitting Americans more than the British. A note of controversy was introduced when the British captain Henry Cotton noticed during practice that the Americans were achieving greater back-spin. He thought the American clubs might have been illegally scuffed up and challenged the players. However, on inspection, they were found to be legal.

When the match began there had been more heavy rainfall. *The Times* wrote: 'There were only a few hundred spectators present when the match opened under threatening skies and with the turf soggy.'

The war-weary British were no match for the Americans. They lost the foursomes and very nearly all the singles, only being saved from a complete whitewash by a Sam King victory over Herman Keiser. Henry Cotton was forced to say: 'I do not think we can ever win a match in your country ... all the same golf is a wonderful game and we all love it.'

The American golfing expert Robert Caldwell said:

They [the British team] drove just as straight as our players, if not quite as far. Their second shots were adequate but lacked the consistent accuracy of the Americans and, consequently, over 36 holes, the British were all under far greater pressure on and around the greens. The modern American professional excels in the trap-shot, the chip of any description and with his putter, which more than earns him his living.

The Times agreed, writing:

The British players ran into most of their troubles on and near the greens, after matching their opponents stroke for stroke from the tees and in the long shots down the fairways. For instance, Cotton and Lees took 54 putts in 27 holes, and in such competitions an average of two putts a hole is not good enough. Cotton himself missed eight putts of between three and nine feet.

1–2 November 1947			
Portland Golf Club, Portland, Oregon, USA			
Captains: T.H. Cotton (Great Britain and Ireland), B. Hogan (USA)			
Great Britain and Ireland		**United States**	
Foursomes			
T.H. Cotton & A. Lees	0	E. Oliver & L. Worsham (10 & 8)	1
F. Daly & C.H. Ward	0	S. Snead & L. Mangrum (6 & 5)	1
J. Adams & M. Faulkner	0	B. Hogan & J. Demaret (2 holes)	1
D.J. Rees & S.L. King	0	B. Nelson & H. Barron (2 & 1)	1
Singles			
F. Daly	0	E.J. Harrison (5 & 4)	1
J. Adams	0	L. Worsham (3 & 2)	1
M. Faulkner	0	L. Mangrum (6 & 5)	1
C.H. Ward	0	E. Oliver (4 & 3)	1
A. Lees	0	B. Nelson (2 & 1)	1
T.H. Cotton	0	S. Snead (5 & 4)	1
D.J. Rees	0	J. Demaret (3 & 2)	1
S.L. King (4 & 3)	1	H. Keiser	0
Great Britain and Ireland 1; USA 11			

The 'Wee Ice Mon'

In 1949, the match was played in England for the first time in twelve years, this time at Ganton in Yorkshire. The American team was again captained by Ben Hogan, though this time he was unable to play.

Born in 1912 – the same year as two other great American golfers, Sam Snead and Byron Nelson – Ben Hogan reached the top of golf the hard way. His father, a blacksmith, committed suicide, supposedly in front of Ben, when his son was only nine, leaving the family in dire financial circumstances. Ben sold newspapers after school and began caddying at the age of eleven. A fellow caddy was Byron Nelson, who was offered junior membership at the club. Caddies over sixteen were not allowed, so Hogan was forced to move to the three poor daily-fee courses. He turned professional at eighteen and secured a low-paying job as a club professional.

He suffered a difficult decade in the 1930s and did not win his first tournament until 1940, when he won three consecutive tournaments in North Carolina. Known as 'The Hawk', Hogan had an iron will and showed fierce determination in curing a hook which was holding back his game. The Scots called him 'Wee Ice Mon' after he won the Open at Carnoustie in 1953.

This win came after he was involved in a near-fatal car accident in 1949. In 1948 he had won no fewer than ten tournaments including the US Open. Not very popular before his accident because of his cold, aloof manner, he nevertheless won over the public by his determination to come back after it. In 1950 he only just lost the Los Angeles Open after a play-off with Sam Snead and, five months later, beat Lloyd Mangrum and George Fazio in an eighteen-hole play-off to win his second US Open at Merion. He then won twelve more PGA Tour tournaments including six Majors.

He received a ticker-tape welcome in New York after winning the Open Championship at Carnoustie in 1953. This made him the second player after Gene Sarazen to win all four of the modern major championships – the US Open, the Masters, the US PGA Championship and the Open Championship (sometimes referred to as the British Open).

Hogan played twice in the Ryder Cup, in 1947 and 1951, and captained it three times – in 1947, in 1949, when he could not play following his accident, and in 1967.

Hogan has been widely acknowledged as the best ever striker of a golf ball. Jack Nicklaus, when asked 'Is Tiger Woods the best ball striker you have ever seen?', replied: 'No, no – Ben Hogan easily.'

The Americans came to Britain on the *Queen Elizabeth* and as they had been alerted to the fact that rationing, including of meat, was still in force, they brought crates of provisions paid for by Robert Hudson. This was seen as patronising by the British, especially when Ben Hogan told the press:

> We aren't eating all those steaks ourselves … we want to do some entertaining and give your British golfers some.

The next bit of controversy was the legality of some of the golf clubs. This time it was Hogan questioning those being used by Dai Rees and Dick Burton. The British PGA took them to a hotel in Scarborough to consult Bernard Darwin who, as well as being *The Times* golf correspondent, was also Chairman of the R&A's Rules of Golf Committee. Darwin's verdict was that 'it was nothing a little filing would not put right'. Consequently, the professional at Ganton, Jack Ballantine, spent the night filing the offending clubs to the correct depth.

All this plus the unwelcome publicity was upsetting the British team, which had already been weakened by the withdrawal of Henry Cotton (who had refused to play after being replaced as captain by Charlie Whitcombe). In spite of all this off-course politics, on the course the British team played well in practice and when the match started in front of large crowds, won the opening foursomes match when Max Faulkner and Jimmy Adams beat 'Dutch' Harrison and Johnny Palmer. The Irishman Fred Daly then helped the newcomer Ken Bousfield to win their game as well and, although Charlie Ward and Sam King lost to Jimmy Demaret and Clayton Haefner, Dick Burton and Arthur Lees beat Sam Snead and Lloyd Mangrum. The British were leading 3–1 at the end of the first day.

That was the end of their hopes as the Americans won the singles 6–2 and ran out winners by 7–5.

The Times summed it up:

> They [the British] played as well as they could, but it was not well enough. No unprejudiced onlooker could doubt that the Americans, playing their own game ... were quite definitely superior ... and their putting, so uniformly smooth, solid, and consistent, was as near as might be invincible.

16–17 September 1949			
Ganton Golf Club, Scarborough, England			
Captains: C.A. Whitcombe (Great Britain and Ireland), B. Hogan (USA)			
Great Britain and Ireland		**United States**	
Foursomes			
M. Faulkner & J. Adams (2 & 1)	1	E.J Harrison & J. Palmer	0
F. Daly & K. Bousfield (4 & 2)	1	R. Hamilton & S. Alexander	0
C.H Ward & S.L. King	0	J. Demaret & C. Heafner (4 & 3)	1
R. Burton & A. Lees (1 hole)	1	S. Snead & L. Mangrum	0

(continued)

16–17 September 1949 (continued)			
Ganton Golf Club, Scarborough, England			
Captains: C.A. Whitcombe (Great Britain and Ireland), B. Hogan (USA)			
Great Britain and Ireland		**United States**	
Singles			
M. Faulkner	0	E.J. Harrison (8 & 7)	1
J. Adams (2 & 1)	1	J. Palmer	0
C.H. Ward	0	S. Snead (6 & 5)	1
D.J. Rees (6 & 4)	1	R. Hamilton	0
R. Burton	0	C. Heafner (3 & 2)	1
S.L. King	0	C. Harbert (4 & 3)	1
A. Lees	0	J. Demaret (7 & 6)	1
F. Daly	0	L. Mangrum (4 & 3)	1
Great Britain and Ireland 5; USA 7			

Little hope of victory

For the match at Pinehurst, North Carolina in November 1951, while the British team travelled with the good wishes of the British press, the latter still expressed little hope of victory.

Bernard Darwin wrote in *The Times*: 'The British team are facing their task with cheerful optimism that warms the heart, and come what may will acquit themselves well.'

Leonard Crawley wrote in the *Daily Telegraph*: 'The British will be output to such an extent that they will be unable to cope with their opponents on such a fearfully long course.'

And Henry Longhurst wrote in *Golf Illustrated*: 'The best the British team can expect is one win in the foursomes and possibly two in the singles.'

The course was certainly long at 7,200 yards, especially as it rained hard the night before the match. The United States team, now with Sam Snead as captain, was strong with a blend of experience and promising youth. The British had now also introduced a system of selection on merit and yet again Henry Cotton did not play, as his tournament appearances had been restricted due to ill health.

The first day, the foursomes, went to the Americans, with only Charlie Ward and Arthur Lees winning for Britain by producing some superb golf and finishing the morning round 3–3–2–5–3–3. The second day, the singles, was just as bad and the eventual result was a humiliating 9½–3½ defeat.

2–4 November 1951			
Pinehurst Country Club, Pinehurst, North Carolina, USA			
Captains: A.J. Lacey (Great Britain and Ireland), S. Snead (USA)			
Great Britain and Ireland		**United States**	
Foursomes			
M. Faulkner & D.J. Rees	0	C. Heafner & J. Burke (5 & 3)	1
C.H. Ward & A. Lees (2 & 1)	1	E. Oliver & H. Ransom	0
J. Adams & J. Panton	0	S. Snead & L. Mangrum (5 & 4)	1
F. Daly & K. Bousfield	0	B. Hogan & J. Demaret (5 & 4)	1
Singles			
J. Adams	0	J. Burke (4 & 3)	1
D.J. Rees	0	J. Demaret (2 holes)	1
F. Daly (halved)	½	C. Heafner (halved)	½
H. Weetman	0	L. Mangrum (6 & 5)	1
A. Lees (2 & 1)	1	E. Oliver	0
C.H. Ward	0	B. Hogan (3 & 2)	1
J. Panton	0	S. Alexander (8 & 7)	1
M. Faulkner	0	S. Snead (4 & 3)	1
Great Britain and Ireland 2½; USA 9½			

'The melancholy fact was ...'

The next match, at Wentworth in October 1953, brought back memories of the first 'unofficial' match in 1926 which the British had won so easily. That victory was not likely to be repeated. At least Britain had Henry Cotton back, and as captain too. There were also some very talented newcomers in Peter Alliss (son of Percy), Eric Brown, Bernard Hunt and Harry Bradshaw. For their part, the USA now had Lloyd Mangrum as captain. Sam Snead was still playing but otherwise the team was steady rather than spectacular.

Born, like those two other great American golfers Ben
Hogan and Byron Nelson, in 1912, Sam Snead was one of
the world's best golfers for almost four decades. He won
seven Majors – three Masters, three PGA Championships
and one Open Championship. He came second in the US
Open four times but never won it.

Many thought he possessed the perfect swing although,
slightly bizarrely, he was known as 'Slammin' Sammy' as if
brute force were the key to his success. Nevertheless he was
an exceptionally long driver into the wind. He was known
for his 'folksy' image, wearing a straw hat and sometimes
playing tournaments barefoot. One of his famous remarks
was: 'Keep close count of your nickels and dimes, stay away
from whiskey, and never concede a putt.'

The peak of his career was just after the Second World
War and in 1950 he won no fewer than eleven events, an
achievement which has not been bettered since. He played
in the Ryder Cup in 1937, 1947, 1949, 1951, 1953, 1955 and
1959 and captained the US team in 1951, 1959 and 1969.

As he grew older he beat his age several times. In 1979
he was the youngest PGA Tour player to shoot his age (67)
in the second round of the 1979 Quad Cities Open. In the
final round he beat that by shooting 66. In 1983, at 71 he
shot a twelve-under par round of 60 and in 1997, at 85, he
shot a round of 78. From 1984 to 2002 he hit the honorary
starting tee shot at the Masters. Until 1999, he was joined by
Gene Sarazen and, until 2001, by Byron Nelson.

As well as being a long driver he was also a superb striker
of long irons. He also possessed an excellent short game,
pioneering the use of the sand wedge for short shots from
grass. His putting deteriorated as he grew older and he
pioneered croquet-style putting in the 1960s. The US Golf
Association banned this style in 1968 and Snead moved to

side-saddle putting, where he crouched and angled his feet towards the hole while holding the club with a split grip.

Other notable quotes from Snead were:

If a lot of people gripped a knife and fork the way they do a golf club, they'd starve to death.

Thinking instead of acting is the number-one golf disease.

Practice puts brains in your muscles.

Correct one fault at a time.

The three things I fear most in golf are lightning, Ben Hogan and a downhill putt.

Jack Nicklaus said of Snead that his was 'the most fluid motion ever to grace a golf course'.

At Wentworth Ben Hogan, who had won the Masters in the spring and the US Open and the Open Championship at Carnoustie in the summer, did not play because he felt his legs would not be able to cope with 36 holes in a day. This was sad for the spectators but good for the prospects of the British team.

The British lost the foursomes 3–1 and their chances looked forlorn; when Dai Rees just lost the opening singles, things looked very bleak indeed. However, some great wins, not least Harry Weetman beating Sam Snead after being four down with five holes to play, put Britain in such a position that if Peter Alliss, one down with one hole to play, could halve, and Bernard Hunt, one up with one to play, could win, Great Britain would win back the Ryder Cup.

Peter Alliss was seemingly suffering from nerves. One up with three to play, he had been unlucky to lose the 16th to Jim Turnesa, but then drove out-of-bounds at the 17th to go one down. On the 18th, Turnesa had hit three bad shots and was struggling to make par while Alliss was just left of the green in two. He was faced with a delicate chip from just in front of a small grandstand (he would later say that his mind 'was full of nothing but feet, rows and rows of feet – brogues, moccasins, sneakers, boots, shoes, spikes, rubbers, the shoes of the people perched on the front of the grand-stand'). Unfortunately, he fluffed the chip but at least then recovered to chip within a yard of the hole. Turnesa missed his putt to score a bogey six. All Alliss had to do was hole his putt to win. He missed!

As Henry Longhurst said:

What ensued made a lasting mark on Alliss. One feels if he had quietly lost his match out in the country, the rest of his golfing life might have been different. As it was in the full ghastly light of publicity, not to be dimmed for many years, he took four from the edge of the green … he was only 22 at the time.

Britain could still tie if Hunt could halve the last hole and win his match, but like Alliss he missed a short putt and lost the hole. The Americans had won one of the most exciting Ryder Cup matches 6½–5½. Lloyd Mangrum said he would 'never, never captain an American team again because of the nine thousand deaths I suffered in the last hour'.

Bernard Darwin wrote in *The Times*:

It was very sad. The melancholy fact must be recorded that par 5s instead of 6s at the home hole in the last two matches to finish would have given Great Britain victory.

That it was the two young members of the team who failed at this point made it the more painful.

2–3 October 1953 Wentworth Golf Club, Virginia Water, Surrey, England *Captains:* T.H. Cotton (Great Britain and Ireland), L. Mangrum (USA)			
Great Britain and Ireland		**United States**	
Foursomes			
H. Weetman & P. Alliss	0	D. Douglas & E. Oliver (2 & 1)	1
E.C. Brown & J. Panton	0	L. Mangrum & S. Snead (8 & 7)	1
J. Adam & B.J. Hunt	0	T. Kroll & J. Burke (7 & 5)	1
F. Daly & H. Bradshaw (1 hole)	1	W. Burkemo & C. Middlecoff	0
Singles			
D.J. Rees	0	J. Burke (2 & 1)	1
F. Daly (9 & 7)	1	T. Kroll	0
E.C. Brown (2 holes)	1	L. Mangrum	0
H. Weetman (1 hole)	1	S. Snead	0
M. Faulkner	0	C. Middlecoff (3 & 1)	1
P. Alliss	0	J .Turnesa (1 hole)	1
B.J. Hunt (halved)	½	D. Douglas (halved)	½
H. Bradshaw (3 & 2)	1	F. Haas	0
Great Britain and Ireland 5½; USA 6½			

'Better than ever before'

These lapses cost Alliss and Hunt their places in the team that went to the Thunderbird Club in Palm Springs, California in 1955. A new selection process had been introduced in Britain whereby a list of tournaments was drawn up in which players were awarded points according to their placings. The top seven would qualify automatically and the British PGA Committee would select the other three. As a result, four new players – John Jacobs, Syd Scott, Christy O'Connor and Johnny Fallon – joined the experienced Harry Bradshaw, Dai Rees, Arthur Lees, Harry Weetman, Ken Bousfield and Eric Brown.

The Thunderbird course was certainly dramatic, its flat, lush expanse of grass contrasting sharply with the surrounding desert landscape. Furthermore, the fairways were narrow and bordered by punishing rough and plenty of water hazards. Very unusually for America, the greens were in poor shape. For once, the British started well, with Jacobs and Fallon winning the top foursomes against Jerry Barber and Chandler Harper in spite of the brilliant chipping of Barber (he holed three times from off the green, even though he had described the greens as being like a piece of asphalt driveway, all bumps, dips and twists). However, although the other matches were reasonably close, the British lost all of them and ended the day 3–1 down. There were some good British performances in the singles, notably John Jacobs' fine round of 65 in the afternoon to beat Dr Cary Middlecroft, and Eric Brown's 3 and 2 victory over Jerry Barber. Arthur Lees also beat Marty Furgol 3 and 2. However, the remaining matches were all won by the USA to give them another easy Ryder Cup victory, this time by 8–4. Nevertheless, Bernard Darwin felt able to write in *The Times*:

> The fact that no match ended before the 34th green indicates how close the issue really was and Britain had certainly done better than ever before.

And that fine aviator Lord Brabazon of Tara, President of the British PGA, said, harking back to Churchill's famous wartime speech:

> We have learnt a lot, although we have lost, and we are going back to practise in the streets and on the beaches.

5–6 November 1955 Thunderbird Golf & Country Club, Palm Springs, California, USA *Captains:* D.J. Rees (Great Britain and Ireland), C. Harbert (USA)			
Great Britain and Ireland		**United States**	
Foursomes			
J. Fallon & J.R.M. Jacobs (1 hole)	1	C. Harper & J. Barber	0
E.C. Brown & S. Scott	0	D. Ford & T. Kroll (5 & 4)	1
A. Lees & H. Weetman	0	J. Burke & T. Bolt (1 hole)	1
H. Bradshaw & D.J. Rees	0	S. Snead & C. Middlecoff (3 & 2)	1
Singles			
C. O'Connor	0	T. Bolt (4 & 2)	1
S. Scott	0	C. Harbert (3 & 2)	1
J.R.M. Jacobs (1 hole)	1	C. Middlecoff	0
D.J. Rees	0	S. Snead (3 & 1)	1
A. Lees (3 & 2)	1	M. Furgol	0
E.C. Brown (3 & 2)	1	J. Barber	0
H. Bradshaw	0	J. Burke (3 & 2)	1
H. Weetman	0	D. Ford (3 & 2)	1
Great Britain and Ireland 4; USA 8			

'You could have knocked us down with a feather'

And so to Lindrick in 1957. Why Lindrick? The answer was money. The British PGA were still struggling to finance the Ryder Cup match and were grateful to a Sheffield businessman, Sir Stuart Goodwin, for giving £10,000 (about £300,000 in today's money) to pay for it. However, he did insist it be played at his home club, Lindrick, a heathland course with tree-lined fairways in south Yorkshire. It was an unpopular choice in Britain as it was thought it would favour the Americans far more than a links course. Furthermore, it was only 6,541 yards long with several holes requiring only a driver and a wedge, again a feature likely to suit the Americans with their renowned short game skills.

The British side was selected by a new system that involved awarding points for finishes in the top twenty in all professional stroke-play tournaments. There were also points for good performances in the Dunlop Masters and

PGA Matchplay events. This resulted in a team considered by most to be the strongest possible though some, including Jacobs himself, considered John Jacobs a surprising omission. In fact Jacobs, later a renowned golf teacher, played in only the 1955 match (in which he won both his matches). In 1953 he had won two of the four qualifying competition rounds around which that year's side was picked, but still did not make the team. In 1957, even though he had grown up at Lindrick and in spite of his fine performance in the 1955 match, again he was not picked. He felt he should have played three times. However, if he had, he might not have kept his 100 per cent record intact!

The team that did face the Americans was a mixture of experience – Dai Rees (captain), Ken Bousfield, Eric Brown, Christy O'Connor, Harry Bradshaw, Max Faulkner and Harry Weetman – and promising youngsters – the recalled Peter Alliss and Bernard Hunt and a newcomer to the Ryder Cup, Peter Mills. For once, the American team did not look as strong as it could have done. Ben Hogan and Sam Snead had turned down invitations to play. Cary Middlecroft and Julius Boros had been omitted because they had played in a lucrative exhibition match rather than the PGA Championship.

Britain made a poor start. Rees sent out Alliss and Hunt as his opening pair, perhaps mindful of their traumatic finishes at Wentworth in 1953. This tactic did not work and they lost 2 and 1 to the supposedly weak pairing of Doug Ford and Dow Finsterwald. However, Rees himself and Bousfield won the second match against Art Wall and Fred Hawkins. In the third match, Faulkner and Weetman played badly and lost to Ted Kroll and Jack Burke. In the final match Brown and O'Connor were overwhelmed by some excellent golf from Tommy Bolt and Dick Mayer. Yet again, the British found themselves 3–1 down at the end of the first day.

The anxious Rees called his team together to discuss tactics for the singles the next day. He discovered that Weetman and Faulkner had played very poorly, and indeed Faulkner, after saying that his playing was 'rubbish', asked to be left out of the singles. Rees also dropped Weetman. This was to have repercussions because Weetman told a journalist that he would never play for Rees again. Needless to say, this appeared as a headline in the next day's newspaper.

In spite of this off-course upset, Britain made a good start to the singles when Eric Brown beat the explosive Tommy Bolt – known at different times as 'Terrible' Tommy Bolt, 'Lightning' Bolt and 'Thunder' Bolt – in a bad-tempered game with the British crowd, sensing Bolt's flawed temperament, winding him up by quietly cheering his wayward drives and missed putts. When Brown eventually won 4 and 3, Bolt said to him: 'You may have won, but I did not enjoy it one little bit.' The tough Scot, Brown, replied: 'After the whipping I gave you, I wouldn't have enjoyed it either.' When Bolt complained further to his team-mate Ed Furgol, Furgol told him to 'pipe down – you were well and truly licked'.

After this start, the British suddenly began to get on top in most of the matches. Alliss lost to Hawkins 2 and 1 but, elsewhere, the young Peter Mills beat the American captain, Jack Burke, 5 and 3, Dai Rees beat Ed Furgol 7 and 6 and Christy O'Connor beat Dow Finsterwald, also 7 and 6. Hunt avenged his Wentworth performance and beat Doug Ford 6 and 5. Finally, Harry Bradshaw halved with Dick May and Great Britain had won 7½–4½, with the Americans gaining only one and half points from a possible eight on the second day. It was unprecedented. What had happened?

First of all, it has to be said that the accommodation for the American team was very poor and, as for their wives, there were not even ladies' lavatories or 'bathrooms' at Lindrick Golf Club. As Henry Longhurst put it:

> The arrangements made for the American team were grossly inadequate and what they must have thought of us I do not care to think. When all was over, some did not even stay for the prize-giving and practically none turned up for the dinner.

Bernard Darwin wrote in *The Times*:

> Frankly you could have knocked us all down with a feather.
> Once they [the USA] were confronted with the possibility of defeat they collapsed. There is no other word for it, and it was something we do not expect from Americans.

In some ways, it was a low point for the Ryder Cup because of the falling-out between Weetman and Rees which received such widespread coverage, and also thanks to the publicity that the American press gave to Bolt's complaints about the behaviour of the crowd. However, the comment by Harry Moffitt, President of the United States PGA, proved to be more prophetic of the future. He said:

> Several of the team came to me and said how the crowd had been very fair. They had applauded their good shots as well as those of their opponents ... The result will prove to be a wonderful boost to the competition and the Ryder Cup will go on for years and years.

4–5 October 1957			
Lindrick Club, Sheffield, Yorkshire, England			
Captains: D.J. Rees (Great Britain and Ireland), J. Burke (USA)			
Great Britain and Ireland		**United States**	
Foursomes			
P. Alliss & B.J. Hunt	0	D. Ford & D. Finsterwald (2 & 1)	1
K. Bousfield & D.J. Rees (3 & 2)	1	A. Wall & F. Hawkins	0
M. Faulkner & H. Weetman	0	T. Kroll & J. Burke (4 & 3)	1
C. O'Connor & E.C. Brown	0	R. Mayer & T. Bolt (7 & 5)	1
Singles			
E.C. Brown (4 & 3)	1	T. Bolt	0
R.P. Mills (5 & 3)	1	J. Burke	0
P. Alliss	0	F. Hawkins (2 & 1)	1
K. Bousfield (4 & 3)	1	L. Herbert	0
D.J Rees (7 & 6)	1	E. Furgol	0
B.J. Hunt (6 & 5)	1	D. Ford	0
C. O'Connor (7 & 6)	1	D. Finsterwald	0
H. Bradshaw (halved)	½	R. Mayer (halved)	½
Great Britain and Ireland 7½; USA 4½			

Crushed again

Needless to say, after the excitement and success of 1957, the British looked forward to the 1959 contest, to be played at the Eldorado Country Club, Palm Springs, California in November, with fresh hope. Unfortunately, things went wrong from the moment the team left Britain.

To help the team to bond it was decided that they should sail to New York on the *Queen Elizabeth* and then take the train across to Los Angeles before flying the last few miles. However, the Atlantic crossing was very rough and nearly all of the team were seasick. The train journey was all right if rather long, but the short trip by air over the San Jacinto Mountains was nearly disastrous. They hit a storm and after juddering violently, the aircraft plunged 5,000 feet. Fortunately, everyone in the team except Bernard Hunt was strapped in. Hunt had gallantly given up his seat to an air hostess and was sent flying into the roof of the aircraft, sustaining severe bruising and a damaged shoulder. Gradually, calm was restored but then the Palm Desert airport was closed and they had to return to Los Angeles. Rather than fly again, the team opted for the Greyhound bus.

When they finally arrived, the British found the course long at 6,823 yards, tight and with many greens guarded by water, a feature few of them were used to.

Slightly surprisingly, though there may have been some gamesmanship on Rees's part behind it, Bernard Darwin wrote in *The Times*:

> D.J. Rees, British Isles captain, is critical of the move here … in removing all out-of-bounds markers on the course … says the change reduces the premium on drives, particularly hooked shots which the original markers made costly … Rees thinks that the tougher the course the better are their chances. He says the Americans are accustomed to easy courses on the tournament circuit.

Not surprisingly, Hunt and Brown lost the first foursome match and Rees and Bousfield the second. However, Christy O'Connor and Peter Alliss beat Art Wall and Doug Ford; and Harry Weetman and newcomer Dave Thomas halved with Sam Snead and Cary Middlecroft. Weetman (obviously the spat and words at Lindrick had been forgiven, if not forgotten) made a terrible blunder at the final hole. He and Thomas were one up and when Snead put his second into the water, victory for the British seemed assured. Instead of playing short and chipping on, Weetman went for the green and also went into the water. The Americans chipped and one-putted, the British chipped and two-putted. Instead of 2–2 it was 2½–1½ to the Americans at the end of the first day.

The singles were a disaster for the British; one American newspaper said correctly that they had been 'crushed'. Only

Eric Brown won, though Alliss and Norman Drew halved.
The final score was: USA 8½, Great Britain 3½.

Leonard Crawley of the *Daily Telegraph* was forgiving of
the British team's performance, writing:

> I regard it as essential that the British party should fly
> out one week beforehand and get rid of the present two
> weeks' unnecessary preliminaries wandering about the
> United States and tiring themselves like the children
> of Israel in the desert before getting to the promised
> land. Travelling, and getting the kindest hospitality, is
> all great fun but nevertheless frightfully tiring.

6–7 November 1959			
Eldorado Country Club, Pal Desert, California, USA			
Captains: D.J. Rees (Great Britain and Ireland), S. Snead (USA)			
Great Britain and Ireland		**United States**	
Foursomes			
B.J. Hunt & E.C. Brown	0	R. Rosburg & M. Souchak (5 & 4)	1
D J Rees & K. Bousfield	0	J. Boros & D. Finsterwald (2 holes)	1
C. O'Connor & P. Alliss (3 & 2)	1	A. Wall & D. Ford	0
H. Weetman & D.C. Thomas (halved)	½	S. Snead & C. Middlecoff (halved)	½
Singles			
N.V. Drew (halved)	½	D. Ford (halved)	½
K. Bousfield	0	M. Souchak (3 & 2)	1
H. Weetman	0	R. Rosburg (6 & 5)	1
D.C. Thomas	0	S. Snead (6 & 5)	1
C. O'Connor	0	A. Wall (7 & 6)	1
D.J. Rees	0	D. Finsterwald (1 hole)	1
P. Alliss (halved)	½	J. Hebert (halved)	½
E.C. Brown (4 & 3)	1	C. Middlecoff	0
Great Britain and Ireland 3½; USA 8½			

Chapter 3

Is this match worth playing?

Must have the captain in control
Royal Lytham 1961

Must include fourballs
Eastlake, Atlanta 1963

The American short game is still superior
Royal Birkdale 1965

'The finest golfers in the world'
Champions, Houston 1967

'I don't think you would have missed that putt, Tony'
Royal Birkdale 1969

Must have the captain in control

Before the next match, at Royal Lytham & St Annes on 13 and 14 October 1961, the two PGAs decided to make changes to the format. Instead of four foursomes over 36 holes on the first day and eight singles, again of 36 holes, on the second day, there would now be eight foursomes of eighteen holes on the first day and two sets of singles, eight in the morning and eight in the afternoon, on the second day. There was a strong feeling among the British that they would stand a better chance over the 'sprints' of eighteen holes. As a result, there were now 24 points at stake instead of twelve.

America brought some new and exciting players in the shape of Billy Casper, Bill Collins, Gene Littler and the redoubtable Arnold Palmer who had won the Open Championship earlier in the year.

Much to the disappointment of most Americans and indeed many British golf fans, they did not bring Sam Snead because the US PGA was offended by his playing in a non-authorised tournament.

Dai Rees, British captain for the fourth time, kept most of his 1959 team but John Panton returned after eight years and Neil Coles began what would be a long Ryder Cup career. The British team did not start well. Used to being 3–1 down after the foursomes, with the new format, true to form they finished 6–2 down. There was criticism of Rees, who picked the same pairings in the afternoon that had lost 3–1 in the morning, and they duly lost 3–1 again. Henry Longhurst said:

> If we have to have 18-hole matches, which I most devoutly hope, then either the order of both morning and afternoon matches must be announced overnight, or we must have a non-playing captain or the captain

must not play himself in the morning. [The US captain, Jerry Barber, had an assistant non-playing captain, Ed Oliver, and furthermore did not play himself in the morning]. Or the captain, if he plays in the morning, must have a sort of assistant-cum-advisor with whom to consult at lunchtime. In the foursomes Rees had hardly got in when the first match was due to go out in the afternoon, and this threw an impossible burden of selection upon him. He could have seen nothing of the other players; he had only minutes to decide; and he had to get his own lunch and rest. He thus made what most critics deemed an error of selection which he later defended on the grounds that the players concerned could hardly play so badly twice running.

Matters did not improve in the first set of singles and with eight singles to go on Sunday afternoon, the Americans were leading 11–5. Only a complete whitewash in the afternoon would bring the Cup back to Britain. They did win four matches and halve one, but it was not good enough and the Americans won by the comfortable margin of 14½ to 9½.

In the criticism of the British performance that followed, Tom Scott wrote in *Golf Illustrated*:

> It's the old story. Our men regard the match as something so special they are unable to play their regular golf at the start and when they come to their senses, their opponents are one or two holes to the good.

13–14 October 1961			
Royal Lytham & St Annes, St Annes, Lancashire, England			
Captains: D.J. Rees (Great Britain and Ireland), J. Barber (USA)			
Great Britain and Ireland		**United States**	
Foursomes: Morning			
C. O'Connor & P. Alliss (4 & 3)	1	D.J. Ford & G. Littler	0
J. Panton & B.J. Hunt	0	A. Wall & J. Hebert (4 & 3)	1
D.J. Rees & K. Bousfield	0	W Casper & A. Palmer (2 & 1)	1
T.B. Haliburton & N.C. Coles	0	W Collins & M. Souchak (1 hole)	1
Foursomes: Afternoon			
C. O'Connor & P. Alliss	0	A. Wall & J. Hebert (1 hole)	1
J .Panton & B.J. Hunt	0	W. Casper & A. Palmer (5 & 4)	1
D.J. Rees & K. Bousfield (2 & 1)	1	W. Collins & M. Souchak	0
T.B. Haliburton & N.C. Coles	0	J. Barber & D. Finsterwald (1 hole)	1
Singles: Morning			
H. Weetman	0	D. Ford (1 hole)	1
R.L. Moffitt	0	M. Souchak (5 & 4)	1
P. Alliss (halved)	½	A. Palmer (halved)	½
K. Bousfield	0	W. Casper 5 & 3)	1
D.J. Rees (2 & 1)	1	J. Hebert	0
N.C. Coles (halved)	½	G. Littler (halved)	½
B.J. Hunt (5 & 4)	1	J. Barber	0
C. O'Connor	0	D. Finsterwald (2 & 1)	1
Singles: Afternoon			
H. Weetman	0	A. Wall (1 hole)	1
P. Alliss (3 & 2)	1	W. Collins	0
B.J. Hunt	0	M. Souchak (2 & 1)	1
T.B. Haliburton	0	A. Palmer (2 & 1)	1
D.J. Rees (4 & 3)	1	D. Ford	0
K. Bousfield (1 hole)	1	J. Barber	0
N.C. Coles (1 hole)	1	D. Finsterwald	0
C. O'Connor (halved)	½	G. Littler (halved)	½
Great Britain and Ireland 9½; USA 14½			

Must include fourballs

After yet another victory, the US PGA now felt in a strong
position to press harder for the inclusion of fourballs in the
match instead of what most Americans call 'Scotch' foursomes. The British did not want to drop the foursomes and
a compromise was reached whereby the match would be

extended to three days and would include two sets of four-somes on the first day, two sets of fourballs on the second day and two sets of singles on the third day. All matches would be over eighteen holes. This increased the number of points on offer from 24 to 32. The new golf correspondent of *The Times*, Peter Ryde, commented that this was 'an encouraging aspect. By the end of tomorrow evening [Friday] only eight of these points will have been settled. Nothing really decisive will have happened.'

The match, at East Lake in Atlanta in October 1963, got off to a good start with the teams level at 2–2 at lunch on the first day. The good news from the British point of view did not last, though, as the Americans won 3–1 in the afternoon. It did not augur well for the fourballs and, in the event, the 5–3 deficit for the British became 12–4 after the fourballs. Under the circumstances, the British did well to win the morning singles 4½–3½ and the match was still just about alive as they went into the afternoon. The highlight, and Peter Alliss felt it was one of the highlights of his career, was his win over Arnold Palmer. However, victory for the US was inevitable and they won every match in the afternoon except Tony Lema's match against Peter Alliss, which was halved. The final score was USA 23 Great Britain 9, a very heavy defeat.

The US captain, Arnold Palmer, summed it up by saying: 'This team could beat the rest of the world combined.'

Peter Ryde wrote in *The Times*:

> The British Isles lost to a better side, but one could per-haps take that remark a step further and say that not for the first time they showed the gap between the two countries to be not so wide as is sometimes imagined … Two factors help to explain the widening of this gap; the brilliant performance in the middle of the contest

by the mainstays of the American side, notably Palmer, Casper and Finsterwald, who played such golf as it was no disgrace to lose to; and secondly the failure of the British players to seize their opportunities with the putter.

Henry Cotton added:

I repeat what I have often said, that we cannot win this match in America. Despite the advantage we have in playing our own small-sized golf ball on these short visits to play in international encounters, we again were outclassed. We know, and have known all along, since the game of golf got under way in the twenties, that good players were in great numbers there, and with the sun throughout the year, practice facilities and huge rewards, we were up against an insoluble problem. The present top home players, by no means poor performers, are leagues outside the tough American ones.

11–13 October 1963			
East Lake Country Club, Atlanta, Georgia, USA			
Captains: J. Fallon (Great Britain and Ireland), A. Palmer (USA)			
Great Britain and Ireland		**United States**	
Foursomes: Morning			
B. Huggett & G. Will (3 & 2)	1	A. Palmer & J. Pott	0
P. Alliss & C. O'Connor	0	W. Casper & D. Ragan (1 hole)	1
N.C. Coles & B.J. Hunt (halved)	½	J. Boros & A. Lema (halved)	½
D. Thomas & H. Weetman (halved)	½	G. Littler & D. Finsterwald (halved)	½
Foursomes: Afternoon			
D. Thomas & H. Weetman	0	W. Maxwell & R. Goalby (4 & 3)	1
B. Huggett & G. Will	0	A. Palmer & W. Casper (5 & 4)	1
N.C. Coles & G.M. Hunt (2 &1)	1	G. Littler & D. Finsterwald	0
T.B. Haliburton & B.J. Hunt	0	J. Boros & A. Lema (1 hole)	1

(continued)

11–13 October 1963 (continued)			
East Lake Country Club, Atlanta, Georgia, USA			
Captains: J. Fallon (Great Britain and Ireland.), A. Palmer (USA)			
Great Britain and Ireland		**United States**	
Fourballs: Morning			
B. Huggett & D. Thomas	0	A. Palmer & D. Finsterwald (5 & 4)	1
P. Alliss & B.J. Hunt (halved)	½	G. Littler & J. Boros (halved)	½
H. Weetman & G. Will	0	W. Casper & W. Maxwell (3 & 2)	1
N.C. Coles & C. O'Connor	0	R. Goalby & D. Ragan (halved)	½
Fourballs: Afternoon			
N.C. Coles & C. O'Connor	0	A. Palmer & D. Finsterwald (3 & 2)	1
P. Alliss & B.J. Hunt	0	A. Lema & J. Pott (1 hole)	1
T.B. Haliburton & G.M. Hunt	0	W. Casper & W. Maxwell (2 & 1)	1
B. Huggett & D. Thomas (halved)	½	R. Goalby & D. Ragan (halved)	½
Singles: Morning			
G.M. Hunt	0	A. Lema (5 & 3)	1
B. Huggett (3 & 1)	1	J. Pott	0
P. Alliss (1 hole)	1	A. Palmer	0
N.C. Coles (halved)	½	W. Casper (halved)	½
D. Thomas	0	R. Goalby (3 & 2)	1
C. O'Connor	0	G. Littler (1 hole)	1
H. Weetman (1 hole)	1	J. Boros	0
B.J. Hunt (2 holes)	1	D. Finsterwald	0
Singles: Afternoon			
G. Will	0	A. Palmer (3 & 2)	1
N.C. Coles	0	D. Ragan (2 & 1)	1
P. Alliss (halved)	½	A. Lema (halved)	½
T.B. Haliburton	0	G. Littler (6 & 5)	1
H. Weetman	0	J. Boros (2 & 1)	1
C. O'Connor	0	W. Maxwell (2 & 1)	1
D. Thomas	0	D. Finsterwald (4 & 3)	1
B.J. Hunt	0	R. Goalby (2 & 1)	1
Great Britain and Ireland 9; USA 23			

The American short game is still superior

Back to Royal Birkdale in England for the 1965 match. It is difficult to believe today but the British PGA was still struggling to finance the event. On this occasion they were helped out by a businessman, Brian Park, who donated

£11,000 (about £200,000 in today's money). Park also knew a bit about marketing and a large tented village was put up with space given for sponsors, restaurants, bars and children's games. For the first time in Britain journalists were given a media centre and young ladies drove round the course in Mini Mokes telling the crowds the scores in all the matches.

Apart from all this razzmatazz, how was the golf? The British retained seven players from the team at East Lake in 1963 – Harry Weetman as captain, Peter Alliss, Bernard Hunt, Christy O'Connor, George Will, Neil Coles and Dave Thomas – and they were joined by newcomers Peter Butler, James Martin, Lionel Platts and Jimmy Hitchcock. The Americans, captained by the legendary Byron Nelson, brought Arnold Palmer, Tony Lema, Billy Casper, Julius Boros and Gene Littler from their 1963 team as well as Ken Venturi, Don January, Dave Marr and Tommy Jacobs.

After the first day the teams were level at 4–4, a much better start than usual for the British team. Furthermore, in the morning the great Arnold Palmer and his partner, Dave Marr, had been beaten 6 and 5 by Will and Thomas which lifted the spirits of both the British team and the home crowd. That said, when the same pairs were matched again the Americans reversed the result exactly – 6 and 5 to them. Alliss and O'Connor were the British heroes, winning both their matches.

How would the British cope on the second day when it was fourballs, supposedly where the Americans were at their strongest? Again it was closer than in the past but even so, the Americans went into the final day of singles 9–7 ahead. There was still hope for the British camp but the Americans won the first four singles matches to stretch their lead to 13–7. That really was a mountain to climb for Britain and it proved too much for them. The British did secure another five and half points but the Americans won comfortably yet again, this time 19½–2½.

Afterwards, when the reasons for this were analysed, it was clear that the large amount of rain there had been meant that three of the long finishing holes, 15, 17 and 18, were not reachable in two. The final shot was going to be a wedge and the Americans had long been superior to the British in this department of the game. Indeed, after the match, as *The Times* said:

> The American captain, Byron Nelson, suggested that pitching from 60 yards was, if anything, the department in which his team were superior … I think that well though our men putted on the first two days, the Americans have developed almost an instinct for recognising the crucial putt and holing it. That is attributable to a tougher competitive spirit. We are not supermen, said Nelson, we just play more tournaments.

Peter Ryde of *The Times* also wrote:

> I offer only two small criticisms; a minor one is the absurd number of people allowed inside the ropes; by the end it would not have surprised me to learn that special armlets had been issued to caddies' mothers-in-law. The other concerns the golf. The 32 matches played seemed to me too much golf – a case of the game suffering for financial considerations. Some reductions in playing could be made without sacrificing any of the three days … A number of players agreed there were too many matches. It puts the emphasis too much on stamina.

7–9 October 1965			
Royal Birkdale, Southport, Lancashire, England			
Captains: H. Weetman (Great Britain and Ireland), B. Nelson (USA)			
Great Britain and Ireland		**United States**	
Foursomes: Morning			
L. Platts & P.J. Butler	0	J. Boros & A. Lema (1 hole)	1
D.C. Thomas & G. Will (6 & 5)	1	A. Palmer & D. Marr	0
B.J. Hunt & N.C. Coles	0	W. Casper & G. Littler (2 & 1)	1
P. Alliss & C. O'Connor (5 & 4)	1	K. Venturi & D. January	0
Foursomes: Afternoon			
D. Thomas & G. Will	0	A. Palmer & D. Marr (6 & 5)	1
P. Alliss & C. O'Connor (2 & 1)	1	W. Casper & G. Littler	0
J. Martin & J. Hitchcock	0	J. Boros & A. Lema (5 & 4)	1
B.J. Hunt & N.C. Coles (3 & 2)	1	K. Venturi & D. January	0
Fourballs: Morning			
D.C. Thomas & G. Will	0	D. January & T. Jacobs (1 hole)	1
L. Platts & P. Butler (halved)	½	W. Casper & G. Littler (halved)	½
P. Alliss & C. O'Connor	0	A. Palmer & D. Marr (6 & 4)	1
B.J. Hunt & N.C. Coles (1 hole)	1	J. Boros & A. Lema	0
Fourballs: Afternoon			
P. Alliss & C. O'Connor (2 holes)	1	A. Palmer & D. Marr	0
D.C. Thomas & G. Will	0	D. January & T. Jacobs (1 hole)	1
L. Platts & P.J. Butler (halved)	½	W. Casper & G. Littler (halved)	½
B.J. Hunt & N.C. Coles	0	K. Venturi & A. Lema (1 hole)	1
Singles: Morning			
J. Hitchcock	0	A. Palmer (3 & 2)	1
L. Platts	0	J. Boros (4 & 2)	1
P.J. Butler	0	A. Lema (1 hole)	1
N.C. Coles	0	D. Marr (2 holes)	1
B.J. Hunt (2 holes)	1	G. Littler	0
D.C. Thomas	0	T. Jacobs (2 & 1)	1
P. Alliss (1 hole)	1	W. Casper	0
G. Will (halved)	½	D. January (halved)	½
Singles: Afternoon			
C. O'Connor	0	A. Lema (6 & 4)	1
J. Hitchcock	0	J. Boros (2 & 1)	1
P.J. Butler	0	A. Palmer (2 holes)	1
P. Alliss (3 & 1)	1	K. Venturi	0
N.C. Coles (3 & 2)	1	W. Casper	0
G. Will	0	G. Littler (2 & 1)	1
B.J. Hunt	0	D. Marr (1 hole)	1
L. Platts (1 hole)	1	T. Jacobs	0
Great Britain and Ireland 12½; USA 19½			

'The finest golfers in the world'

From the British point of view, matters did not improve in 1967 when the Americans won very convincingly, 23½–8½, at the Champions Golf Club, Houston. The tough Ben Hogan, non-playing captain of the United States team, set the tone at the pre-match dinner. Following a long and tedious speech by the British non-playing captain Dai Rees, in which he had detailed all the achievements of his team, Ben Hogan merely said:

> Ladies and gentlemen, the United States Ryder Cup team – the finest golfers in the world.

He played the role of captain like he played golf; with utter determination and discipline. To him, everyone in his team was equal and when Arnold Palmer, on being told that the US team would play the small British ball, said 'But I don't play the small ball,' Hogan replied: 'Who says you are playing?'

Hogan seemed to have a problem with Palmer. As *The Times* reported:

> The dropping of Palmer in the previous series had not been explained. When asked the reason, their captain Ben Hogan said, 'Because I chose not to play him', and when approached by a suitably deferential reporter with, 'Mr Hogan, may I ask you why you made that choice?' The reply came, 'You may ask, but I shall not tell you.'

Whatever Hogan thought of Palmer, the rest of the world was in awe of him. Learning the game from his father, Deacon Palmer, head professional and greenkeeper at Latrobe Country Club, he won the 1955 Cavendish Open in his rookie season and his first Major, the Masters in 1958. In

1960 he became the first client of the peerless sports agent Mark McCormack, who said that Palmer was especially easy to market thanks to his good looks, his relatively modest background, the way he played whereby he was never afraid to take risks, his involvement in a string of close finishes in televised events and his affability. He is also credited for putting the Open Championship on the map as far as American golfers were concerned. McCormack should also be credited for convincing Palmer that if he emulated Bobby Jones, Sam Snead and Ben Hogan by winning the Open, he would become a truly global star. In the end he won seven Majors – the Masters in 1958, 1960, 1962 and 1964, the US Open in 1960 and the Open Championship in 1961 and 1962.

He made many quotable comments such as:

What other people may find in poetry, I find in the flight of a good drive.

Golf is deceptively simple and endlessly complicated.

Putting is a fascinating, aggravating, wonderful, terrible and almost incomprehensible part of the game of golf.

One thing I've learnt over time is, if you hit a ball into water, it won't float.

When I was in college I thought about becoming an attorney. But I wasn't smart enough; I hate being cooped up indoors; and I'm too nice a guy.

The only really unplayable lie I can think of is when you're supposed to be playing golf and come home with lipstick on your collar.

Once the match started the manifestly better American team soon imposed their superiority, winning the foursomes 5½–2½. Of the British team only the fresh young Tony Jacklin, playing with the experienced Dave Thomas, won both his matches. He confessed to being very nervous and said that Thomas had been a huge help in steadying him. The fourballs were won by the Americans, who were victorious in the first seven matches before Jacklin and Thomas scrambled a half in the final match against Littler and Geiberger. Now, unfortunately for Britain, the Americans were leading 12½–3½ going into the singles. And then they won the first three singles to make it 15½–3½, effectively closing the British out. The final score was a triumphant – or for the British humiliating – 23½–8½. Only Huggett, Coles (twice) and Alliss managed to secure victories for Great Britain and Ireland.

Since the matches had been restarted in 1947, the Americans had won ten of the eleven contests and the matter of whether or not the matches should continue was being seriously questioned. Peter Ryde wrote in *The Times*:

> There has been more talk than usual of ending Ryder Cup matches because public interest in the United States is dying and because some of the players would rather spend the time earning money elsewhere ... My impression is that, among American Ryder Cup players, pride and interest still have the upper hand ... and they would not bring it to an end unless that is what the players want.

There was much criticism in the British press. To counter it, Rees said that the British must do three things if they were going to compete with the Americans:

1. Water the greens
2. Improve their short game and hit the ball instead of flicking it
3. Use the American size of golf ball.

The British PGA had long resisted this last suggestion and indeed there was much opposition throughout the British golfing world. However, the PGA finally agreed to a three-year experiment of using the American ball in professional tournaments.

20–22 October 1967			
Champions Golf Club, Houston, Texas, USA			
Captains: D.J. Rees (Great Britain and Ireland), B. Hogan (USA)			
Great Britain and Ireland		**United States**	
Foursomes: Morning			
B. Huggett & G. Will (halved)	½	W. Casper & J. Boros (halved)	½
P. Alliss & C. O'Connor	0	A. Palmer & G. Dickinson (2 & 1)	1
A. Jacklin & D.C Thomas (4 & 3)	1	D. Sanders & G. Brewer	0
B.J. Hunt & N.C Coles	0	R. Nichols & J. Pott (6& 5)	1
Foursomes: Afternoon			
B. Huggett & G. Will	0	W. Casper & J. Boros (1 hole)	1
M. Gregson & H. Boyle	0	G. Dickinson & A. Palmer (5 & 6)	1
A. Jacklin & D.C. Thomas (3 & 2)	1	G. Littler & A. Geiberger	0
P. Alliss & C. O'Connor	0	R. Nichols & J. Pott (2 & 1)	1
Fourballs: Morning			
P. Alliss & C. O'Connor	0	W. Casper & G. Brewer (3 & 2)	1
B.J. Hunt & N.C. Coles	0	R. Nichols & J. Pott (1 hole)	1
A. Jacklin & D.C. Thomas	0	G. Littler & A. Geiberger (1 hole)	1
B. Huggett & G. Will	0	G. Dickinson & D. Sanders (3 & 2)	1
Fourballs: Afternoon			
B.J. Hunt & N.C. Coles	0	W. Casper & G. Brewer (5 & 3)	1
P. Alliss & M. Gregson	0	G. Dickinson & D. Sanders (3 & 2)	1
G. Will & H. Boyle	0	A. Palmer & J. Boros (1 hole)	1
A. Jacklin & D.C. Thomas (halved)	½	G. Littler & A. Geiberger (halved)	½

(continued)

20–22 October 1967 (continued)			
Champions Golf Club, Houston, Texas, USA			
Captains: D.J. Rees (Great Britain and Ireland), B. Hogan (USA)			
Great Britain and Ireland		**United States**	
Singles: Morning			
H. Boyle	0	G. Brewer (4 & 3)	1
P. Alliss	0	W. Casper (2 & 1)	1
A. Jacklin	0	A. Palmer (3 & 2)	1
B. Huggett (1 hole)	1	J. Boros	0
N.C. Coles (2 & 1)	1	D. Sanders	0
M. Gregson	0	A. Geiberger (4 & 2)	1
D.C. Thomas (halved)	½	G. Littler (halved)	½
B.J. Hunt (halved)	½	R. Nichols (halved)	½
Singles: Afternoon			
B. Huggett	0	A. Palmer (5 & 3)	1
P. Alliss (2 & 1)	1	G. Brewer	0
A. Jacklin	0	G. Dickinson (3 & 2)	1
C. O'Connor	0	R. Nichols (3 & 2)	1
G. Will	0	J. Pott (3 & 1)	1
M. Gregson	0	A. Geiberger (2 & 1)	1
B.J. Hunt (halved)	½	J. Boros (halved)	½
N.C. Coles (2 & 1)	1	D. Sanders	0
Great Britain and Ireland 8½; USA 23½			

'I don't think you would have missed that putt, Tony'

For the moment the Ryder Cup survived and fortunately the 1969 match, held again at Royal Birkdale, proved to be a memorable one.

The Americans were clearly favourites but maybe not as much of a red-hot certainty as the bookies were suggesting with their odds. *The Times* asked their captain Sam Snead how he felt about his team being 5 to 1 favourites:

He expressed surprise and added thoughtfully 'I don't see it quite like that' ... Recalling that Byron Nelson's assessment of the match here four years ago was that the Americans won because from 60 yards in they were setting up the birdie putts, Snead reminded us that for the past two years the British had been playing with the bigger ball and that their short pitching might well have closed the gap.

At last, the great Jack Nicklaus was able to play and, on the British side, Tony Jacklin had just become the first Englishman to win the Open Championship since Max Faulkner at Royal Portrush as long ago as 1951.

For once, the British started well, winning the opening foursomes 3½–½. The Americans hit back in the afternoon by winning 3–1. Nevertheless, at the end of day one the British were leading 4½–3½. Jacklin, playing with the newcomer Peter Townsend, had won both his matches. Nicklaus, not playing in the morning, just won on the 18th partnering Dan Sikes against Peter Butler and Bernard Hunt. The second day was just as close and in the afternoon controversy arose when, in the match between Brian Huggett and Bernard Gallacher and the Americans Dave Hill and Ken Still, the British claimed that Hill had putted out of turn.

This is how it happened: on the seventh green Hill, further away than any of the others and the only player to reach the green in two, putted and left his putt two feet short. He then walked up and tapped it in for a four. Still, realising he could not improve on this, picked up his ball, and the Americans waited to see if either of the British could hole his putt to secure a half. At this point, Gallacher claimed that Hill had putted out of turn. Strictly according to the rules, Gallacher was correct, but the Americans felt he was being overly pedantic. Nevertheless, the referee had no option but to award the hole to the British pair. Apparently Still became furious, argued with the referee and then picked up Gallacher's ball marker, saying: 'You can have the hole and the goddamn Cup.' As the argument continued on the next tee, Hill hit his tee-shot and then told Gallacher that if he did not shut up he would get his iron wrapped round his neck. The bad feeling continued but the Americans managed to win 2 and 1.

The day finished with the two teams level at 8–8. It had been quite an eventful couple of days. Out of sixteen matches, twelve had gone to the last green, three to the 17th and one to the 16th. What a final day lay in prospect! The singles started badly for the British with both Alliss and Townsend losing the first two matches to Trevino and Hill. However, Coles beat Tommy Aaron before Brian Barnes lost to Billy Casper. Then the British came good with Christy O'Connor, Maurice Bembridge, Peter Butler and Tony Jacklin all winning against Beard, Still, Floyd and Nicklaus. Jacklin's 4 and 3 victory over Nicklaus was a particular cause for celebration. Coming into the final eight singles, the British were leading 13–11. They only needed 3½ points from the last eight. They won two and lost two of the first four matches, so they now only needed 1½ points from the last four. Unfortunately they then lost the next two matches so, with two matches to go, the score was 15–15.

The last two matches were between the powerful Billy Casper and the tough little Welshman Brian Huggett and, in the very final match, the legendary Jack Nicklaus and the rising star, Tony Jacklin. Huggett had been trailing Casper by one hole for most of the round but on the 16th Casper's drive finished in a bunker, as did his second shot. Huggett kept his cool and won the hole. All square with two to go. Casper got a birdie at 17 but Huggett, under enormous pressure, holed a seven-foot putt to secure a half. On the 18th both reached the green in two and Casper two-putted for a birdie 4. Huggett had a four-footer for a half. Just as he was about to putt there was a huge roar from the crowd around the 17th green. Jacklin had just holed a 40-foot putt for a half, but Huggett assumed he had won his match against

Nicklaus and that therefore his putt for a half with Casper would win the Cup for Britain. To his credit he holed it, only to be told that Britain were not quite there yet.

Down the 18th came Nicklaus and Jacklin. Both drove down the middle and Nicklaus, playing first, made the green and finished about 25 feet from the hole on the right of the green. Jacklin also made the green but was right at the back, leaving him a slightly longer putt. Jacklin putted well to within two feet of the hole, while Nicklaus did not play safe but went for the hole. He very nearly made it but the ball lipped out and finished five feet away. Now it was Nicklaus to putt: a deathly silence. He holed it. Jacklin to putt, to halve both his match and the whole match. But, as everyone knows, Nicklaus did not give him the chance. He spoke the oft-repeated words: 'I don't think you would have missed that putt, Tony, but, in the circumstances I wasn't going to give you that opportunity.'

Typical Nicklaus, the true gentleman of golf. Not surprisingly, in view of some of the tensions during the three days, some of the Americans were not best pleased with this generous gesture. But who remembers the others? Everyone remembers Jack Nicklaus.

Jack Nicklaus, the 'Golden Bear', is still considered by many to be the greatest golfer of all time. Will Tiger Woods ever overtake his record eighteen Majors? After victories in the US Amateur Championship in 1959 (at the age of nineteen) and 1961 he turned professional at the end of 1961. His first Major win was the US Open in 1962. This was followed by the Masters and PGA in 1963, the Masters in 1965 and 1966 and also the Open Championship in 1966, the US Open in 1967, the Open Championship in 1970, the PGA in 1971, the Masters and US Open in 1972, the PGA in 1973 and 1975 and also the Masters in 1975, the Open Championship in 1978, the US Open and PGA in 1980 and finally, at the age of 46, the Masters in 1986. For 25 years he was the man to beat.

His early rivalry was with Arnold Palmer and in those days Palmer seemed to be the golfers' favourite. One commentary encapsulated this with a saying that became famous:

> When God created Jack Nicklaus and Arnold Palmer, He turned to Nicklaus and said: 'You will be the greatest the game has ever seen.' Then he turned to Palmer, adding: 'But they will love you more.'

The truth is that Jack Nicklaus was a winner. As Ken Bowden wrote:

> There have been prettier swings of the club than Jack Nicklaus. There may have been better ball-strikers than Jack Nicklaus. There have definitely been better short-game exponents than Jack Nicklaus. Other golfers have putted as well as Jack Nicklaus. There may have been golfers as dedicated and fiercely competitive as Jack Nicklaus. But no individual has been able to develop and combine and sustain all of the complex physical skills and the immense mental and emotional resources the game demands at its highest level as well as Jack Nicklaus has for as long as he has.

There was, of course, much euphoria about this result, especially in Britain – though some, on reflection, felt that perhaps Britain had lost an opportunity to win and bring back the Cup to Britain (as the holders, the USA, retained the Cup). In *The Times* Peter Ryde said, under the headline 'Test of stamina should not be overdone':

Only one fault stands out from the splendour of last week's Ryder Cup match. There was, in my opinion, too much golf. I have always opposed the introduction of the four-ball matches on the second day, and if I do so again it is only because nothing but a superb day of weather stood between the programme of that day and a shambles. Even with maximum daylight which on the past three occasions we have had for those matches, crucial putts have had to be holed, and more often missed, in semi-darkness.

This year the Professional Golfers' Association, in defending the possibility that play would be incomplete on Friday and matches resumed first thing Saturday, said they had not counted on so many matches coming to the 18th; but in drawing up a programme for a match of this stature they have no right to gamble on the weather or the length of matches.

There is a more serious objection to these four and a half hour matches inserted into the programmes. They restrict the power of the two captains to manoeuvre their order of play and indeed their choice of player.

Townsend was neither making excuses nor complaining when he said: 'After seven holes in the afternoon of the second day, my legs just turned to jelly: I had nothing on which to base my swing. After all, if you include time spent on the practice ground, I and others were out there for the best part of 11 hours on four-ball day.' Trevino was another whose game suffered from sheer fatigue; no American gave more to the contest than he did; he simply wore himself out.

Some survive; Jacklin showed us how basically tough he is by not only surviving, but triumphing; his counterpart on the American team was Hill, who played all six. He may have been spurred on to great deeds on the last day by the unfavourable light in which certain incidents on the second day left him, and he won both times by a comfortable margin. It was a fine performance, for his figures against Townsend were of the best, but it hardly proves a case for exhausting most of the players.

Four-ball matches can be defended on the grounds that they increase profits from the match and that they make a good subject for television. But is there any golfing reason for having them? The Ryder Cup is, to a certain extent, a spectacle, a public entertainment, but so long as it remains in any degree a contest between two countries, and not just a money-making project, considerations of profit and television should be secondary to the game.

18–20 September 1969 Royal Birkdale, Southport, Lancashire, England *Captains:* E.C. Brown (Great Britain and Ireland), S. Snead (USA)			
Great Britain and Ireland		**United States**	
Foursomes: Morning			
N.C. Coles & B.G Huggett (3 & 2)	1	M. Barber & R. Floyd	0
B. Gallacher & M. Bembridge (2 & 1)	1	L. Trevino & K. Still	0
A. Jacklin & P. Townsend (3 & 1)	1	D. Hill & T. Aaron	0
C. O'Connor & P. Alliss (halved)	½	W. Casper & F. Beard (halved)	½
Foursomes: Afternoon			
N.C. Coles & B. Huggett	0	D. Hill & T. Aaron (1 hole)	1
B. Gallacher & M. Bembridge	0	L. Trevino & G. Littler (1 hole)	1
A. Jacklin & P. Townsend (1 hole)	1	W. Casper & F. Beard	0
P.J. Butler & B.J. Hunt	0	J. Nicklaus & D. Sikes (1 hole)	1
Fourballs: Morning			
C. O'Connor & P. Townsend (1 hole)	1	D. Hill & D. Douglass	0
B. Huggett & G.A. Caygill (halved)	½	R. Floyd & M. Barber (halved)	½
B. Barnes & P. Alliss	0	L. Trevino & G. Littler (1 hole)	1
A. Jacklin & N.C. Coles (1 hole)	1	J. Nicklaus & D. Sikes	0

(continued)

18–20 September 1969 (continued)			
Royal Birkdale, Southport, Lancashire, England			
Captains: E.C. Brown (Great Britain and Ireland), S. Snead (USA)			
Great Britain and Ireland		**United States**	
Fourballs: Afternoon			
P.J. Butler & P. Townsend	0	W. Casper & F. Beard (2 holes)	1
B. Huggett & B. Gallacher	0	D. Hill & K. Still (2 & 1)	1
M. Bembridge & B.J. Hunt (halved)	½	T. Aaron & R. Floyd (halved)	½
A. Jacklin & N.C. Coles (halved)	½	L. Trevino & M. Barber (halved)	½
Singles: Morning			
P. Alliss	0	L. Trevino (2 & 1)	1
P. Townsend	0	D. Hill (5 & 4)	1
N.C. Coles (1 hole)	1	T. Aaron	0
B. Barnes	0	W. Casper (1 hole)	1
C. O'Connor (5 & 4)	1	F. Beard	0
M. Bembridge (1 hole)	1	K. Still	0
P.J. Butler (1 hole)	1	R. Floyd	0
A. Jacklin (4 & 3)	1	J. Nicklaus	0
Singles: Afternoon			
B. Barnes	0	D. Hill (4 & 2)	1
B. Gallacher (4 & 3)	1	L. Trevino	0
M. Bembridge	0	M. Barber (7 & 6)	1
P.J. Butler (3 & 2)	1	D. Douglass	0
N.C. Coles	0	D. Sikes (4 & 3)	1
C. O'Connor	0	G. Littler (2 & 1)	1
B. Huggett (halved)	½	W. Casper (halved)	½
A. Jacklin (halved)	½	J. Nicklaus (halved)	½
Great Britain and Ireland 16; USA 16			

Chapter 4

'Something has to be done to make it more of a match'

Same old story

On into the 1970s. Would Britain prove itself a match for the Americans or was 1969 just a blip? At least the close match in 1969, allied to Tony Jacklin's victory in the US Open Championship in 1970, persuaded American broadcasters to televise the 1971 match at Old Warson, St Louis, nationally for the first time. Certainly the British, with the combative Scot Eric Brown re-appointed as its non-playing captain, went out to America full of hope. He had personally enjoyed a remarkable singles record in the four matches he played from 1953 to 1959. The singles were still played over 36 holes and Brown won all four of his, beating Lloyd Mangrum in 1953, Jerry Barber in 1955, Tommy 'Lightning' Bolt in the surprise British victory at Lindrick in 1957 and Cary Middlecoff in 1959. Never one to miss a chance to wind up the enemy, Brown said that the rolling ground, narrow fairways and tight drives would suit his team better than it would the Americans.

Defying the hot weather, the British again won the foursomes on the first morning and, in spite of a US fightback in the afternoon, led 4½–3½ at the end of the first day.

Indeed, one American had said at lunch: 'I'm glad it's working out this way. Palmer said it was a cinch. He shouldn't shoot his mouth off.' Captain Eric Brown was delighted with his team's work, saying: 'This is the first time a British team in America has gone into the second day's play ahead.'

Nevertheless, he knew that the fourball series would be 'the toughest day of all'. No one needed to remind him that the British had never won the fourball series since it had been introduced in 1963.

And, in the event, the second day was a disaster for the British as they won only one and a half points all day and went into the final day's singles 10–6 down. For some reason known only to the captain, Eric Brown, the winning combination of Jacklin and Huggett did not play in the morning. After a good start in the singles when Brian Barnes beat Rudolph and Peter Oosterhuis beat Littler, the rest fell away so that the Americans increased their lead and went into the final eight singles matches five points in the lead. The first two matches in the afternoon settled the match when Trevino thrashed Huggett 7 and 6 and Jacklin lost to J.C. Snead (nephew of Sam) by one hole. Britain did at least win four of the remaining six matches but, nevertheless, the Americans were comfortable winners at 18½–13½.

16–18 September 1971 Old Warson Country Club, St Louis, Missouri, USA *Captains:* E.C. Brown (Great Britain and Ireland), J. Hebert (USA)			
Great Britain and Ireland		**United States**	
Foursomes: Morning			
N.C. Coles & C. O'Connor (2 & 1)	1	W. Casper & M. Barber	0
P. Townsend & P. Oosterhuis	0	A. Palmer & G. Dickinson (1 hole)	1
B. Huggett & A. Jacklin (3 & 2)	1	J. Nicklaus & D. Stockton	0
M. Bembridge & P.J. Butler (1 hole)	1	C. Coody & F. Beard	0
Foursomes: Afternoon			
H. Bannerman & B. Gallacher (2 & 1)	1	W. Casper & M. Barber	0
P. Townsend & P. Oosterhuis	0	A. Palmer & G. Dickinson (1 hole)	1
B. Huggett & A. Jacklin (halved)	½	L. Trevino & M. Rudolph (halved)	½
M. Bembridge & P.J. Butler	0	J. Nicklaus & J.C. Snead (5 & 3)	1
Fourballs: Morning			
C. O'Connor & B. Barnes	0	L. Trevino & M. Rudolph (2 & 1)	1
N. C Coles & J. Garner	0	F. Beard & J.C. Snead (2 & 1)	1
P. Oosterhuis & B. Gallacher	0	A. Palmer & G. Dickinson (5 & 4)	1
P. Townsend & H. Bannerman	0	J. Nicklaus & G. Littler (2 & 1)	1

(continued)

1. *(above)* The Great Britain
Ryder Cup team in 1929
(back row, l to r): Henry Cotton,
Fred Robson, Archie Compston,
Ernest Whitcombe, Stewart Burns;
(front row, l to r): Aubrey Boomer,
Abe Mitchell, George Duncan (captain),
Charles Whitcombe.

2. Fred Daly, the Open Champion (left) and
Charlie Ward discuss the larger American
ball that they used in the match between
Great Britain and the Oxford & Cambridge
Golfing Society before the 1947 Ryder Cup
so that they could get used to it.

3. *(above)* The Great Britain team at Waterloo station before leaving for the 1947 match (l to r): Arthur Lees, Eric Green, Charlie Ward, Henry Cotton, Reg Home, Fred Daly, Max Faulkner, Dai Rees, Commander Roe, Jimmy Adams and Sam King.

4. *(below)* Sam Snead drives at the 5th at Ganton watched by Charlie Ward in the 1949 match.

5. Great Britain's Bernard Hunt driving in the 1953 match at Wentworth.

6. Great Britain's Eric Brown drives from the 3rd tee on his way to victory at Lindrick in 1957. Brown played a total of four 36-hole singles in his Ryder Cup career, winning them all.

7. Captain Dai Rees held aloft by Bernard Hunt and Ken Bousfield following the British victory at Lindrick in 1957, the first British victory for 24 years.

8. *(below)* Peter Alliss and Christy O'Connor in the 1965 Ryder Cup match at Royal Birkdale

9. The 1969 match at Royal Birkdale finished in an exciting draw as Jack Nicklaus conceded a two-and-a-half-foot putt to Tony Jacklin on the final green. A number of the American team questioned that decision.

10. Jack Nicklaus driving in his match against Maurice Bembridge in the 1973 Ryder Cup at Muirfield.

11. Brian Barnes and Bernard Gallacher look on disconsolately as the Americans win another match at Royal Lytham in 1977.

12. Peter Oosterhuis and a young Nick Faldo just after they had beaten Jack Nicklaus and Ray Floyd at Royal Lytham in 1977.

13. *(above)* Nicklaus advises Tom Watson in their match against Bernhard Langer and Manuel Piñero at Walton Heath in 1981.

14. Sam Torrance has the honour of holing the putt that brings Europe its first Ryder Cup victory at The Belfry in 1985.

15. The European team celebrate their famous victory at The Belfry in 1985 (back row, l to r) José Rivero, Bernhard Langer, Nick Faldo, Sam Torrance, Tony Jacklin (captain), Sandy Lyle, Paul Way, Ken Brown, Seve Ballesteros; (front row, l to r): Howard Clark, Ian Woosnam, José María Cañizares, Manuel Piñero.

16. Seve Ballesteros making a point to captain Tony Jacklin and Mark James in the 1989 match at The Belfry.

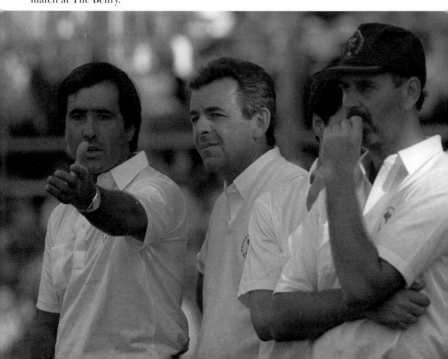

16–18 September 1971 (continued)			
Old Warson Country Club, St Louis, Missouri, USA			
Captains: E.C. Brown (Great Britain and Ireland), J. Hebert (USA)			
Great Britain and Ireland		**United States**	
Fourballs: Afternoon			
B. Gallacher & P. Oosterhuis (1 hole)	1	L. Trevino & W. Casper	0
A. Jacklin & B. Huggett	0	G. Littler & J.C. Snead (2 & 1)	1
P. Townsend & H. Bannerman	0	A. Palmer & J. Nicklaus (1 hole)	1
N.C. Coles & C. O'Connor (halved)	½	C. Coody & F. Beard (halved)	½
Singles: Morning			
A. Jacklin	0	L. Trevino (1 hole)	1
B. Gallacher (halved)	½	D. Stockton (halved)	½
B. Barnes (1 hole)	1	M. Rudolph	0
P. Oosterhuis (4 & 3)	1	G. Littler	0
P. Townsend	0	J. Nicklaus (3 & 2)	1
C. O'Connor	0	G. Dickinson (5 & 4)	1
H. Bannerman (halved)	½	A. Palmer (halved)	½
N.C. Coles (halved)	½	F. Beard (halved)	½
Singles: Afternoon			
B. Huggett	0	L. Trevino (7 & 6)	1
A. Jacklin	0	J.C. Snead (1 hole)	1
B. Barnes (2 & 1)	1	M. Barber	0
P. Townsend	0	D. Stockton (1 hole)	1
B. Gallacher (2 & 1)	1	C. Coody	0
N.C. Coles	0	J. Nicklaus (5 & 3)	1
P. Oosterhuis (3 & 2)	1	A. Palmer	0
H. Bannerman (2 & 1)	1	G. Dickinson	0
Great Britain and Ireland 13½; USA 18½			

Change of format, same result

Back to England, or rather Scotland, as the 1973 match was played at Muirfield. The unofficial inaugural match had been played at Gleneagles in 1921 but none of the subsequent matches had been played in what was considered by many to be 'the home of golf'. Would this first time there help the British team?

In spite of the undoubted strength of the American team – Nicklaus, Palmer, Casper, Aaron, Brewer, Weiskopf,

Graham, Blancas and Chi Chi Rodriguez – the British were reasonably hopeful and indeed, after the first two days, the teams were tied at 8–8. The format had been slightly changed so that instead of two lots of foursomes on the first day and two lots of fourballs on the second, there were now foursomes on each morning followed by fourballs in the afternoon. Barnes and Gallacher did well on the first day, winning both their matches, though on the second day Barnes and Butler lost both their matches. Oddly, after garnering two points on the first day, Bernard Gallacher was rested on the second day. Jacklin had a reasonable two days, picking up two and half points out of a possible four, as did Peter Oosterhuis and Maurice Bembridge. On the American side, Nicklaus won three times.

Unfortunately, the British made a poor start to the singles, losing the first three matches. Indeed the only British winner on the Sunday morning was Tony Jacklin and, with three matches halved, the Americans went into the final eight singles leading 13½–10½. Britain won the first match in the afternoon, but lost the next four and that was it. The final score was 19–13.

20–22 September 1973			
Muirfield, Gullane, Scotland			
Captains: B.J. Hunt (Great Britain and Ireland), J. Burke (USA)			
Great Britain and Ireland		**United States**	
Foursomes: Morning			
B. Barnes & B. Gallacher (1 hole)	1	L. Trevino & W.J. Casper	0
C. O'Connor & N.C. Coles (3 & 2)	1	T. Weiskopf & J.C. Snead	0
A. Jacklin & P. Oosterhuis (halved)	½	J. Rodriguez & L. Graham (halved)	½
M. Bembridge & P.J. Butler	0	J. Nicklaus & A. Palmer (6 & 5)	1

(continued)

20–22 September 1973 (continued)			
Muirfield, Gullane, Scotland			
Captains: B.J. Hunt (Great Britain and Ireland), J. Burke (USA)			
Great Britain and Ireland		**United States**	
Fourballs: Afternoon			
B. Barnes & B. Gallacher (5 & 4)	1	T. Aaron & G. Brewer	0
M. Bembridge & B. Huggett (3 & 1)	1	A. Palmer & J. Nicklaus	0
A. Jacklin & P. Oosterhuis (3 & 1)	1	T. Weiskopf & W. Casper	0
C. O'Connor & N.C. Coles	0	L. Trevino & H. Blancas (2 & 1)	1
Foursomes: Morning			
B. Barnes & P.J. Butler	0	J. Nicklaus & T. Weiskopf (1 hole)	1
P. Oosterhuis & A. Jacklin (2 holes)	1	A. Palmer & D. Hill	0
M. Bembridge & B. Huggett (5 & 4)	1	J. Rodriguez & L. Graham	0
N.C. Coles & C. O Connor	0	L. Trevino & W. Casper (2 & 1)	1
Fourballs: Afternoon			
B. Barnes &. P J Butler	0	J.C. Snead & A. Palmer (2 holes)	1
A. Jacklin &. P. Oosterhuis	0	G. Brewer & W. Casper (3 & 2)	1
C. Clark & E. Polland	0	J. Nicklaus & T. Weiskopf (3 & 2)	1
M. Bembridge & B. Huggett (halved)	½	L. Trevino & H. Blancas (halved)	½
Singles: Morning			
B. Barnes	0	W. Casper (2 & 1)	1
B. Gallacher	0	T. Weiskopf (3 & 1)	1
P.J. Butler	0	H. Blancas (5 & 4)	1
A. Jacklin (3 & 1)	1	T. Aaron	0
N.C. Coles (halved)	½	G. Brewer (halved)	½
C. O'Connor	0	J.C. Snead (1 hole)	1
M. Bembridge (halved)	½	J. Nicklaus (halved)	½
P. Oosterhuis (halved)	½	L. Trevino (halved)	½
Singles: Afternoon			
B. Huggett (4 & 2)	1	H. Blancas	0
B. Barnes	0	J.C. Snead (3 & 1)	1
B. Gallacher	0	G. Brewer (6 & 5)	1
A. Jacklin	0	W. Casper (2 & 1)	1
N.C. Coles	0	L. Trevino (6 & 5)	1
C. O'Connor (halved)	½	T. Weiskopf (halved)	½
M. Bembridge	0	J. Nicklaus (2 holes)	1
P. Oosterhuis (4 & 2)	1	A. Palmer	0
Great Britain and Ireland 13; USA 19			

'Well done, Barnesy'

Back to America in 1975, this time to the Laurel Valley
Golf Club in Pennsylvania. Heavy rain again preceded the
match making an already long course, with ten holes of
more than 430 yards, even longer. This probably helped the
Americans, not that they needed it. In spite of the emerg-
ing South African golfer Gary Player, who won the Masters
and the Open in 1974, the Americans dominated world golf
to the extent that they had won twenty of the 24 Majors
played since 1970. The Americans were very relaxed about
the match and even organised a celebrity pro-am for the
day before it, much to the disgust of Peter Ryde who wrote
in *The Times*:

> We are threatened with a celebrity pro-am tomorrow,
> involving the rival captain and inevitably, Bob Hope. I
> dislike the idea of dressing up this match, which should
> stand or fall on its own quality and tradition.

The British team was not one of the country's strongest. Tony
Jacklin was almost certainly past his best, and Gallacher,
Barnes, Bembridge, Oosterhuis and Huggett (playing for
the sixth and last time) were joined by newcomers Tommy
Horton, Guy Hunt, John O'Leary, Norman Wood, Christy
O'Connor Jr. and Eamonn D'Arcy. Only the last two had a
Ryder Cup future in front of them.

Arnold Palmer suggested that the USA might win all 32
matches, and when Britain lost all four of the first morning
foursomes this did not seem entirely far-fetched. However,
Britain and Ireland secured one and a half points in the
afternoon. The second day was just as one-sided, and the
British went into the singles trailing 12½–3½.

On the final day the Americans had won by lunch-time
and the real point of interest was Brian Barnes beating Jack

Nicklaus 4 and 2 in the morning. As it happened, the pair were matched against each other again in the afternoon. Some thought that perhaps Nicklaus had not really been trying. That may or may not have been the case, but he was certainly going to try in the afternoon. He arrived on the first tee and said to Barnes:

> Well done this morning, Barnesy, but there's no way you're gonna beat me this afternoon.

Nicklaus won the first two holes, but Barnes hung in there and eventually beat the great man 2 and 1 with a birdie at the 17th. It was the one bright spot for the British in an otherwise overwhelming, almost humiliating, defeat of 21–11.

19–21 September 1975 Laurel Valley, Pennsylvania, USA *Captains:* B.J. Hunt (Great Britain and Ireland), A. Palmer (USA)			
Great Britain and Ireland		**United States**	
Foursomes: Morning			
B. Barnes & B. Gallacher	0	J. Nicklaus & T. Weiskopf (5 & 4)	1
N. Wood & M. Bembridge	0	G. Littler & H. Irwin (4 & 3)	1
A. Jacklin & P. Oosterhuis	0	A. Geiberger & J. Miller (3 & 1)	1
T. Horton & J. O'Leary	0	L. Trevino & J.C. Snead (2 & 1)	1
Fourballs: Afternoon			
P. Oosterhuis & A. Jacklin (2 & 1)	1	W. Casper & R. Floyd	0
E. Darcy & C. O'Connor Jr.	0	T. Weiskopf & L. Graham (3 & 2)	1
B. Barnes & B. Gallacher (halved)	½	J. Nicklaus & R. Murphy (halved)	½
T. Horton & J. O'Leary	0	L. Trevino & H. Irwin (2 & 1)	1
Fourballs: Morning			
P. Oosterhuis & A. Jacklin (halved)	½	W. Casper & J. Miller (halved)	½
T. Horton & N. Wood	0	J. Nicklaus & J.C. Snead (4 & 2)	1
B. Barnes & B. Gallacher	0	G. Littler & L. Graham (5 & 3)	1
E. Darcy & G.L. Hunt (halved)	½	A. Geiberger & R. Floyd (halved)	½

(continued)

19–21 September 1975 (continued)				
Laurel Valley, Pennsylvania, USA				
Captains: B.J. Hunt (Great Britain and Ireland), A. Palmer (USA)				
Great Britain and Ireland		**United States**		
Foursomes: Afternoon				
A. Jacklin & B. Barnes (3 & 2)	1	L. Trevino & R. Murphy		0
C. O'Connor Jr. & J. O'Leary	0	T. Weiskopf & J. Miller (5 & 3)		1
P. Oosterhuis & M. Bembridge	0	H. Irwin & W. Casper (3 & 2)		1
E. Darcy & G.L. Hunt	0	A. Geiberger & L. Graham (3 & 2)		1
Singles: Morning				
A. Jacklin	0	R. Murphy (2 & 1)		1
P. Oosterhuis (2 holes)	1	J. Miller		0
B. Gallacher (halved)	½	L. Trevino (halved)		½
T. Horton (halved)	½	H. Irwin (halved)		½
B. Huggett	0	G. Littler (4 & 2)		1
E. Darcy	0	W. Casper (3 & 2)		1
G.L. Hunt	0	T. Weiskopf (5 & 3)		1
B. Barnes (4 & 2)	1	J. Nicklaus		0
Singles: Afternoon				
A. Jacklin	0	R. Floyd (1 hole)		1
P. Oosterhuis (3 & 2)	1	C. Snead		0
B. Gallacher (halved)	½	A. Geiberger (halved)		½
T. Horton (2 & 1)	1	L. Graham		0
J. O'Leary	0	H. Irwin (2 & 1)		1
M. Bembridge	0	R. Murphy (2 & 1)		1
N. Wood (2 & 1)	1	L. Trevino		0
B. Barnes (2 & 1)	1	J. Nicklaus		0
Great Britain and United States Ireland 11; USA 21				

Faldo on the scene

In 1977 it was back to Royal Lytham and St Annes. The US PGA suggested that the Great Britain and Ireland team should invite the rest of the world to join them. The PGA did not like this but did make another change to the format, which was to reduce the number of points at stake from 32 to twenty. The new programme was five foursomes on the first day, five fourballs on the second and ten singles on the third. This did not turn out to be a good move and meant that there was not enough golf for the spectators to watch.

Fortunately, the experiment was abandoned after this one match.

Fortunately, the match was remembered for another reason: two great players played for the first time. For the Americans it was Tom Watson who had just beaten Jack Nicklaus in the famous 'duel in the sun' at Turnberry in the Open Championship and who would go on to win five Open Championships. On the British side, Nick Faldo played for the first time. He would go on to play in eleven Ryder Cup matches and win no fewer than 25 points, more than any other player. Also making their debut at Royal Lytham were three other British players who would have interesting, not to say exciting, futures in the Cup: Ken Brown, Mark James and Howard Clark.

The new format did not help the British as they had hoped. They garnered only 2½ points out of ten on the first two days and, although they halved the singles 5–5, they lost the match 12½–7½. There were a few positives for the British, however. Faldo and Oosterhuis, playing together, won both their foursome and fourball matches, and then both won their singles. Between them, they won four of the team's seven and a half points.

15–17 September 1977			
Royal Lytham & St Annes, St Annes, Lancashire, England			
Captains: B. Huggett (Great Britain and Ireland), D. Finsterwald (USA)			
Great Britain and Ireland		**United States**	
Foursomes:			
B. Gallacher & B. Barnes	0	L. Wadkins & H. Irwin (3 & 1)	1
N.C. Coles & P. Dawson	0	D. Stockton & M. McGee (1 hole)	1
N. Faldo & P. Oosterhuis (2 & 1)	1	R. Floyd & L. Graham	0
E. Darcy & A. Jacklin (halved)	½	E. Sneed & D. January (halved)	½
T. Horton & M. James	0	J. Nicklaus & T. Weiskopf (5 & 4)	1

(continued)

15–17 September 1977 (continued)			
Royal Lytham & St Annes, St Annes, Lancashire, England			
Captains: B. Huggett (Great Britain and Ireland), D. Finsterwald (USA)			
Great Britain and Ireland		**United States**	
Fourballs:			
B. Barnes & T. Horton	0	T. Watson & H. Green (5 & 4)	1
N.C Coles & P. Dawson	0	E. Sneed & L. Wadkins (5 & 3)	1
N. Faldo & P. Oosterhuis (3 & 1)	1	J. Nicklaus & R. Floyd	0
A. Jacklin & E. Darcy	0	D. Hill & D. Stockton (5 & 3)	1
M. James & K. Brown	0	H. Irwin & L. Graham (1 hole)	1
Singles			
H. Clark	0	L. Wadkins (4 & 3)	1
N.C. Coles	0	L. Graham (5 & 3)	1
P. Dawson (5 & 4)	1	D. January	0
B. Barnes (1 hole)	1	H. Irwin	0
T. Horton	0	D. Hill (5 & 4)	1
B. Gallacher (1 hole)	1	J. Nicklaus	0
E. Darcy	0	H. Green (1 hole)	1
M. James	0	R. Floyd (2 & 1)	1
N. Faldo (1 hole)	1	T. Watson	0
P. Oosterhuis (2 holes)	1	J. McGee	0
Great Britain and Ireland 11; USA 21			

Bring in the Europeans

One of the best things to come out of the 1977 contest was that the British PGA finally felt forced to act on taking realistic steps to strengthen their team. As we have seen, there had already been pressure from the US PGA to make changes; but maybe it was this comment by Jack Nicklaus, after yet another comfortable US victory at Lytham, that finally persuaded the PGA to make a move:

> The Americans are quite happy to treat this match as a goodwill gesture, a get together, a bit of fun. But here in Britain it's treated differently. The people here seem to want a serious, knock-em-down match. If that's what's wanted, there has to be a stronger opposition.

Something has to be done to make it more of a match
for the Americans.

And Nicklaus followed up his remark by writing a letter to
Lord Derby, President of the British PGA, in which he said,
'amongst other things', that it was:

vital to widen the selection procedures if the Ryder Cup
is to continued to enjoy its past prestige.

The 'rest of the world' seemed a nebulous concept and
might entail having to play the match in faraway places like
Australia, New Zealand and South Africa. But what about
Europe? The European tour was beginning to emerge as
an important part of the golfing calendar. Furthermore, a
handsome, effervescent young Spanish golfer, Severiano
Ballesteros, had burst on to the scene at Royal Birkdale in
the 1976 Open Championship when he had nearly caught
up the eventual winner, Johnny Miller. None who saw it will
ever forget the deft little chip Ballesteros played along a
path between two bunkers to the final green.

In early 1978 two former Ryder Cup team stalwarts who
were now members of the British Ryder Cup Committee,
Brian Huggett and Peter Butler, flew to the USA and
secured the PGA's approval for the British team to include
Europeans. They probably did not realise it at the time, but
this was to prove an immensely important decision.

However, this fact was not immediately apparent. For
the 1979 match, which was to be played at Greenbrier, West
Virginia, the new Great Britain and Europe team included
only two players from Europe: Seve Ballesteros and
Antonio Garrido, both Spaniards. They were joined by six
Englishmen – Tony Jacklin, Nick Faldo, Peter Oosterhuis,
Mark James, Ken Brown and Michael King; three Scots

– Bernard Gallacher, Sandy Lyle and Brian Barnes – and an Irishman, Des Smyth. The diplomatic John Jacobs was selected as non-playing captain.

Jacobs might have expected that his main task would be integrating the two Spaniards into the team. In the event, his main problems arose from the poor, not to say juvenile, behaviour of two Englishmen, Mark James and Ken Brown. This was the era of punk rock and rebellious youth and they were going to show that they were 'with it'. An early sign of trouble ahead was flagged up by the two appearing at Heathrow wearing casual clothes instead of the official uniform of suit and tie as worn by the rest of the team. Once in the USA the two missed a team meeting because they had gone shopping and, at the opening ceremony, both behaved as though the whole thing was a waste of time.

One element that pleased everyone was the abandonment of the format introduced at Lytham and the reintroduction of two sets of foursomes and fourballs, now followed by twelve singles on the third day. Jacobs entered into the spirit of the new Great Britain and Europe team by pairing the two Spaniards and sending them out as the top foursomes pair. This tactic did not work very well; they lost, as did the next two pairs, so that by mid-morning the USA were leading 3–0. Bernard Gallacher and Brian Barnes beat Hale Irwin and John Mahaffey to make it 3–1 by lunch. In the afternoon, Ballesteros and Garrido beat Fuzzy Zoeller and Hubert Green, and Jacklin and Sandy Lyle halved with Lee Trevino and Gill Morgan, but the Americans won the other two matches to lead 5½–2½ at the end of the first day. Ken Brown and Mark James lost their match playing together (some people suggested to John Jacobs that he leave them out altogether as punishment for their bad behaviour); Brown again behaved badly during his match partnering

Des Smyth in the afternoon, and the pair were thrashed 7 and 6 by Hale Irwin and Tom Kite.

The foursomes on the second morning went better for the Europeans. James was injured and could not play, so Jacobs found it easy to drop Brown and that improved team morale. They won the first three matches to level the scores before Ballesteros and Garrido lost to Lanny Wadkins and Larry Nelson. The afternoon fourballs were drawn 2–2 so the Europeans were only one behind going into the singles, the closest margin at that stage in any of the matches played in the United States so far.

As James could not play, the Americans would have to drop one of their players and call that non-played match a half. The possibility of this happening had been foreseen; both captains had put a name in an envelope before the match started, and that person would be the one to stand down. The American captain, Billy Casper, must have misunderstood because the name he put in the envelope was one of his best and most experienced players, Lee Trevino. Casper told Jacobs of his mistake and, to his credit, the diplomatic Jacobs allowed him to substitute Trevino with Gil Morgan.

The Europeans got off to a great start when Gallacher beat Lanny Wadkins 3 and 2. But that was the peak of their achievement, as the Americans then won all five of the remaining morning singles to lead 13½–8½. The afternoon was a formality and with the Americans winning 3½–2½, the final score was again a comfortable victory for the USA: 17–11. The one irony was that the consistently badly behaved Ken Brown won his single against Fuzzy Zoeller. PB 'Laddie' Lucas would write later:

The fact that Ken Brown, pursuing his young, idiosyncratic way, was eventually one of the only three British and European winners in the singles (the other two were Gallacher and Faldo) only compounded the wretchedness of the whole affair.

It was not a great start for the new Great Britain and Europe team and, two years later, Seve Ballesteros would refuse to play following a long-running argument with the British PGA over appearance money. The truth was that Ballesteros did not, at first, get into the spirit of the Ryder Cup. Obviously, it had no tradition in Spain and Ballesteros had not been brought up on a diet of foursomes and fourballs matchplay, but rather on stroke-play where golfers played for money.

14–16 September 1979			
The Greenbrier, West Virginia, USA			
Captains: J. Jacobs (Europe) W. Casper (USA)			
Europe		**United States**	
Foursomes: Morning			
A. Garrido & S. Ballesteros	0	L. Wadkins & L. Nelson (2 & 1)	1
K. Brown & M. James	0	L. Trevino & F. Zoeller (3 & 2)	1
P. Oosterhuis & N. Faldo	0	A. Bean & L. Elder (2 & 1)	1
B. Gallacher & B. Barnes (2 & 1)	1	H. Irwin & J. Mahaffey	0
Fourballs: Afternoon			
K. Brown & D. Smyth	0	H. Irwin & T. Kite (7 & 6)	1
S. Ballesteros & A. Garrido (3 & 2)	1	F. Zoeller & H. Green	0
A. Lyle & A. Jacklin (halved)	½	L. Trevino & G. Morgan (halved)	½
B. Gallacher & B. Barnes	0	L. Wadkins & L. Nelson (3 & 2)	1
Foursomes: Morning			
A. Jacklin & A. Lyle (5 & 4)	1	L. Elder & J. Mahaffey	0
N. Faldo & P. Oosterhuis (6 & 5)	1	A. Bean & T. Kite	0
B. Gallacher & B. Barnes (2 & 1)	1	F. Zoeller & M. Hayes	0
S. Ballesteros & A. Garrido	0	L. Wadkins & L. Nelson (3 & 2)	1
Fourballs: Afternoon			
S. Ballesteros & A. Garrido	0	L. Wadkins & L. Nelson (5 & 4)	1
A. Jacklin & A. Lyle	0	H. Irwin & T. Kite (1 hole)	1
B. Gallacher & B. Barnes (3 & 2)	1	L. Trevino & F. Zoeller	0
N. Faldo & P. Oosterhuis (1 hole)	1	L. Elder & M. Hayes	0

(continued)

14–16 September 1979 (continued)			
The Greenbrier, West Virginia, USA			
Captains: J. Jacobs (Europe) W. Casper (USA)			
Europe		**United States**	
Singles: Morning			
B. Gallacher (3 & 2)	1	L. Wadkins	0
S. Ballesteros	0	L. Nelson (3 & 2)	1
A. Jacklin	0	T. Kite (1 hole)	1
A. Garrido	0	M. Hayes (1 hole	1
M. King	0	A. Bean (4 & 3)	1
B. Barnes	0	J. Mahaffey (1 hole)	1
Singles: Afternoon			
N. Faldo (3 & 2)	1	L. Elder	0
D. Smyth	0	H. Irwin (5 & 3)	1
P. Oosterhuis	0	H. Green (2 holes)	1
K. Brown (1 hole)	1	F. Zoeller	0
A. Lyle	0	L. Trevino (2 & 1)	1
M. James (injured, halved)	½	G. Morgan (halved, match not played)	½
Europe 11; USA 21			

Jacklin was insulted

The usual Ryder Cup controversy came to the fore in the run-up to the 1981 match. The PGA had chosen The Belfry in the Midlands, the location of their new headquarters, as the venue. The course, designed by Peter Alliss and Dave Thomas, was relatively new and was not really ready. For example, Brian Barnes described it as being like a 'ploughed field' and many other professionals told the PGA that the course was not yet ready for the Ryder Cup. The PGA gave way and the venue was changed to Walton Heath, the choice of the sponsors, Sun Alliance, and their chairman Lord Aldington, who was a member of the club.

The controversy did not end with the rows over Ballesteros, appearance money and the choice of venue. Next was the dropping of Tony Jacklin in favour of bad boy Mark James, who had been fined £1,500 for his behaviour in 1979 (Brown had been fined £1,000 and also banned from playing in 1981). Jacklin was insulted and vowed to have nothing to do with the Ryder Cup again.

He declined John Jacobs' invitation to be one of his assistants. As far as Jacklin was concerned, he was finished with the Ryder Cup:

By then I was totally disenchanted and particularly with the attitude of those in charge, not just of the Ryder Cup, but golf in Europe generally. For a dozen years or so I have been playing mostly in the States, and was constantly aware of how much higher standards were over there. I am not talking about players' skills, but about the running of tournaments, the excellence of events week after week. The conditioning of the courses was far superior; they felt it important to get the greens as good as they could be. All the facilities were first class, the locker rooms, practice grounds, food in the clubhouse, all were absolutely as good as they could make them.

Of course all this costs money and in those days the European Tour was nowhere near as well off as the US, but this wasn't just about money. No one was trying to raise standards and without raising those, then the standard of play wasn't going to improve either. And it wasn't just on the European Tour. I remember playing in the (British) Open Championship back then, and they didn't see the need to change the pin positions during the practice rounds. For three days you played to the same hole, which was always on the front of the green. For someone who played regularly in America, it all looked so unprofessional.

The PGA [the club professionals' body, rather than the European Tour, as it became after tournament players and club pros went their separate ways in 1973] headed up the Ryder Cup in those days, and it seemed to me they left so much to chance in putting a team together. It was travel as cheaply as possible – no wives or girlfriends then – find a company – any company – that might give you a few shirts, and off you go. If you wanted to take your caddy, then you had to pay for him.

I particularly remember one year, 1975 at Arnold Palmer's home club, Laurel Valley, we were all given Stylo's plastic shoes, and one of my soles came completely off during my singles against Ray Floyd. Meanwhile, there they were, travelling by Concorde, looking a million dollars, wives to match and the best of everything laid on. In those days we really were second-class citizens and like lambs to the slaughter.

Obviously, being me, I spoke my mind, but I was a lone voice and was always seen as something of a whinger. Once Peter Oosterhuis came along and later Nick Faldo, and started saying the same things, then they started listening, but throughout my playing days, despite what I had achieved, nothing changed. Then when Mark James was preferred to me in 1981, despite his dreadful behaviour at the Greenbrier, and then banning Seve, well I thought I was done with the Ryder Cup. They just weren't serious about trying to win the match.

So Europe would go into the match without the only two players who had won a Major (Ballesteros had won the Masters to add to his Open victory at Lytham) and would face an immensely strong American team – Jack Nicklaus, Tom Watson, Lee Trevino, Larry Nelson, Hale Irwin, Ray Floyd, Johnny Miller, Ben Crenshaw, Jerry Pate, Bill Rogers, Tom Kite and Bruce Lietzke. (Only Bruce Lietzke would fail to win a Major in his career.) There were now three continental Europeans in the Europe team – Manuel Piñero and José Maria Cañizares from Spain and Bernhard Langer from Germany. Langer had burst on to the scene by coming second to Bill Rogers in that year's Open Championship.

The first morning foursomes finished even at 2–2 with notable European wins for Sandy Lyle and Mark James over Rogers and Lietzke, and by Gallacher (the most experienced Ryder Cup performer on the team) and Des Smyth over Irwin and Floyd. The proven partnership of Oosterhuis and Faldo could not prevent Watson and Nicklaus winning 4 and 3. And the Europeans did even better in the afternoon, winning two and halving one of the four fourball matches. Lyle and James won again, as did Smyth and the newcomer, Cañizares. At the end of the first day, the Europeans were leading 4½–3½ and hopes were high.

The euphoria soon evaporated on the second day as the Americans stamped their authority on the match by winning three of the morning fourballs and all the afternoon foursomes. Going into the singles the Americans led 10½–5½ and proceeded to win the first two matches to make it 12½–5½. When Gallacher halved with Rogers and then Nelson and Crenshaw both won it was all over. Langer managed a half and Piñero, Faldo and Howard Clark (beating Tom Watson 4 and 3) all won but, yet again, the Americans won by the comfortable margin of 18½–9½. At least the continental Europeans had contributed three and a half points. The quality of some of the golf was extremely high. For example, Sandy Lyle secured no fewer than eight birdies in the sixteen holes he played against Tom Kite but still lost 3 and 2. Kite had ten birdies and was on his way to a round of 63. Larry Nelson, the 1981 United States PGA champion, was too good for Mark James and created a new Ryder Cup record by winning his first nine matches.

Dave Marr, the American captain, said after the match that maybe the Europeans had made a tactical mistake by leading at the end of the first day and thereby wounding

American pride. For his part, the European captain John Jacobs said he was proud of the courage of his players, adding:

> None of them was intimidated but they were not all able to produce their best.

18–20 September 1981			
Walton Heath, Surrey, England			
Captains: J. Jacobs (Europe), D. Marr (USA)			
Europe		**United States**	
Foursomes: Morning			
B. Langer & M. Piñero	0	L. Trevino & L. Nelson (1 hole)	1
A. Lyle & M. James (2 & 1)	1	B. Rogers & B. Lietzke	0
B. Gallacher & D. Smyth (3 & 2)	1	H. Irwin & R. Floyd	0
P. Oosterhuis & N. Faldo	0	T. Watson & J. Nicklaus (4 & 3)	1
Fourballs: Afternoon			
S. Torrance & H. Clark (halved)	½	T. Kite & J. Miller (halved)	½
A. Lyle & M. James (3 & 2)	1	B. Crenshaw & J. Pate	0
D. Smyth & J.M. Cañizares (6 & 5)	1	B. Rogers & B. Lietzke	0
B. Gallacher & E. Darcy	0	H. Irwin & R. Floyd (2 & 1)	1
Fourballs: Morning			
N. Faldo & S. Torrance	0	L. Trevino & J. Pate (7 & 5)	1
A. Lyle & M. James	0	L. Nelson & T. Kite (1 hole)	1
B. Langer & M. Piñero (2 & 1)	1	R. Floyd & H. Irwin	0
J.M. Cañizares & D. Smyth	0	J. Nicklaus & T. Watson (3 & 2)	1
Foursomes: Afternoon			
P. Oosterhuis & S. Torrance	0	L. Trevino & J. Pate (2 & 1)	1
B. Langer & M. Piñero	0	J. Nicklaus & T. Watson (3 & 2)	1
A. Lyle & M. James	0	B. Rogers & R. Floyd (3 & 2)	1
D. Smyth & B. Gallacher	0	T. Kite & L. Nelson (3 & 2)	1

(continued)

18–20 September 1981 (continued)
Walton Heath, Surrey, England
Captains: J. Jacobs (Europe), D. Marr (USA)

Europe		United States	
Singles:			
S. Torrance	0	L. Trevino (5 & 3)	1
A. Lyle	0	T. Kite (3 & 2)	1
B. Gallacher (halved)	½	B. Rogers (halved)	½
M. James	0	L. Nelson (2 holes)	1
D. Smyth	0	B. Crenshaw (6 & 4)	1
B. Langer (halved)	½	B. Lietzke (halved)	½
M. Piñero (4 & 2)	1	J. Pate	0
J.M Cañizares	0	H. Irwin (1 hole)	1
N. Faldo (2 & 1)	1	J. Miller	0
H. Clark (4 & 3)	1	T. Watson	0
P. Oosterhuis	0	R. Floyd (1 hole)	1
E. Darcy	0	J. Nicklaus (5 & 3)	1
Europe 9½; USA 18½			

Chapter 5
The Tony Jacklin Era

'This wasn't a loss'
Palm Beach Gardens, Florida 1983

'I didn't come the heavy stuff'
The Belfry 1985

Superior golf from the Europeans
Muirfield Village 1987

'Spectators clapping us all the way'
The Belfry 1989

'This wasn't a loss'

Perish the thought, but at that point Tony Jacklin was almost lost to the Ryder Cup matches forever. He said later:

Then in 1983 they came and asked me to be captain. I was in shock! It wasn't something I had anticipated; indeed I'd love to have known how they came to the decision. It was within a few months of the match and at the time I thought I must have been the choice of last resort. My first inclination, what with the way they went about putting the team into the field, and how little communication there was when I was left out, was to tell them to get lost. Overnight, though, I thought about how important the future of the European Tour was, how good it could be, and I didn't want to end my days in dispute with them and certainly not do anything that would drag them down.

So I gave a lot of thought to all the things I felt should happen if our team was to go into the matches at least on a level footing. It wasn't that difficult. You looked how they travelled, flying Concorde, and that would be how we should go. We should be properly dressed, plenty of shirts and trousers, good quality materials and suppliers. Of course you should have your own caddy and it should not cost you to have him there.

The team room was something I instigated. For me, it was absolutely vital to have a room at the club or hotel where the team could get together and away from all the people who are inevitably around. Only there could a good team spirit be created and nurtured. In my day, playing under Eric Brown or Bernard Hunt, team get-togethers used to take place in some corner of the locker room; a quick huddle there, hope nobody was listening, and we all went our separate ways, some to eat on their own, or with a chum, others to hit a few shots; the absolute opposite of creating camaraderie and a sense of unity and purpose.

A day or so after I had been asked to be the next captain, I put all these issues on the table to Ken [Schofield, executive director of the Tour] and Colin [Snape, his opposite number at the PGA]. All the way through they kept saying 'OK' and when I got through nothing had been refused. Frankly, if they had said no to any of the big issues, then I would have just walked away, and with a clear conscience.

The team was being picked straight from the Order of Merit, the European tour's money list, but Jacklin accepted the captaincy on the condition that he would be able to pick three players regardless of their position in the Order of Merit. The one person he really wanted was Seve Ballesteros, who was still deeply upset about his treatment by the British PGA. Lord Derby suggested Jacklin talk to him, and this was how Jacklin remembered their meeting:

I met with him at the Prince of Wales Hotel in Southport during the Open Championship at Royal Birkdale that year. He was still very much at odds with the European Tour and their attitude to appearance fees. He wasn't right on everything, but the Tour made very little effort to talk to him, to try and understand his point of view, and remember, he was their greatest asset, already had two Majors under his belt, and Faldo and the rest hadn't come forward yet.

I was passionate about the issue – him on the course and me doing all the other stuff – I thought we could make a real difference. I said to him, 'Apart from anything else, your public relations in the UK are at rock bottom right now. If we can pull this off, turn this thing around, you will be seen by the British public as the greatest thing that ever happened.' The long and the short of it was he saw sense in what I said, recognised that however much he played in America, Europe would always be his base and this was a real opportunity to start moving forward rather than just looking back. From that chat in Southport he came aboard.

Jacklin's other demands, mainly his stipulation that the players be treated as first-class VIPs in every way, was going to be tricky in that it involved heavy expenditure. However, Ken Schofield and Colin Snape did all they could to meet Jacklin's requests.

Jacklin gave credit to Snape especially:

Colin started by going to BA and did a deal whereby if they laid on Concorde at a reasonable price, we would find 50 or so wealthy golf fanatics who would pay good money to fly Concorde, be with the team, included in photos, a sort of elite band of supporters, then that would take care of the cost of that; and it did. It became very much a joint effort; I was doing my bit on the team front, they did theirs making all things possible.

Then they went to Austin Reed, who were happy to help out with the clothing; not free, but at a good price and in turn they got some good publicity out of it. That was the start. A few years later it was Burberry, and by now, with the match really taking off, they were most anxious for us to have their gear and then got Lord Lichfield to take the publicity pictures. And never forget, all this attention did wonders for the team's self-awareness and self-assurance; it was a case of I'd better pull my finger out if everyone's taking such an interest.

To me, the amazing thing is that no one had ever bothered to try and make these sorts of things happen in the past; in the States it had been standard practice for years. Colin Snape, as I said, did most of it and was, I suppose, surprised and delighted he was able to achieve so much.

I put a lot of thought into the team uniform, made sure the colours I chose, and the combinations, would look good on television. Vivien [Jacklin, Tony's first wife who sadly died of a brain haemorrhage in 1988] helped me a lot with that, as she did in all areas where her knowledge was better than mine. I didn't discuss it with the players, this had to be put in place long before the final team was sorted; I just told them there were various outfits and which colours to wear on which day. Bearing in mind in the past they had been lucky to have more than a couple of shirts for the week, I suppose they were delighted. I certainly felt I had left no stone unturned.

Approaching everything in his usual professional way, Jacklin then went to Palm Beach Gardens where the 1983 match was due to be played, to check on the accommodation and, when he got back, made sure he saw every member of the team individually. He said later:

I wanted them to understand that they could and must approach me if there was any issue on which they had a problem; that I was there for them to sort anything out that wasn't right. They had to know that was what I could do for them as captain.

As for working out pairings and partnerships, in the beginning it was just close observation of people to see their reactions to one another. That was very important to me, knowing they were going out there together under great pressure, some under the greatest pressure they were ever likely to face. If two people liked one another, got on well, then for me they had the makings of a good partnership, the whole could become greater than the sum of the parts, whether it be foursomes or fourball.

In 1983, I had no particular view as to how we might shape up against the Americans. I hadn't quite got the team I wanted because of the selection process, but with Seve on board once again, I felt we had the nucleus of a good team with some really good players coming through. Sandy Lyle was winning regularly, and often posting very low scores; Nick Faldo was clearly of a different class to much that had gone before in Europe; and Bernhard Langer could be among the very best if he could sort out his putting problems.

Ian Woosnam, who had by then won a couple of tournaments and was a wonderful striker of the ball, looked to be a cut above the rest as well.

The United States team, with Jack Nicklaus as captain, also had the five-times Open winner Tom Watson, Lanny Wadkins, Fuzzy Zoeller, Ben Crenshaw and Craig Stadler (winner of the Masters in 1982). Because of their slightly odd selection system, the team would not contain the reigning USA Open and US PGA champions, Larry Nelson and Hal Sutton, but it was still a very strong team.

When the match started, Watson and Crenshaw easily beat Gallacher and Lyle in the first foursome but Faldo and Langer beat Wadkins and Stadler 4 and 2, and Cañizares and Torrance beat Ray Floyd and Bob Gilder 4 and 3. Ballesteros, playing with young Paul Way, lost to Tom Kite and Carl Peete and the match was tied 2–2 at lunchtime. Ballesteros had wanted to play with his fellow Spaniard,

Cañizares, but after Jacklin told him at lunchtime that it was up to him to help Paul Way, Ballesteros did just that and the pair won in the afternoon against Ray Floyd and Curtis Strange. Brian Waites and Ken Brown beat Gill Morgan and Fuzzy Zoeller and, when Torrance and Woosnam managed to halve with Crenshaw and Peete, the Europeans finished the day ahead by 4½–3½.

On the second day, as always, the Americans came back. Nevertheless, the Europeans fought hard and only lost the day 4½–3½. The teams were therefore level going into the singles. Jacklin said he put a lot of thought into the order, knowing that the Americans usually put their strongest players at the bottom. He decided not to go down that route but to lead off with Seve Ballesteros, followed by Faldo and Langer. When the envelopes were opened Nicklaus was astonished and said: 'You can't do that!'

Jacklin replied: 'Why not? What's the point of having Seve at the bottom, if the match is already over? I want his point to count, and count early.'

For a time it looked as though the Jacklin strategy was working. Ballesteros was soon two up against Zoeller, and Faldo and Langer were up as well. However, at three up with seven to play, Ballesteros suddenly seemed to lose his touch and slumped to one down going down the 18th. Even after driving into a bunker, Ballesteros recovered to win his hole and halve the match. Faldo and Langer duly won, but then came three American victories as Gilder beat Brand, Crenshaw beat Lyle and Peete beat Waites. The Americans were one ahead with six matches to go.

The young but pugnacious Way won his match against Curtis Strange, Torrance and Kite halved but then Stadler beat Woosnam to put the Americans ahead again. Cañizares and Wadkins halved before Brown beat Floyd 4 and 3. It was all down to the last match between Tom Watson and

Bernard Gallacher. Gallacher made a mess of the 17th to lose 2 and 1 and the Americans had squeezed home by one point. So relieved was Jack Nicklaus to have avoided being the first American captain to lose on home soil that he kissed the spot from which Wadkins had hit a magnificent approach to save his match.

Jacklin would say later:

We went very close that day and frankly were unlucky to lose. Deep down we all felt it was a match we'd let get away. Look at the photographs taken afterwards, and there we all are with glum faces. Perhaps in the end we hadn't really believed enough it was possible. But the great thing was we had shown ourselves that this match really was winnable with the players we had; it was definitely a springboard for the next match at The Belfry. As Seve said at the end, 'This wasn't a loss, this was a win, just to have got so close.'

Mitchell Platts wrote in *The Times*:

What is certain is that everyone in the team deserves to be welcomed home as a hero because as a team they produced the most exciting Ryder Cup match to unfold on American soil. They illustrated how fast the gulf in standards is closing between the two sides.

Nicklaus insisted that when the next match takes place, at The Belfry in 1985, Europe will probably start as favourites. There can be no greater accolade. With Severiano Ballesteros, Nick Faldo and Bernhard Langer, the European team possesses three world-class players.

In two years' time Paul Way might well have emerged as another. Way gathered three and a half points in his first Ryder Cup. That was a remarkable effort by the twenty-year-old from Kent, and afterwards Nicklaus said,

'He's a tremendous prospect. For a little guy he knocks the cover off the ball.'

14–16 October 1983

PGA National Golf Club, Palm Beach Gardens, Florida, USA

Captains: A. Jacklin (Europe), J. Nicklaus (USA)

Europe		United States	
Foursomes: Morning			
B. Gallacher & A. Lyle	0	T. Watson & B. Crenshaw (5 & 4)	1
N. Faldo & B. Langer (4 & 2)	1	L. Wadkins & C. Stadler	0
J.M. Cañizares & S. Torrance (4 & 3)	1	R. Floyd & B. Gilder	0
S. Ballesteros & P. Way	0	T. Kite & C. Peete (2 & 1)	1
Fourballs: Afternoon			
B. Waites & K. Brown (2 & 1)	1	G. Morgan & F. Zoeller	0
N. Faldo & B. Langer	0	T. Watson & J. Haas (2 & 1)	1
S. Ballesteros & P. Way (1 hole)	1	R. Floyd & C. Strange	0
S. Torrance & I. Woosnam (halved)	½	B. Crenshaw & C. Peete (halved)	½
Fourballs: Morning			
B. Waites & K. Brown	0	L. Wadkins & C. Stadler (1 hole)	1
N. Faldo & B. Langer (4 & 2)	1	B. Crenshaw & C. Peete	0
S. Ballesteros & P. Way (halved)	½	G. Morgan & J. Haas (halved)	½
S. Torrance & I. Woosnam	0	T. Watson & B. Gilder (5 & 4)	1
Foursomes: Afternoon			
N. Faldo & B. Langer (3 & 2)	1	T. Kite & R. Floyd	0
S. Torrance & J.M. Cañizares	0	G. Morgan & L. Wadkins (7 & 5)	1
S. Ballesteros & P. Way (2 & 1)	1	T. Watson & B. Gilder	0
B. Waites & K. Brown	0	J. Haas & C. Strange (3 & 2)	1

(continued)

14–16 October 1983 (continued)				
PGA National Golf Club, Palm Beach Gardens, Florida, USA				
Captains: A. Jacklin (Europe), J. Nicklaus (USA)				
Europe		**United States**		
Singles:				
S. Ballesteros (halved)	½	F. Zoeller (halved)	½	
N. Faldo (2 & 1)	1	J. Haas	0	
B. Langer (2 holes)	1	G. Morgan	0	
G.J. Brand	0	B. Gilder (2 holes)	1	
A. Lyle	0	B. Crenshaw (3 & 1)	1	
B. Waites	0	C. Peete (1 hole)	1	
P. Way (2 & 1)	1	C. Strange	0	
S. Torrance (halved)	½	T. Kite (halved)	½	
I. Woosnam	0	C. Stadler (3 & 2)	1	
J.M. Cañizares (halved)	½	L. Wadkins (halved)	½	
K. Brown (4 & 3)	1	R. Floyd	0	
B. Gallacher	0	T. Watson (2 & 1)	1	
Europe 13½; USA 14½				

'I didn't come the heavy stuff'

Having done a great job in 1983, Jacklin was asked to continue as captain of the European team for the 1985 match to be played at The Belfry. Again he approached the match with meticulous care, saying later:

I worked with Brian Cash, chief executive of The Belfry, for the best part of eight months setting up an atmosphere which guaranteed we had our own rooms to eat together, relax together and above all, complete privacy; almost a family atmosphere you might say.

Brian was a great help. He believed in excellence as much as I did. He understood that the better we did, the better it would reflect on his hotel. He provided everything I asked for and more. We got the rooms we asked for and he provided every sort of food and drinks the players wanted. Of course there was no reason for the players not to gravitate to the team room and it was there that the team came together.

Right from the start I felt it important that the players' wives should be part of what we were doing. I am certain their presence at The Belfry was a big factor in creating the atmosphere of togetherness I believed so essential. I could never have achieved what I did without the help and support of my wife Vivien, and after she so sadly died, with Astrid. One of the reasons I accepted the captain's job a fourth time in 1989 was so Astrid could experience this extraordinary event and see why it meant so much to me.

First of all, he set the course up to suit the Europeans as much as possible. As he said:

There wasn't a great deal to do, but I made sure there would be none of that fluffy long grass close to the greens that was the staple diet for Americans; I had all the areas round the greens shaved so you could chip, something they don't get to do very often. Then I made sure the speed of the greens was right for our side, so quite a bit slower than they were used to.

Nevertheless, the very layout of the course, with its narrow fairways, thick rough and plenty of water hazards, was very similar to most of the tournament courses in the USA. The US captain, Lee Trevino, would say:

My guys love this course! It's so Americanised. It's what they're used to – with water hazards to fire over, rather than bump-and-run golf we get at your Open.

For this match, the European team had plenty of continental Europeans. Ballesteros' influence is probably what led to there being three Spaniards; José Rivero, Manuel Piñero and José Maria Cañizares. And, of course, there was the German, Bernhard Langer, who had won the Masters at Augusta in the spring. Joining the five continentals were two Scots, Sam Torrance and Sandy Lyle; a Welshman, Ian Woosnam and four Englishmen; Nick Faldo, Ken Brown, Howard Clark and Paul Way.

The foursomes began well for the Europeans with Ballesteros and Piñero beating Curtis Strange and Mark O'Meara. At the famous par-four, but driveable, 10th where the front of the green is guarded by water, Ballesteros did what he had in 1978 to become the first professional to drive the green. Nevertheless, in spite of this early victory, the Europeans went into lunch 3–1 down as the Americans won the remainder of the foursomes.

The successful partnership of Faldo and Langer, which had won three out of four matches in 1983, failed this time largely because Faldo was going through a radical swing change. Jacklin asked if he wanted to continue and when he declined, Faldo did not play again until the singles where he lost again. It would be a Ryder Cup match for Faldo to forget, so far as his own performance was concerned.

Jacklin did not panic, saying:

> I didn't come the heavy stuff. There were no pep talks, no recriminations. We just had a frank discussion about the way every player was feeling inside. Quite a few players were not fond of foursomes and were looking forward to hitting their own ball in the afternoon. Despite the scoreline, I felt we went out optimistic and determined.

Woosnam and Way led off for Europe in the fourballs and played perfect fourball golf, going round in a better-ball 64. Even so, it was only just good enough to beat Fuzzy Zoeller and Hubert Green on the last green. The two Spaniards, Ballesteros and Cañizares, halved with Craig Stadler and Hal Sutton. Clark and Torrance played well but lost on the last green to Ray Floyd and Lanny Wadkins, so the position at the end of the first day was USA 4½, Europe 3½.

The second morning – fourballs instead of foursomes – was very close and, at the end, provided a moment which would never be forgotten by those who saw it, whether live and in person or on television. Before that, Way and Woosnam beat Green and Zoeller 4 and 3, and Torrance and Clark beat Kite and North 2 and 1. The two Spaniards, Ballesteros and Piñero, finally lost a match, by 3 and 2, to O'Meara and Wadkins. And so to the final match where Stadler and Strange seemed to have the measure of Langer and Lyle, standing two up on the 17th tee. The Europeans would surely have to finish eagle or birdie to save the match. Lyle duly delivered the eagle at the par-five 17th. At the 18th Strange bunkered his tee shot but Stadler made the green in two, and a par would probably win the match for the US. Lyle and Langer both had birdie putts but missed. Two putts from Stadler and the match would be won. He lagged his first to within eighteen inches. It was almost a 'gimme' but somehow Stadler contrived to miss it. As everyone gasped and Stadler squirmed with embarrassment there was a palpable sense that this was a turning point. The score was now Europe 6, USA 6.

And the Europeans, their tails up, soon rammed home the advantage with a new Spanish pairing, Cañizares and Rivero, beating Kite and Peete 4 and 3, and Ballesteros and Piñero finding their form again to beat Stadler and Sutton 5 and 4. Strange and Jacobsen hit back for the Americans, beating Way and Woosnam 4 and 2, but Langer and Brown completed a very good day for the Europeans by beating

Floyd and Wadkins 3 and 2. The Europeans had gone from 4½–3½ down at the beginning of the day to 9–7 up.

For the singles, Jacklin changed his strategy from the one he had used in 1983 and put his strongest players in the middle of the order. He would say afterwards:

> I have always felt the right philosophy for the singles is to put most of your best players out early to get their result and hopefully their win on the board quickly. Then keep some strength and experience at the end, should things get tight. That's what I did in1983, but at The Belfry I put most of the cream in the middle. I was sure Trevino would put his best players out first to try and get back into the match as soon as possible. That is exactly how it worked out.

Even so, Piñero secured a 3 and 1 victory over Lanny Wadkins in the top match. Stadler, who must have felt very relieved afterwards, won his match against Woosnam before Paul Way, who had suffered an attack of tonsillitis before the match and whose form was therefore uncertain, won his match against Ray Floyd. It was now 11–8 to the Europeans and Europe's strongest players – Ballesteros, Lyle and Langer – were playing the next three matches against Kite, Jacobsen and Sutton. Ballesteros, playing erratically, found himself three down with five to play. However, in characteristic Ballesteros style, he produced some spectacular birdies and managed to secure a half. Lyle was also somewhat erratic but managed to beat Jacobsen 3 and 2 to make it Europe 12½, USA 8½ with seven matches still out on the course. Langer duly delivered the win everyone expected, beating Hal Sutton easily 5 and 4. It was now 13½–8½ to Europe.

By this time, it seemed just a question of who would have the honour of making the winning putt. In the event, Howard Clark had the chance on the 17th to beat Mark O'Meara 2 and 1. His putt lipped out (he won the match at the 18th). The glory went to the match in front where Torrance and North drove off the 18th tee all square. Torrance had a perfect drive and played an equally sound second into the middle of the green. Meanwhile North had found the water. Torrance therefore had two putts for a personal win and a historic win for Europe. He did not need two putts. He holed the first and raised his arm in triumph as the deliriously happy spectators went wild with delight. The Americans won three of the last four matches but it was too late. Europe had won and the final score was a comfortable 16½–11½.

To cap it all, Concorde flew low over The Belfry to acknowledge the victory.

To their relief, Europe had won the Ryder Cup back but there was still one more challenge for the team and their successful captain, Tony Jacklin. They needed to win in America. Roll on 1987.

13–15 September 1985			
The Belfry Golf & Country Club, Sutton Coldfield, West Midlands, England			
Captains: A. Jacklin (Europe), L. Trevino (USA)			
Europe		**United States**	
Foursomes: Morning			
S. Ballesteros & M. Piñero (2 & 1)	1	C. Strange & M. O'Meara	0
B. Langer & N. Faldo	0	C. Peete & T. Kite (3 & 2)	1
A. Lyle & K. Brown	0	L. Wadkins & R. Floyd (4 & 3)	1
H. Clark & S. Torrance	0	C. Stadler & H. Sutton (3 & 2)	1

(continued)

13–15 September 1985 (continued)				
The Belfry Golf & Country Club, Sutton Coldfield, West Midlands, England				
Captains: A. Jacklin (Europe), L. Trevino (USA)				
Europe		**United States**		
Fourballs: Afternoon				
P. Way & I. Woosnam (1 hole)	1	F. Zoeller & H. Green	0	
S. Ballesteros & M. Piñero (2 & 1)	1	A. North & P. Jacobsen	0	
B. Langer & J.M. Cañizares (halved)	½	C. Stadler & H. Sutton (halved)	½	
S. Torrance & H. Clark	0	R. Floyd & L. Wadkins (1 hole)	1	
Fourballs: Morning				
S. Torrance & H. Clark (2 & 1)	1	T. Kite & A. North	0	
P. Way & I. Woosnam (4 & 3)	1	H. Green & F. Zoeller	0	
S. Ballesteros & M. Piñero	0	M. O'Meara & L. Wadkins (3 & 2)	1	
B. Langer & A. Lyle (halved)	½	C. Stadler & C. Strange (halved)	½	
Foursomes: Afternoon				
J.M. Cañizares & J. Rivero (4 & 3)	1	T. Kite & C. Peete	0	
S. Ballesteros & M. Piñero (5 & 4)	1	C. Stadler & H. Sutton	0	
P. Way & I. Woosnam	0	C. Strange & P. Jacobsen (4 & 2)	1	
B. Langer & K. Brown (3 & 2)	1	R. Floyd & L. Wadkins	0	
Singles:				
M. Piñero (3 & 1)	1	L. Wadkins	0	
I. Woosnam	0	C. Stadler (2 & 1)	1	
P. Way (2 holes)	1	R. Floyd	0	
S. Ballesteros (halved)	½	T. Kite (halved)	½	
A. Lyle (3 & 2)	1	P. Jacobsen	0	
B. Langer (5 & 4)	1	H. Sutton	0	
S. Torrance (1 hole)	1	A. North	0	
H. Clark (1 hole)	1	M. O'Meara	0	
J. Rivero	0	C. Peete (1 hole)	1	
N. Faldo	0	H. Green (3 & 1)	1	
J.M. Cañizares (2 holes)	1	F. Zoeller	0	
K. Brown	0	C. Strange (4 & 2)	1	
Europe 16½; USA 11½				

Superior golf from the Europeans

The Americans, to be led again by Jack Nicklaus at his home course, Muirfield Village, made some changes to their selection system. Nicklaus argued successfully that the selection period should be stretched to two years. Furthermore, Nicklaus suggested the match be extended to four days and include two days of singles. In this he was unsuccessful, as Jacklin and the British PGA rejected these latter suggestions.

There was no doubting the challenge of the occasion or the splendour of the setting. Jack Nicklaus had bought the plot of land near his home town of Columbus, Ohio shortly after his first Open Championship victory at Muirfield in 1966. He gradually transformed it into a magnificent golf course which he named Muirfield Village. *The Times* described it as 'truly a sporting Garden of Eden, simultaneously voluptuous and sinister' where the greens 'were set like banqueting tables, surrounded by quicksand'. Some said it was 'the Augusta of the North'.

For once the Europeans seemed to have the best players in the world – Ballesteros, Langer, Faldo and Lyle – though, as always, the Americans appeared to have greater depth, with all twelve of their team in the top 40 of the world rankings compared with only six of the Europeans. Some of the Americans became irritated by the media's talk of a shift in power away from America to Europe. For example, Lanny Wadkins said:

I get sick and tired of reading all that stuff about Ballesteros and Langer being the best. If they are the best why haven't they won in America in two years?

And Payne Stewart added, 'We've got the best tour in the world and we've got the best players.'

The Europeans picked nine of the successful Belfry team, added two new players, José Maria Olazábal and Gordon Brand Jr., and brought back Eamonn Darcy. The Americans brought in five newcomers; Larry Mize, who had famously won the Masters with a chip-in, Dan Pohl,

Mark Calcavecchia, Payne Stewart and Scott Simpson. And it was the Americans who made a cracking start to the foursomes on the first day. At one point they were up in all four matches and soon won the first two. However, the Europeans hit back to win the remaining two and at lunch the teams were level at 2–2.

Jacklin reacted sharply. Of the two beaten pairs, he dropped Torrance, Clark and Brown, retaining only Bernhard Langer for the afternoon fourballs. First out in the afternoon fourballs would go the young and inexperienced Gordon Brand Jr. partnered by José Rivero. Partnering Langer would be an out-of-form Sandy Lyle. The two successful pairs, Faldo and Woosnam and Ballesteros and Olazábal, were retained. For his part, and continuing his policy of playing all of his team before the singles, Nicklaus produced four new pairings. The result was that Europe won all four of the fourball matches in the afternoon and at the end of the first day led 6–2.

Jacklin said later:

Quite simply I have never seen such fantastic golf in foursomes or fourball; it was just birdies all the way. In all the years I was captain, I never had as easy a time as I had at Muirfield Village in putting pairings together, as after the first series, those three pairs picked themselves.

The new Spanish partnership, Ballesteros and young José Maria Olazábal, had won both their matches, as had Faldo (with his new swing) and Woosnam. There was much for the Europeans, along with the 2,000 supporters who had made the trip to support them, to feel happy about.

This situation was unprecedented, and there was much jubilation in the Europeans' bungalow before Jacklin pointed out that there were still two days to go.

On the second day, the Europeans went further ahead by lunch, winning two matches and halving one, and then in the afternoon held on to their five-point lead by winning two more matches. Wadkins may have questioned whether Langer was really one of the best players in the world, and had to suffer two defeats by him for his temerity.

The quality of the golf was outstanding. It was calculated that of the 65 holes played that afternoon, the Europeans were cumulatively 29 under par while the Americans were 22 under. Nicklaus said:

> I have seen the superior golf played by the European team. We fought to the end but our best simply was not good enough today.

And Jacklin added: 'I never thought I would live to see the day when I would see golf played like this.' With a lead of 10½–5½ going into the singles, surely Europe's first victory in the USA was at hand.

Much to everyone's surprise Nicklaus did not put his strongest players out first in an attempt to reduce the deficit quickly. For example, he sent Andy Bean out first but, again to most people's surprise, he beat Ian Woosnam.

The first three singles were split evenly, with the USA winning one when Andy Bean secured that victory over Ian Woosnam, Europe winning one when Howard Clark just beat Dan Pohl, and a half between Sam Torrance and Larry Mize. Then, with Europe needing only two points from the remaining nine, the Americans made their long-expected fightback, winning the next four matches and reducing the deficit to one point with five matches still to be decided.

The first of these five was Eamonn Darcy against the redoubtable American Ben Crenshaw. On this occasion Crenshaw did not help himself by slamming his putter into the ground after missing a putt at the 6th, breaking it. He had to putt with his three-iron for the rest of the round. To his credit, Crenshaw fought like a tiger and, even though Darcy quickly went three up, Crenshaw got it all back and even went one up at the 16th. Darcy squared the match on the 17th and at the 18th Crenshaw hit a poor drive and finished with a bogey 5. Darcy also suffered, as his second to the green finished in a bunker. He played a great shot from there to four feet from the hole. The putt would win the match. However, it was a very fast downhill putt and a miss could easily leave him further away than he was already. His nerve held and he holed it. It was all the more admirable because it gave him his first Ryder Cup victory in eleven attempts.

Years later, and the memory still brought tears to Darcy's eyes. In his words:

> It was all downhill and oh, so fast. I thought I could hole it, but if I didn't, I didn't think I would be able to get the one back; there would be just nothing to stop it. There was a little break from the left and I just kissed it, and in it went.

Now Europe really was on the brink of a famous victory. Langer was all square with Nelson going down the last, and he made the green in two. Nelson was short and would have to chip and putt for his par. He chipped to within three feet and Langer had a long putt for a birdie and to win the match. He did not go for it, instead putting just outside Nelson's marker, and suggested a half. To many people's surprise, with the USA needing every point, Nelson accepted it. Minutes later, Ballesteros clinched the European victory by beating Curtis Strange 2 and 1. Gordon Brand Jr. halved with Hal Sutton to make the final score Europe 15, USA 13.

So Nicklaus had now suffered what he had dreaded. He was the first American captain to lead his team to defeat on home soil. Needless to say, he was gracious in that defeat, saying: 'The Europeans were tougher coming down the final hole today.'

Tony Jacklin, who in six years had succeeded in turning the perennial losers into winners, was tearful and almost speechless, confining himself to: 'It is the greatest week of my life.'

Ian Woosnam stood up and said what many were thinking: 'I'm not one for making speeches, but what this man has done today, he deserves a knighthood. And he's got to be captain again in 1989.' Two years earlier, Peter Jacobsen had said much the same at The Belfry: 'You should make Jacklin captain for the next 30 years; if not, you can send him over to us.' Twenty years later, Paul Azinger, on being asked at his own coronation as captain who his vice captains would be, said 'to start with … probably Tony Jacklin'. That's how highly even his opponents rated his performance.

Unfortunately, the greatest week of Jacklin's life was followed shortly by the terrible tragedy of the death of his beloved wife, Vivien, from a brain haemorrhage. She had always been a great support to him and had been critical in securing the support of the players' wives who had done so much, both at the Belfry and Muirfield Village, to whip up support for the European team among the spectators.

There had been considerable debate as to whether or not Jacklin should continue as captain. He made it clear he was happy to do so when he said:

Already I am being asked whether I will captain again. Of course it would be presumptuous of me to speculate; it is up to others to decide … But if everyone who mattered was to suggest that they felt the best chance of another win was with me again, I would not shirk the responsibility.

In the event, Jacklin was asked to carry on as captain and accepted the invitation. Fortunately he met another very competent and charming lady, Astrid Waagen, whom he married at Christmas in 1988, and who would prove to be just as helpful as Vivien. She had previously been married to Alan Kendall, a guitarist with the Bee Gees, so she knew all about showbiz and how to cope with the sometimes difficult and eccentric personalities involved. When the American team came to The Belfry again in 1989 she struck up a friendship with Maria, the wife of the new American captain, Ray Floyd, and together they made sure that their respective teams' wives had a good time and were an asset to their team.

25–27 September 1987 Muirfield Village, Columbus, Ohio, USA *Captains:* A. Jacklin (Europe), J. Nicklaus (USA)			
Europe		**United States**	
Foursomes: Morning			
S. Torrance & H. Clark	0	C. Strange & T. Kite (4 & 2)	1
K. Brown & B. Langer	0	H. Sutton & D. Pohl (2 & 1)	1
N. Faldo & I. Woosnam (2 holes)	1	L. Wadkins & I. Mize	0
S. Ballesteros & J.M. Olazábal (1 hole)	1	L. Nelson & P. Stewart	0
Fourballs: Afternoon			
C. Brand Jr. & J. Rivero (3 & 2)	1	B. Crenshaw & S. Simpson	0
A. Lyle & B. Langer (1 hole)	1	A. Bean & M. Calcavecchia	0
N. Faldo & I. Woosnam (2 & 1)	1	H. Sutton & D. Pohl	0
S. Ballesteros & J.M. Olazábal (2 & 1)	1	C. Strange & T. Kite	0

(continued)

25–27 September 1987 (continued)			
Muirfield Village, Columbus, Ohio, USA			
Captains: A. Jacklin (Europe), J. Nicklaus (USA)			
Europe		**United States**	
Foursomes: Morning			
J. Rivero & G. Brand Jr.	0	C. Strange & T. Kite (3 & 1)	1
N. Faldo & I. Woosnam (halved)	½	H. Sutton & L. Mize (halved)	½
A. Lyle & B. Langer (2 & 1)	1	L. Wadkins & L. Nelson	0
S. Ballesteros & J.M. Olazábal (1 hole)	1	B. Crenshaw & P. Stewart	0
Fourballs: Afternoon			
N. Faldo & I. Woosnam (5 & 4)	1	C. Strange & T. Kite	0
E. Darcy & G. Brand Jr.	0	A. Bean & P. Stewart (3 & 2)	1
S. Ballesteros & J.M. Olazábal	0	H. Sutton & L. Mize (2 & 1)	1
S. Lyle & B. Langer (1 hole)	1	L. Wadkins & L. Nelson	0
Singles:			
I. Woosnam	0	A. Bean (1 hole)	1
H. Clark (1 hole)	1	D. Pohl	0
S. Torrance (halved)	½	L. Mize (halved)	½
N. Faldo	0	M. Calcavecchia (1 hole)	1
J.M. Olazábal	0	P. Stewart (2 holes)	1
J. Rivero	0	S. Simpson (2 & 1)	1
A. Lyle	0	T. Kite (3 & 2)	1
E. Darcy (1 hole)	1	B. Crenshaw	0
B. Langer (halved)	½	L. Nelson (halved)	½
S. Ballesteros (2 & 1)	1	C. Strange	0
K. Brown	0	L. Wadkins (3 & 2)	1
G. Brand Jr. (halved)	½	H. Sutton (halved)	½
Europe 15; USA 13			

'Spectators clapping us all the way'

Beaten twice in a row, the Americans had now lost all sense of complacency about the Ryder Cup and for the next match Floyd brought probably the strongest team Jacklin had faced. Nicklaus had impressed on the team that the Europeans were hardened 'winners' now. 'Winning is winning,' he said, 'it doesn't matter if it's the Hong Kong fourball. The Europeans are more used to it than we are.'

This was the team the Americans chose to make sure they did not lose three matches in a row:

The ten who qualified automatically were Tom Kite, Curtis Strange, Mark Calcavecchia, Payne Stewart, Mark O'Meara – all with Ryder Cup experience – and Paul Azinger, Chip Beck, Mark McCumber, Ken Green and Fred Couples – all newcomers. To make up the twelve, Floyd picked the very experienced Tom Watson and Lanny Wadkins. (He was heavily criticised for his selection of Wadkins, who had suffered a poor season.)

Thanks to the European victories, and also because the game of golf was exploding in popularity around the world, publicity surrounding the match reached unprecedented heights, and not only in Europe and the USA but also in places like Japan and South Africa. The Americans raced off to a good start in the foursomes on the first morning. Wadkins and Stewart beat Howard Clark and Mark James, while Calcavecchia and Green beat Langer and Ronan Rafferty. Kite and Strange halved with Faldo and Woosnam, while Watson and Beck also halved with the formidable partnership of Ballesteros and Olazábal. 3–1 to the USA and not a single victory for the Europeans.

Jacklin did not panic and kept three of the pairs together. He replaced Langer and Rafferty with Torrance and Gordon Brand Jr. The result was four wins for the Europeans and a score at the end of day one of Europe 5, USA 3. The support from the spectators had been tremendous. Gordon Brand Jr., playing in his first match on home soil, said:

> The spectators were clapping us all the way. You feel two
> up before you start.

The Americans came back in the fourballs in the second morning but, even so, only won two of the four matches. Beck and Azinger and Calcavecchia and Green enjoyed relatively easy victories over Gordon Brand Jr. and Torrance and

Christy O'Connor Jr. and Rafferty, but Wadkins and Stewart were not good enough to beat the strong and proven partnership of Faldo and Woosnam. Kite and Strange made a valiant effort against that other proven European partnership, Ballesteros and Olazábal, but just lost by one hole. In the afternoon, it was again two wins for each side. For once, the Faldo/Woosnam partnership failed against Beck and Azinger and so did that of Langer and Cañizares against Kite and McCumber. By mid-afternoon the match stood at 7–7. Then the Europeans reasserted themselves with victories by Clark and James over Stewart and Strange – just, by one hole – and another easy one by Ballesteros and Olazábal, this time over Calcavecchia and Green. And so the Europeans once again went into the final day leading 9–7.

This time for the singles, Jacklin split his best players, putting Ballesteros, Langer and Olazábal at the top and Faldo and Woosnam at the bottom. Unfortunately, the plan did not work. Before Ballesteros had lost to Azinger by one hole and Langer had been beaten 3 and 2 by Beck, news came through that, further down the order, Howard Clark had been overwhelmed by Tom Kite by 8 and 7. In short, the Europeans had slumped from 9–7 up to 10–9 down.

As the crowd became increasingly anxious, the Europeans recovered their poise when Olazábal just beat Payne Stewart by one hole and Rafferty beat Calcavecchia by the same margin.

Stewart was the first of four Americans to drive into the water at the 18th, effectively throwing away matches they could have won or halved. The cheering of the partisan crowd that greeted these mishaps did not go down well with the Americans; some said it contributed to similar behaviour by American spectators at the 'battle' of Kiawah Island two years later, of which more in the next chapter.

Back to 12–10 in Europe's favour. Christy O'Connor Jr. moved them one point nearer ultimate victory when he hit the most magnificent two-iron all of 200 yards to within four feet of the hole at the 18th. Disconcerted, Fred Couples pushed the approach from his much longer drive, chipped poorly and conceded the hole and the win. Ten minutes later Cañizares beat Green, and the Europeans had achieved the fourteen points they needed to retain the trophy.

At this point they were leading 14–10 but then contrived to lose the last four singles to make the final score 14–14. So, the Europeans, as the holders, retained the Cup but losing the last four matches made for something of an anti-climax. Nevertheless, Tony Jacklin could be immensely proud of what he had achieved and he immediately announced his retirement, saying:

> You have got to know when to quit and this is that moment. It's been an honour and a privilege but the players now need someone who is closer to their own age.

Jacklin recommended that his successor be Bernard Gallacher who had been an assistant, and a first-rate assistant, to him. Within weeks the PGA confirmed that they had indeed asked Gallacher to be captain.

Jacklin was going to be a hard act to follow.

22–24 September 1989
The Belfry Golf & Country Club, Sutton Coldfield, West Midlands, England
Captains: A. Jacklin (Europe), D. Stockton (USA)

Europe		United States	
Foursomes: Morning			
N. Faldo & I. Woosnam (halved)	½	T. Kite & C. Strange (halved)	½
H. Clark & M. James	0	L. Wadkins & P. Stewart (1 hole)	1
S. Ballesteros & J.M. Olazábal (halved)	½	T. Watson & C. Beck (halved)	½
B. Langer & R. Rafferty	0	M. Calcavecchia & K. Green (2 & 1)	1
Fourballs: Afternoon			
S. Torrance & G. Brand Jr. (1 hole)	1	C. Strange & P. Azinger	0
H. Clark & M. James (3 & 2)	1	F. Couples & L. Wadkins	0
N. Faldo & I. Woosnam (2 holes)	1	M. Calcavecchia & M. McCumber	0
S. Ballesteros & J.M. Olazábal (6 & 5)	1	T. Watson & M. O'Meara	0
Foursomes: Morning			
I. Woosnam & N. Faldo (3 & 2)	1	L. Wadkins & P. Stewart	0
G. Brand Jr. & S. Torrance	0	C. Beck & P. Azinger (4 & 3)	1
C. O'Connor Jr. & R. Rafferty	0	M. Calcavecchia & K. Green (3 & 2)	1
S. Ballesteros & J.M. Olazábal (1 hole)	1	T. Kite & C. Strange	0
Fourballs: Afternoon			
N. Faldo & I. Woosnam	0	C. Beck & P. Azinger (& 1)	1
B. Langer & J.M. Cañizares	0	T. Kite & M. McCumber (2 & 1)	1
H. Clark & M. James (1 hole)	1	P. Stewart & C. Strange	0
S. Ballesteros & J.M. Olazábal (4 & 2)	1	M. Calcavecchia & K. Green	0
Singles:			
S. Ballesteros	0	P. Azinger (1 hole)	1
B. Langer	0	C. Beck (3 & 2)	1
J.M. Olazábal (1 hole)	1	P. Stewart	0
R. Rafferty (1 hole)	1	M. Calcavecchia	0
H. Clark	0	T. Kite (8 & 7)	1
M. James (3 & 2)	1	M. O'Meara	0
C. O'Connor Jr. (1 hole)	1	F. Couples	0
J.M. Cañizares (1 hole)	1	K. Green	0
G. Brand Jr.	0	M. McCumber (1 hole)	1
S. Torrance	0	T. Watson (3 & 1)	1
N. Faldo	0	L. Wadkins (1 hole)	1
I. Woosnam	0	C. Strange (2 holes)	1
Europe 14; USA 14			

Chapter 6
Over to you, Bernard

'War on the Shore'
Kiawah Island 1991

'I had to split up two winning partnerships'
The Belfry 1993

'I tried to keep the pressure on the golf course'
Oak Hill, Rochester 1995

'War on the Shore'

Taking over from Jacklin was an intimidating prospect. He had achieved so much, even if he had been fortunate to have first-class golfers of the calibre of Seve Ballesteros, Bernhard Langer, Nick Faldo, Sandy Lyle and Ian Woosnam. Compounding the challenge was the fact that these stars were beginning to show their age and there were not too many obvious successors.

Certainly Gallacher was very experienced. He had played in the eight Ryder Cup matches between 1969 and 1983 and served as Jacklin's assistant in the next three. He always insisted he was an assistant and not vice-captain, saying:

> That was something we never had in those days, in fact I don't know where that came from. I was only there to help. I never attended team meetings, indeed never went in the team room. Tony and I would have a meeting in the mornings and anything logistical I would sort out for him, but as for pairings or tactics that was up to Tony and the players, I never got involved.

He may not have been as inspirational as Jacklin and, of course, he never won a Major, but he carried on most of Jacklin's initiatives such as the pursuit of excellence and having the best of everything in support. He said later:

> Compared with times I played, Tony introduced a more relaxed style of captaincy. The players didn't have to dress up for formal team dinners, as had been the case in my day. His first concern was always for the team, and to cut out everything that might interfere with the best possible preparation.

Initially, apart from Sandy Lyle, who had completely lost his form, Gallacher still had the stars and José Maria Olazábal was a fine replacement for Lyle. Indeed, he and Ballesteros were almost unbeatable when playing together. But unfortunately, although they had been successful together in the 1980s, Faldo and Woosnam did not gel at Kiawah Island. As Gallacher put it:

> They had been successful in both the last two matches. So, along with Seve and Ollie, we had two cast-in-stone partnerships. But Nick and Ian didn't gel and it wasn't till later I found out they didn't really want to play together. By then they had lost two matches on the first day.
>
> Successful partnerships occur when one player is more assertive than the other, a sort of team leader if you like. In the past, Woosnam had looked up to Faldo, who made all the decisions; Nick always made the decisions! By 1991, Ian had won the Masters, was number one in the world and instead of working together, they competed with one another.

Gallacher was unlucky in the choice of Kiawah Island as the venue in that the course was not really ready. Furthermore, it was designed to be the secluded jewel in the island's crown, or in other words an exclusive club for the most privileged. The clubhouse was not much more than a locker room on stilts and could not cater for the people associated with the modern Ryder Cup match (shades of Lindrick 1957!) Even the teams had to change in a Portakabin.

Then there was a severe setback for the European supporters. As Gallacher said:

The support we had at Muirfield Village had been tremendous; a shock for the Americans and a great boost for us. Unfortunately at Kiawah, Keith Prowse was in charge of travel and transport at the UK end, and just before the match, they went bust. They'd already taken all the money, but that was then tied up in the courts, so a lot of people couldn't go who had wanted to go. Keith Prowse had been responsible for chartering Concorde, and it was only because Johnnie Walker stepped in and paid for it, that we could go by Concorde.

And for those that did go, it was hard work. The nearest town with any decent hotels was Charleston, almost an hour away. The course was designed to be used with buggies. Anyone walking round was faced with long walks between greens and tees, especially that between the 9th green and 10th tee which measured no less than 900 yards!

But if the Europeans' support was a bit muted, that given to the Americans was not. The new captain, Dave Stockton, realised that he would need all the help he could get, saying:

> We had just lost six straight years, hadn't seen the cup, probably forgotten what it looked like. So there was a sense of urgency. When Nicklaus lost at Muirfield Village, it became apparent to me, and every captain after me, if Nicklaus can lose on his own course then anybody can get beat. If you're going to be successful you're going to have to dot the 'I's and cross the 'T's of this thing.
>
> I knew I had to get the team to bond. I did a number of things to try and ensure it wasn't just one or two individuals that were going to carry it. I worked on getting them all to have a whole team concept.

The first Gulf War was still going on, so there was a lot of pride in America at that time. That certainly brought the guys together. The old forage caps might have looked a bit aggressive, but it was the symbol of pride we felt at that time.

I got the Tour to play shoot-outs on Tuesday at tournaments, not just the usual old practice rounds. At half a dozen events I was able to put various players together, to see how they got on, what worked and what didn't. A couple of times we even had a Ryder Cup format, a little match if you like. There were about four of us who used to meet up and talk Ryder Cup stuff; that was Paul Azinger, Payne Stewart, Lanny Wadkins and myself. We talked strategy, psychology, different things like that, and when we got Kiawah I felt the team was ready to play, to win. It still blows me away that Lanny is one of the ones that didn't win when it was his turn in 1995, because he understood what we were about.

And the Americans, still perhaps somewhat sore after what they perceived as unsportsmanlike support for the Europeans at The Belfry, continued their aggressive approach at the pre-match dinner where a 40-minute film of the history of the Ryder Cup, depicting only American triumphs, was shown.

Even worse, a local disc jockey had read out the British team's hotel phone number on his show and encouraged his listeners to 'wake up the enemy' by telephoning the players in the middle of the night. Many did, in some cases making obscene remarks to players' wives.

Once play started, Ballesteros and Olazábal gained their usual victory beating Azinger and Beck 2 and 1, though not before an argument over the Americans wrongly changing their ball to one with a different compression. Then the Europeans lost the remainder of the morning four-somes, with Langer and James losing to Floyd and Couples, newcomers David Gilford and Colin Montgomerie losing to Wadkins and Irwin and, much to Gallacher's disappointment, Faldo and Woosnam losing to Stewart and Calcavecchia.

Gallacher made changes in his pairings for the afternoon and opened with Sam Torrance and David Feherty. The Irishman was very nervous and scuffed his first putt. His old friend Torrance said to him:

> If you don't pull yourself together, I'm going to join them [their opponents, Wadkins and O'Meara] and you can play all three of us, you useless bastard!

This treatment worked. Feherty went on to play well and they secured a half. Ballesteros and Olazábal beat Azinger and Beck again and newcomer Steven Richardson, partnering Mark James, beat Corey Pine and Calcavecchia by one half. As in the morning, Faldo and Woosnam lost again – this time heavily, 5 and 3, to Floyd and Couples. The result of all this was that, at the end of the first day of the 'war on the shore', the Americans were leading 4½–3½.

On the second day, poor old Gallacher made another tactical error regarding Faldo. If Faldo could not play with Woosnam any more, he reasoned, why not pair him with the newcomer, David Gilford, in the hope that he would guide him. Guide him? As the golf commentator Lauren St John wrote:

> Faldo's surliness and Gilford's painful shyness ensured a pairing with less conversation than Trappist monks.

The pair were slaughtered 7 and 6 by Azinger and O'Meara. Needless to say, the British press strongly criticised Faldo for not encouraging Gilford enough and, also needless to say, Faldo brushed off this criticism by saying that he should not have been paired with Gilford in the first place.

Gallacher beat himself up somewhat over the decision, saying later:

> He [Faldo] was playing all right when he arrived, hitting the ball very well, but like most of the team found the new strain of grass on the greens, Tiftdwarf, difficult to read. He couldn't hole a putt for love nor money. He let it affect the rest of his game. By now I realised what I should have known from the start. He and Woosie no longer wanted to play together. I thought to give Nick some responsibility for shepherding one of the newcomers. I still felt David Gilford was basically playing well; his game was ideal for foursomes, so sent the pair of them out on the second morning. It was a disaster. Nick by now was so deep inside his own shell, he never made the effort to communicate with his partner, let alone help him through the rigours of a Ryder Cup. That was another bit of inspiration that went wrong!

> If I have any anxiety over that first Ryder Cup, it is for David Gilford. In hindsight two rookies going out on the first morning is not a good thing. Obviously putting him with Faldo was a mistake, and then there was the brown envelope. [As mentioned earlier, in the Ryder Cup, when it comes to the singles and every player is involved, each captain puts the name of one player in the 'brown envelope' – the man who would not play in the event that one of the other side could not play due to ill health.]

I had put David's name in the envelope because he had played twice and lost twice, but never thought it would be used. In all the years I had played, and the years of Tony's captaincy, the brown envelope had never been an issue and who was in it never discussed or divulged. Steve Pate had played the previous afternoon, so the thought he might not play never entered my mind.

Again, one of the failings of Kiawah as a venue was that we had no team room back at the hotel, some had breakfast there, some at the course. When I saw the draw, and that Stockton had pulled Pate out, David was already on his way out there, and it was Tony Jacklin who gave him the news. I certainly should have been there for that and felt really bad about it.

This time both Feherty and Torrance failed, as did James and Richardson, and yet again it was left to Ballesteros and Olazábal to salvage a point by beating Couples and Floyd. By lunchtime on the second day, the Americans were leading 7½–4½ and things were starting to look serious for the Europeans.

Fortunately, they fought back very strongly in the afternoon fourballs. Woosnam and newcomer Paul Broadhurst got them off to a good start with a fine 2 and 1 win against Azinger and Irwin. Langer helped Montgomerie secure his first Ryder Cup point when they beat Corey Pavin and Steve Pate. Mark James and Steve Richardson found their winning touch again and beat Wadkins and Wayne Levi, while Ballesteros and Olazábal secured a half against Stewart and Couples. It was 8–8 with just the singles to come.

How would the Europeans cope? In 28 Ryder Cup matches the Americans had lost the singles only four times. They certainly made a good start when the grumpy Faldo beat Floyd. Gallacher was pleased he got this tactic right when he surmised that Faldo would pull himself together if given the responsibility of leading the team out. Then the originally nervous Feherty beat Payne Stewart 2 and 1. Montgomerie secured an unlikely half against Calcavecchia after the American had been four up with four to play. Calcavecchia then imploded to allow Montgomerie to win the last four holes.

The Europeans were now leading 11–9 (adding in the halves for the unplayed match), but the Americans won the next two matches when Azinger beat Olazábal and Pavin beat Richardson. Both Americans behaved rather badly, enticing the crowds to make more noise. Beck beat Woosnam but Ballesteros steadied things for Europe by beating Levi. 12–12 with four matches to go. Paul Broadhurst secured another point for Europe, beating Mark O'Meara 3 and 1, but then Couples and Wadkins beat Torrance and James, in both cases 3 and 2. It was 14–13 to the USA with just Bernhard Langer and Hale Irwin on the course.

After fourteen holes Irwin was two up, but at the 15th Langer holed a six-foot putt to make it only one down and, when Irwin three-putted the 17th, they were all-square on the 18th tee. This would be one of the holes in the Ryder Cup that would stick in everyone's memory. Langer drove and hit a solid drive into the middle of the fairway while Irwin clearly pulled his drive into the rough, only for the ball to reappear on the edge of the fairway. However, Irwin missed the green while Langer made it, even if he was thirteen feet from the hole. Irwin then hit a poor chip and was still 25 feet away in three. Langer putted and was then six feet away. Irwin putted to within two feet and Langer gave him the putt.

Langer now had his putt to win his match and retain the Ryder Cup. He took a long time over it, and much later would say that he did not take the line he wanted to take because of spike marks.

The memory of Langer's putt is etched on the minds of all who saw it, as it is on Langer's. In his words:

> The line of the putt was the left edge of the hole. Pete Colman [Langer's caddy] pointed to a pair of spike marks right on that line and they weren't so little. I was sure if I hit it at them the ball might go anywhere. So we determined that it might be better to putt it straight and hope it wouldn't break too much. I made a pretty good stroke, but it did break too much and the ball went right over the side of the hole.
>
> I was shocked, sad for the team, but didn't feel I had let anyone down. I had made a good stroke and the ball hadn't gone in. Faced with the same situation, I would probably make the same decision. I didn't mention the spike marks for some time as I felt it might sound like an excuse, that I'd yipped it or something. But the truth came out in time.

Whatever the full story, the upshot was that after much agonising he putted and missed. Europe had lost the Ryder Cup.

What did Gallacher learn from this exciting introduction to captaining the European Ryder Cup team? This was his answer:

> The one thing I learned from Kiawah Island was to think more deeply about the pairings, talk more to the players about who they would like to play with, even who they wouldn't want to play with. I still had Seve and Ollie, who never imagined they wouldn't be playing together. Other than that I still had a great side, we were back

at The Belfry, a tried and tested venue, where we were guaranteed great support, where everything was sure to work well.

13–15 September 1991			
Ocean Course, Kiawah Island, South Carolina, USA			
Captains: B. Gallacher (Europe), D. Stockton (USA)			
Europe		**United States**	
Foursomes: Morning			
S. Ballesteros & J.M. Olazábal (2 & 1)	1	P. Azinger & C. Beck	0
B. Langer & M. James	0	R. Floyd & F. Couples (2 & 1)	1
D. Gilford & C. Montgomerie	0	L. Wadkins & H. Irwin (4 & 2)	1
N. Faldo & I. Woosnam	0	P. Stewart & M. Calcavecchia (1 hole)	1
Fourballs: Afternoon			
S. Torrance & D. Feherty (halved)	½	L. Wadkins & M. O'Meara (halved)	½
S. Ballesteros & J.M. Olazábal (2 & 1)	1	P. Azinger & C. Beck	0
S. Richardson & M. James (5 & 4)	1	C. Pavin & M. Calcavecchia	0
N. Faldo & I. Woosnam	0	R. Floyd & F. Couples (5 & 3)	1
Foursomes: Morning			
D. Feherty & S. Torrance	0	H. Irwin & L. Wadkins (4 & 2)	1
M. James & S. Richardson	0	M. Calcavecchia & P. Stewart (1 hole)	1
N. Faldo & D. Gifford	0	P. Azinger & M. O'Meara (7 & 6)	1
S. Ballesteros & J.M. Olazábal (3 & 2)	1	F. Couples & R. Floyd	0
Fourballs: Afternoon			
I. Woosnam & P. Broadhurst (2 & 1)	1	P. Azinger & H. Irwin	0
B. Langer & C. Montgomerie (2 & 1)	1	C. Pavin & S. Pate	0
M. James & S. Richardson (3 & 1)	1	L. Wadkins & W. Levi	0
S. Ballesteros & J.M. Olazábal (halved)	½	P. Stewart & F. Couples (halved)	½

(continued)

Europe		United States	
13–15 September 1991 (continued)			
Ocean Course, Kiawah Island, South Carolina, USA			
Captains: B. Gallacher (Europe), D. Stockton (USA)			
Europe		**United States**	
Singles:			
N. Faldo (2 holes)	1	R. Floyd	0
D. Feherty (2 & 1)	1	P. Stewart	0
C. Montgomerie (halved)	½	M. Calcavecchia (halved)	½
J.M. Olazábal	0	P. Azinger (2 holes)	1
S.R. Richardson	0	C. Pavin (2 & 1)	1
S. Ballesteros (3 & 2)	1	W. Levi	0
I. Woosnam	0	C. Beck (3 & 1)	1
P. Broadhurst (3 & 1)	1	M. O'Meara	0
S. Torrance	0	F. Couples (3 & 2)	1
M. James	0	L. Wadkins (3 & 2)	1
B. Langer (halved)	½	H. Irwin (halved)	½
D. Gilford (halved)	½	S. Pate (halved – Pate withdrew through injury)	½
Europe 13½; US 14½			

'I had to split up two winning partnerships'

In the run-up to the match in Britain in 1993, which was to be held again at The Belfry, there was much comment about the lack of sportsmanship and the overt aggression that had been shown at Kiawah Island. One journalist wrote:

> American professionals sporting army fatigues, unruly crowds influencing the play and accusations of games-manship have no place in the Ryder Cup. What next? Arm-wrestling to decide who has the honour on each tee?

The British and American PGAs got together to discuss measures that could be put in place to prevent a repetition of some of the worst excesses at Kiawah Island. First, crowd numbers would be limited and certain restrictions would be placed on those who were allowed to walk inside the ropes.

As far as the players were concerned, they would be given instructions on what they could say to the media.

The new captain of the American team was Tom Watson and he was determined to try to restore what he saw as the right spirit in which the match should be played. Before he left America he said:

> This isn't war, this is golf. We're going over there and will try like hell to kick their butts. And they're going to try like hell to kick ours. That's as it should be. But when it's over, we should be able to get together, lift a glass and toast one another. That's what the Ryder Cup is all about.

As always, the American team was formidable on paper. Experienced players such as Payne Stewart, Paul Azinger, Chip Beck, Corey Pavin, Tom Kite and Fred Couples qualified, as did newcomers Lee Janzen, Davis Love III, Jim Gallagher Jr. and John Cook. For his two captain's choices, Watson went for the very experienced and battle-hardened Ray Floyd and Lanny Wadkins.

Meanwhile, Bernard Gallacher, who had had to be persuaded to continue as European captain, had some worries. As we have seen, the originally successful partnership of Woosnam and Faldo had foundered in the Kiawah Island match, and now an equally promising one of Faldo and Montgomerie seemed to be there for the taking. For the moment, Faldo could again be the dominant partner. And dominant he was, especially when it came to putting. As Montgomerie said:

> It started in the practice rounds. I would look at a putt and think it was right or left lip, but Nick would say that was far too casual, and between us, particularly in four-

somes, we would have to work out the four or five points over which the ball had to travel to get to the hole; sort of golfing dot-to-dot, you might say.

Gallacher was also concerned about Bernhard Langer, who had not played for six weeks because of a neck injury. Ballesteros had also suffered a poor year and Gallacher said later:

> I had to give him a captain's pick; back then a side without Seve was unthinkable and with four out of the five series fourballs or foursomes, he was a vital part of that great partnership with Olazábal. Because of his poor form, what I didn't get from him that year was his work with the rookies, his captain's role on the course; he was too wrapped up in trying to sort out his own game.

When the match began Gallacher picked those whom he considered to be his eight best players for the opening foursomes. Torrance and James (who would play Pavin and Wadkins) in match one, to be followed by Ballesteros and Olazábal (playing Kite and Love), Langer and Woosnam (playing Couples and Floyd) and Faldo and Montgomerie (playing Azinger and Stewart). Pavin and Wadkins won easily and then Langer and Woosnam overwhelmed Couples and Floyd 7 and 5 – a record margin for a European pair in the foursomes. The big surprise was a defeat for the Spanish pair, Ballesteros and Olazábal. Seve was definitely not his usual self and even declined to go for the 10th green off the tee. Very surprised, Kite then hit a beautiful shot into the middle of the green. Olazábal's chip was still outside the Americans', but Ballesteros duly holed it for a birdie three. Could Davis Love hole his for an eagle? 'Yes' was the answer, and the Americans held their lead to win 2 and 1. In the last game Faldo and Montgomerie beat Floyd and Couples comfortably 4 and 3.

In the afternoon the Spanish pair exacted their revenge on Kite and Love, winning 4 and 3. The final match, between Faldo and Montgomerie and Azinger and Couples, had to be halted on the 17th green because the light was fading. Before that, newcomer Peter Baker had played well with Woosnam and they just beat Jim Gallagher and Lee Janzen, while Wadkins and Pavin had a reasonably comfortable victory over Langer and Barry Lane. So it was 4–3 to the Europeans with one match to be settled early the next morning.

Faldo and Montgomerie had birdied the 17th to bring them to all square and at 8:00am the next morning there were two good drives and two poor new ones. The shoot-out was now effectively between Faldo and Azinger. Both made the green with their approaches but Faldo left his long putt ten feet short of the hole. Azinger almost holed for a birdie for a definite win, but his putt slid past and he had to settle for a par. Could Faldo hole that ten-footer? Of course he could, and the match was halved: Europe 4½, USA 3½.

By lunch that day the score was Europe 7½, USA 4½. Faldo and Montgomerie had beaten Wadkins and Pavin fairly comfortably, Langer and Woosnam beat Couples and Azinger and yet again Ballesteros and Olazábal beat Love and Kite. The only American win was a comfortable one by Floyd and Stewart over Baker and Lane.

The Americans were going to need to do well in the afternoon or they would have a mountain to climb in the singles. As it happened, though, things had started to go wrong for Europe during the morning. Captain Bernard Gallacher recalled later:

I was beginning to think about winning the Ryder Cup that Saturday afternoon, then at 11.45 I got word that Seve wanted to see me on the 14th fairway. He was in the bottom foursome and he and Ollie were 2 up. He knew I had to have the afternoon pairings in at 12.00, but he wanted to say he didn't want to play that afternoon. 'But you're 2 up, you're going to win again and this partnership can always get points,' I told him. But he was adamant, he was dragging Olazábal down, his own play was too poor and he wanted to work on the practice ground to be ready to play in the singles. He wouldn't change his mind.

Moments later, Langer called in to say he wouldn't be able to play in the afternoon; his neck was too sore, and he wanted to rest to be ready for the singles. So with just two minutes to go, I had to split up two winning partnerships and put two new pairings together, with little or no warning.

The two newcomers, Constantino Rocca and Joakim Haegmann (the first Italian and first Swede to play in the European team) were called up to play with Mark James and Olazábal respectively. Unfortunately both lost as, surprisingly, did Faldo and Montgomerie. Ian Woosnam and Peter Baker won easily 6 and 5 against Couples and Azinger (Woosnam was performing brilliantly – this was his fourth win in the two days) but the 3–1 to Europe in the morning was matched 3–1 by the Americans in the afternoon. Europe would go into the singles leading by just one point.

Adding to Europe's concerns were the form of Ballesteros and the fitness of Langer. Finally, Torrance had a toe injury which was getting worse and he could not play. At least that meant a half, as Wadkins sportingly offered to stand down on the American side, saving Watson a tough decision as to whom he should leave out.

Gallacher stuck to the policy for the singles line-up he had employed at Kiawah Island, saying:

> I like the team to have a balanced look about it for the singles, with some strength at the top, a bit in the middle and some old hands down at the bottom, should it get tight.

Tom Watson, apart from Fred Couples at the top, put most of his heavyweights at the bottom. Europe started well, securing 3½ points from the first five matches as Woosnam halved with Couple while Montgomerie, Baker and Haegmann beat Janzen, Pavin and Cook. Only Lane just lost to Beck after being three up with five to play. A similar poor finish by Rocca, where he was one up with two to play against Love and lost, meant that Europe lost two matches that they had looked like winning.

Then came an avalanche of American wins as Stewart beat James, Gallagher beat Ballesteros, Floyd beat Olazábal and Kite beat Langer. The last match, between Faldo and Azinger, was halved, but by then Europe had lost once again with a final score of 15–13 to the USA.

26–28 September 1993			
The Belfry Golf & Country Club, Sutton Coldfield, West Midlands, England			
Captains: B. Gallacher (Europe), T. Watson (USA)			
Europe		**United States**	
Foursomes: Morning			
S. Torrance & M. James	0	L. Wadkins & C. Pavin (4 & 3)	1
I. Woosnam & B. Langer (7 & 5)	1	P. Azinger & P. Stewart	0
S. Ballesteros & J.M. Olazábal	0	T. Kite & D. Love III (2 & 1)	1
N. Faldo & C. Montgomerie (4 & 3)	1	R. Floyd & F. Couples	0

(continued)

Europe		United States	
26–28 September 1993			
The Belfry Golf & Country Club, Sutton Coldfield, West Midlands, England			
Captains: B. Gallacher (Europe), T. Watson (USA)			
Fourballs: Afternoon			
I. Woosnam & P. Baker (1 hole)	1	J. Gallagher Jr. & L. Janzen	0
B. Langer & B. Lane	0	L. Wadkins & C. Pavin (4 & 2)	1
N. Faldo & C. Montgomerie (halved)	½	P. Azinger & F. Couples (halved)	½
S. Ballesteros & J.M. Olazábal (4 & 3)	1	D. Love III & T. Kite	0
Foursomes: Morning			
N. Faldo & C. Montgomerie (3 & 2)	1	L. Wadkins & C. Pavin	0
B. Langer & I. Woosnam (2 & 1)	1	F. Couples & P. Azinger	0
P. Baker & B. Lane	0	R. Floyd & P. Stewart (3 & 2)	1
S. Ballesteros & J.M. Olazábal (2 & 1)	1	D. Love III & T. Kite	0
Fourballs: Afternoon			
N. Faldo & C. Montgomerie	0	J. Cook & C. Beck (1 hole)	1
M. James & C. Rocca	0	C. Pavin & J. Gallagher Jr. (5 & 4)	1
I. Woosnam & P. Baker (6 & 5)	1	F. Couples & P. Azinger	0
J.M. Olazábal & J. Haeggman	0	R. Floyd & P. Stewart (2 & 1)	1
Singles:			
I. Woosnam (halved)	½	F. Couples (halved)	½
B. Lane	0	C. Beck (1 hole)	1
C. Montgomerie (1 hole)	1	L. Janzen	0
P. Baker (2 holes)	1	C. Pavin	0
J. Haeggman (1 hole)	1	J. Cook	0
M. James	0	P. Stewart (3 & 2)	1
C. Rocca	0	D. Love III (1 hole)	1
S. Ballesteros	0	J. Gallagher Jr. (3 & 2)	1
J.M. Olazábal	0	R. Floyd (2 holes)	1
B. Langer	0	T. Kite (2 holes)	1
N. Faldo (halved)	½	P. Azinger (halved)	½
S. Torrance (halved; S. Torrance retired due to injury; match halved)	½	L. Wadkins (halved)	½
Europe 13; USA 15			

'I tried to keep the pressure on the golf course'

So Gallacher had captained the European team twice and lost twice. Surely that was enough and someone else should be given a chance. Ballesteros was the obvious choice, but he was still playing so he was pencilled in for 1997. Other candidates ruled themselves out for one reason or another. Peter Oosterhuis and Sandy Lyle were both spending nearly all their time in America and furthermore, if Ballesteros was going to take over in 1997, whoever took command in 1995 would only get one match.

In the end the PGA turned again to Gallacher who, after all, had done a pretty good job. Gallacher himself was happy to have one more go, saying later:

> Before I ever started, I made up my mind to enjoy it, and I had done. I always, as a player, enjoyed the Ryder Cups, the camaraderie, the forming of partnerships, friendships, and I found the same as captain. I never found it stressful, like Sam Torrance or Seve did. I'm not as emotional as those guys – Sam, Seve and Tony Jacklin. I tried to keep the pressure to the golf course, and not to still have it around off the course. I tried to instil that in the players.

The 1995 match was to be played at Oak Hill Country Club, Rochester, New York, and before the Europeans made their now customary flight on Concorde, trouble broke out.

Just as the team was about to board Concorde for the flight to America, the press broke a story concerning Nick Faldo's marital problems. He had been playing almost exclusively in America, basing himself in Orlando, while his wife Gill was back in England bringing up the children. That summer he had formed a relationship that was to bring their marriage to an end. Faldo wasn't on Concorde, as he was already in America. Gill, being completely in the dark until the news broke, travelled with the team, but in floods of tears. Faldo greeted the team as it came off Concorde, embraced some of the wives and girlfriends, and shook his wife by the hand. It didn't get any better: 'It is amazing how well Nick played, considering what was going on in his private life,' reflects Gallacher. 'Gill and Lesley [Bernard's wife] are best friends and neither of them knew what was going on until it broke in the press just as we were leaving.'

Compounding these woes was the problem Olazábal was having with his fitness; some ailment was attacking his legs and back. At least he could be replaced by Woosnam as an alternative wild card. The European team was experienced – some said 'too old' – with only the newcomer, Per-Ulrik Johansson from Sweden, aged under 30. Apart from the other newcomer, Philip Watson, in Woosnam, Faldo, Clark, James, Torrance, Montgomerie, Rocca and Gilford there were plenty who had been round the block a few times.

Nor was the American team quite up to the usual high standard. There were only three survivors from their victorious 1993 team – Fred Couples, Davis Love III and Corey Pavin. There were five rookies – Tom Lehman, Jeff Maggart, Brad Faxon, Lauren Roberts and Phil Mickelson. Captain Lanny Wadkins received some criticism for his wild-card choice of Couples and Curtis Strange, who appeared to have been picked on the basis that they were long-standing friends of Wadkins rather than on their current golfing form.

The first morning foursomes went reasonably well for Europe, especially taking into account the problems Gallacher was facing on the final practice day. This was how he remembered it:

I wasn't totally without established pairings. I had Bernhard Langer and Ian Woosnam, who had played well together two years previously, winning twice in foursomes, and I intended putting them together again. Then I was going to put Philip Walton out with Sam Torrance, as both of them were taught by Sam's dad, Bob Torrance, and know one another well. Then in the practice round Philip's game began to go off, and I asked him if he was still happy about opening up in the first set of foursomes. He said he wasn't really ready and would prefer to wait till the fourballs. No sooner that, than Ian came to me and said he didn't want to play tomorrow, 'You know, my game's not really there.' Now all this came up in the final practice. I always insist that the final nine holes of practice be played as strict foursomes, no second shots, so we all go into the first morning in foursome mode. Now I really was starting from scratch, and I ended up putting Langer with Per-Ulrik Johansson, and Sam Torrance with Constantino Rocca; where that came from I've no idea! And they both came off!

So those pairs won, against Crenshaw and Strange and Jay Haas and Couples respectively. Unfortunately the formerly sound Faldo/Montgomerie pairing had had its day. Faldo had his marital problems and Montgomerie was now too good to be pushed around by Faldo. They lost to Pavin and Lehman while Clark and James lost to Love and Maggart. So, it was 2–2 at lunch.

In the afternoon, the Americans were dominant and Gallacher certainly blamed himself for one of the losses, saying:

Then I made my one real mistake. I had one or two other pairings for the fourballs that afternoon, but as the time approached to put in the afternoon line-up [midday], Bernhard and Per-Ulrik were something like 3 or 4 up with just five to play. Now, when I played in the Ryder Cup and won, I just couldn't wait to get out there and do it all again, so I put them together again. What a disaster.

No sooner had I put my pairings in than it started to rain and they [Langer and Johansson] started losing holes; more than an hour later they scraped home on the last green, but were soaked through, cold, and only half an hour for a sandwich and a change of clothes. They were no match for a fresh, dry and fit Pavin and Mickelson. When I went into the team room that evening I told the team that if we lose the Ryder Cup by a point, they can blame me. It was my mistake; I got that one completely wrong.

He may have got that one wrong but, more by luck perhaps, he got his one victorious pair of the afternoon, Ballesteros and David Gilford, right. This was how he remembered that choice:

David is a very straight hitter, so he could get the pars and maybe Seve might come in with a birdie or two. Anyway, Seve inspired David. David played way above himself, he would say so himself, and Seve did what Seve does best, annoying the opposition, getting in the way, getting even an American crowd on their side and they won handsomely.

As well as Langer and Johansson getting hammered, Torrance and Rocca were also overwhelmed by Maggert and Roberts 6 and 5 and when Faldo and Montgomerie lost again, this time 3 and 2 to Couples and Love, the Europeans ended the first day 5–3 down. A good performance the next morning was essential and they achieved it, with Faldo and Montgomerie finally finding their winning form again and beating Strange and Haas 4 and 2. Torrance and Rocca avenged their 6 and 5 defeat of the previous afternoon by beating Love and Maggert by the same margin. Woosnam and Walton just lost to Roberts and Jacobsen but Langer and Gilford easily beat Pavin and Lehman 4 and 3. So, 6–6 at lunch.

The afternoon fourballs were going to be critical and, unfortunately for the Europeans, the Americans came back strongly and won them 3–1, with only Woosnam and Rocca securing a European point when they beat Love and Crenshaw 3 and 2.

It was 9–7 to the Americans and they had rarely lost the singles. Was poor Gallacher going down to his third defeat? He must have feared so, but still he said:

The Americans can have their cheers on Saturday, we're going to have ours on Sunday! I really liked to have a balanced spread, some power at the start, experience near the end as well as a bit here and there in the middle. I didn't want to put a batch of first time players all out together anywhere in the draw. This time I didn't have as many rookies and really tried to work out what Lanny would do and react accordingly.

Being two ahead, and being the hard competitor that he is, I thought Wadkins would try and go out and win this thing quickly, have some good players out early, and keep a couple back to the end if things got tight. And that's what he did. I decided to put what I felt at the time to be my best and most experienced players in the middle. My biggest problem was what to do with Seve. Despite his short game, there is no way he could win a point and in the end I decided to put him out first. There was a fair chance he would get one of their good players, and that year Tom Lehman was very much one of the best, and if Seve was to go down, then let him make a big name for himself.

Seve was not best pleased with the idea at the time, but he preferred it to the other berth I suggested, going last. The thought that it might all come down to him, with the way his game was, really didn't appeal! He knew in his heart I had to get rid of his point early on, so first it was and what a fantastic job he did. He was still all square after 10 holes, and what a fillip to the team that was, as they set off; it really gave them a boost to think that he could keep such a player as Lehman tied up for that long.

Seve eventually lost 4 and 3 but then Howard Clark and Mark James both won, a considerable achievement as neither had played since the Friday morning. Woosnam secured a half with Couples before Rocca lost 3 and 2 to Love. The score was now 11½–9½ to the USA with seven matches still on the course. Now the Europeans started to come good. Montgomerie beat Crenshaw 3 and 1 and Torrance beat Roberts 2 and 1. Then came the first of some critical moments.

Gilford was one up playing the last against Brad Faxon and, as might be expected, found the fairway off the tee. Faxon did not, and with no option but to lay up 100 yards short, it looked like it would be a relatively simple task for Gilford to put another point on the board for Europe. However, while he is straight, Gilford is not long and he still had over 200 yards to go with his second. A long iron is hardly the ideal club with which to tackle the 18th at Oak Hill, especially with the greens firm and this one perched up on the hill. He hit a fine shot, but it skipped just through the green and into some long grass.

Now, Gilford cannot chip, or at least he certainly could not back then. He was a mere fifteen feet from the putting surface, with the pin just another ten feet away on the green and all downhill, the surface glassy. In some ways it was a shot similar to the one Pavin had holed the night before against Faldo and Langer, but Gilford's lie was far worse. By now it was apparent that a five might well be good enough, Faxon having played a good but not great third to some fifteen feet.

Seve, and possibly only Seve, might have managed to flick the ball up from Gilford's lie and somehow get it to stop somewhere close on that slippery green. It was certainly beyond Gilford's capabilities. He took a seven-iron, his aim being somehow to dribble the ball through the rough and trickle onto the green. If he were to try a normal shot, there was a better than even chance he would not keep it on the green.

Seve, watching from behind the green, could not believe it. 'Bernard,' he said to Gallacher, 'go and tell him he cannot run that through the rough; he must chip it.' Seve was already rehearsing the role of interfering captain that he was to play in Spain two years later! Gallacher, of course, did no such thing. Gilford's destiny was literally in his own hands. Failing to get to the green was the lesser of two evils: too strong and he was bound to be miles away. He duly scuffed it, but got through most of the rough and, to his credit, was able to get the next one within ten feet. Faxon, the great putter, missed and Gilford, again with all the fortunes of the Ryder Cup on his shoulders, somehow managed to hole it. One of the vital tasks, from Europe's point of view, had been achieved but there were still to be a couple more.

This contest was followed by Faldo holding his nerve and just beating Strange with a tricky putt on the last green.

That left Philip Walton, whose game had fallen away during the week of the match. He did have one outing, a foursome, with Ian Woosnam on the second morning but lost that, so his confidence was not high. He was in the penultimate match and, with Johansson by now down to Phil Mickelson immediately behind, Walton came to the 17th two up with two to play against Jay Haas, the whole match his to win or lose. With the Americans holding the trophy, only an outright win would bring it back to Europe. Walton had a put for the match from five feet at 17, but missed. Haas was never going to make four at 18, but from the fairway Walton came up short, into deep grass on the bank in front of the green; far better than being long and up where David Gilford had been. For an agonising moment or two it seemed he might have lost his ball. He hadn't, but the lie was poor and he chipped modestly, still some fifteen feet short. Somehow, shaking all over, he got close enough to be conceded.

There was no shame in Walton having the shakes – grown men were crying, and even in the context of this astonishing series of contests, this surely was the most amazing of them all. It almost passed unnoticed that for the first time, the Americans had lost the singles on their own soil. Perhaps they had been a bit too relaxed once they had a lead going into the final day.

Walton was the hero of the hour – the man who had won the Ryder Cup – and he received a magnificent welcome when he got back to his native Ireland. He then disappeared into obscurity and never played in the Ryder Cup again.

22–24 September 1995			
Oak Hill Country Club, Rochester, New York, USA			
Captains: B. Gallacher (Europe), L. Wadkins (USA)			
Europe		**United States**	
Foursomes: Morning			
N. Faldo & C. Montgomerie	0	C. Pavin & T. Lehman (1 hole)	1
S. Torrance & C. Rocca (3 & 2)	1	J. Haas & R. Couples	0
H. Clark & M. James	0	D. Love III & J. Maggert (4 & 3)	1
B. Langer & P.-U. Johansson (1 hole)	1	B. Crenshaw & C. Strange	0
Fourballs: Afternoon			
D. Gilford & S. Ballesteros (4 & 3)	1	B. Faxon & P. Jacobsen	0
S. Torrance & C. Rocca	0	J. Maggert & L. Roberts (6 & 5)	1
N. Faldo & C. Montgomerie	0	F. Couples & D. Love III (3 & 2)	1
B. Langer & P.-U. Johansson	0	C. Pavin & P. Mickelson (6 & 4)	1
Foursomes: Morning			
N. Faldo & C. Montgomerie (4 & 2)	1	C. Strange & J. Haas	0
S. Torrance & C. Rocca (6 & 5)	1	D. Love III & J. Maggert	0
I. Woosnam & P. Walton	0	L. Roberts & P. Jacobsen (1 hole)	1
B. Langer & D. Gilford (4 & 3)	1	C. Pavin & T. Lehman	0
Fourballs: Afternoon			
S. Torrance & C. Montgomerie	0	B. Faxon & F. Couples (4 & 2)	1
I. Woosnam & C. Rocca (3 & 2)	1	D. Love III & B. Crenshaw	0
S. Ballesteros & D. Gilford	0	J. Haas & P. Mickelson (3 & 2)	1
N. Faldo & B. Langer	0	C. Pavin & L. Roberts (1 hole)	1
Singles:			
S. Ballesteros	0	T. Lehman (4 & 3)	1
M. Clark (1 hole)	1	P. Jacobsen	0
M. James (4 & 3)	1	J. Maggert	0
I. Woosnam (halved)	½	F. Couples (halved)	½
C. Rocca	0	D. Love III (3 & 2)	1
D. Gilford (1 hole)	1	B. Faxon	0
C. Montgomerie (3 & 1)	1	B. Crenshaw	0
N. Faldo (1 hole)	1	C. Strange	0
S. Torrance (2 & 1)	1	L. Roberts	0
B. Langer	0	C. Pavin (3 & 2)	1
P. Walton (1 hole)	1	J. Haas	0
P.–U. Johansson	0	P. Mickelson (2 & 1)	1
Europe 14½; USA 13½			

Chapter 7

The irrepressible Seve

'I tried to get to the tee before they drove'
Valderrama 1997

The Bear Pit at Brookline
Brookline, Boston, Massachusetts 1999

'I tried to get to the tee before they drove'

The first Ryder Cup match in Europe outside Britain was always going to be in Spain and the captain of the European team was always going to be Seve Ballesteros. Spain had always been a great supporter of the European tour and had consistently supplied more members of the European team than any other country besides Britain. As for Seve, what other Spaniard could have been selected before him?

The truth is that as captain he displayed as many weaknesses as strengths, but Europe ended up winning so the weaknesses are now mentioned only to be laughed about and forgiven. His man management was poor. He interfered too much with the seasoned players and barely spoke to the newcomers, thereby increasing their nervousness. Colin Montgomerie, by this time one of the seasoned team members, said:

> Seve was always the leader, just couldn't help himself. Here we were in Spain; losing just wasn't an option. It was Seve and the King of Spain; you felt you were part of an irresistible force.

On the other hand, the Swedish newcomer, Thomas Björn, was not impressed with Seve's captaincy. Speaking about his singles game with Justin Leonard in which he lost the first four holes but then rallied to be one up with one to play, only to lose the last hole to halve his match, he said:

> Seve walked with me those first four holes, then fortunately went somewhere else. So what happened at the last? Seve reappeared!

That Seve wanted, and would get, his own way was apparent before the match. First, there was the question of which club in Spain would have the honour of hosting the match. A club near Madrid was the obvious choice but the logistical problems of the crowded capital itself counted against it. Of the other courses, Valderrama seemed to stand out. It had an excellent record of hosting tournaments and the course, although not long, was tricky and testing thanks to its narrow fairways, small greens and exposure to the varied winds of southern Spain. Its owner, Jaime Ortiz-Patiño, offered Ballesteros a deal whereby he would receive a percentage of the extra green fees generated by the club's hosting the match and Ballesteros would earn nearly $1 million from this arrangement. Nevertheless, Ballesteros decided at the last minute to support the bid of Novo Sancti Petri, a course near Cádiz, which he had designed. However, after all this it turned out to be unsuitable and, in spite of other bids, Valderrama won the day.

Second, Ballesteros was not happy that he only had two captain's picks to add to the ten players who would qualify automatically. There were three powerful contenders – Nick Faldo, Jesper Parnevik and José Maria Olazábal. Ballesteros picked Faldo and Parnevik and then sought a way to include his former partner Olazábal, now recovered from his leg and back ailment. As it happened, the person who had qualified tenth, largely thanks to his winning the Heineken Classic in Australia months earlier, was another Spaniard, Miguel Angel Martín. During the summer, Martín had injured his wrist and Ballesteros, sensing an opportunity to drop him, insisted on a fitness test. Martín refused to take the test so Ballesteros deselected him. Martín threatened legal action and, in the end, Ballesteros got his way by picking Martín as a thirteenth man so that he would be in the team but would not play. Olazábal was in.

Third, Ballesteros worked with the head greenkeeper and John Paramour, the tournament referee, on the course at Valderrama to make sure it suited the Europeans rather than the Americans. The fairways were narrowed at around 300 yards where the big-hitting Americans liked to hit their drives. On the par-five 17th, they even put rough across the fairway at that distance from the tee.

The Americans were soon complaining on the practice days. Phil Mickelson said, 'I'm not a fan of rough in the middle of the fairway,' and Tom Lehman added: 'I never much cared for a par five where you hit driver, sand wedge, sand wedge.'

On the practice days, Ballesteros was everywhere advising and cajoling and his captaincy was not the democratic rule of Gallacher; it was much closer to a dictatorship. In one of the practice rounds the seasoned quartet of Faldo, Woosnam, Langer and Montgomerie were on the 17th green, a hole that Seve had recently redesigned. Up came Seve in his buggy, leapt out and questioned the group on how they had played the hole; had they laid up, had they gone for the green in two, where had they driven to, that sort of thing. He did not like the answers, and had this illustrious quartet buggied back to the tee to play it all over again, the way he felt it should be played!

And during the match he certainly used the captain's prerogative to tell his players what to do. Montgomerie recalled his appearing at the 17th during his fourball match with the young Darren Clarke when they were all square with two to play against Couples and Love. Clarke had driven into the rough while Montgomerie was on the fairway. Montgomerie said later:

> Darren's ball was lying quite well but the obvious play was for him to lay up and then I could go for the green; I was well within range. But no, Seve insisted that Darren have a go for it, which he did, and well as he hit it, it

didn't make the carry. I now had to lay up; the risk of both of us going in the pond was too great. I hit it to 58 yards, the fairways still sopping wet, and there's Seve at my side telling me, 'hit it in softly, feel it in.' In the end I had to tell him to p... off. Fortunately I did hit a good shot and holed the putt to go one up, and a half at the last was good enough.

The team that Ballesteros led was solid with a mixture of the experienced – Faldo, Lange, Woosnam, Olazábal, Parnevik, Montgomerie, Johansson and Rocca – and the up-and-coming Björn, Garrido, Clarke and Westwood. For the first time, more than half the team were from continental Europe.

The Americans looked strong with six Major champions – Justin Leonard, Lee Janzen, Tom Lehman, Fred Couples, Davis Love and Tiger Woods. The captain was Tom Kite.

They were playing well and the American media were confident they would win back the cup. One journalist wrote:

To think Europe will win the Ryder Cup is to think the moon is made of cheese and Mickey Mouse will make it to the White House one day.

Once the match started, Ballesteros' fight to secure Olazábal paid off immediately when he and Constantine Rocca beat Love and Mickelson in the first fourball (Ballesteros had exercised his right to change the format so that the fourballs were played in the morning).

Then Faldo, fathering Westwood, just lost to Couples and Faxon, but Parnevik and Johansson scraped home against Lehman and Furyk before Woods and O'Meara beat Montgomerie and Langer fairly easily by 3 and 2. It was 2–2 at lunch on the first day.

In the afternoon Olazábal and Rocca just lost to Hoch and Janzen but Langer and Montgomerie avenged their defeat by Woods and O'Meara by beating them easily 5 and 3. As far as Woods was concerned it was bad enough not playing for money, let alone having to play 'Scotch' foursomes! At this point a halt was called, with the final two matches to be finished the next morning. When they were, Westwood secured his first Ryder Cup point when he and Faldo beat Leonard and Maggert 3 and 2. Finally Garrido and Parnevik secured a half against Lehman and Mickelson and the Europeans were leading 4½ and 3½. Perhaps Mickey Mouse would need to start learning the American Constitution.

When the second day's fourballs began at 10:40am, the Americans charged into the lead encouraged by the presence of former President George Bush and basketball hero Michael Jordan. They led in three matches and were square in the other. They took a break for lunch and afterwards the Europeans fought back so that, at one point, all the matches were level. The putts were really dropping for the Europeans and they won the first three matches, with Faldo and Westwood giving Woods and O'Meara their second defeat at the 17th, where Woods managed to putt into the water. In the last match Olazábal holed a twenty-foot putt on the 18th for him and Garrido to secure a half against Mickelson and Lehman. The Europeans were now leading by four points and Ballesteros was leaping about in delight.

It was to get better in the afternoon when Europe won another 2½ points. The weather continued to cause delays and only one of the afternoon matches was finished on the Saturday. At that point the score was 9–4 and when play resumed on the Saturday morning Europe's five-point lead was retained, each side winning one match while the other was halved.

Ballesteros was charging from match to match handing out advice. In the top match, with Montgomerie and Langer one up and one to play against Janzen and Furyk, Montgomerie missed the 18th fairway with his drive and it settled on the right under the trees. Montgomerie recalled later:

> Seve was there waiting, even before Langer could get to the ball. He had already seen some impossible escape route, a sort of high-flying 3-iron, between branches and with a couple of changes of direction, that would get the ball to the green. Only Seve could have thought such a shot possible, and certainly only Seve might have brought it off! Even while he was trying to convince Bernhard that this was the shot to play, Bernhard chipped out on to the fairway.
>
> The American meanwhile found the front of the green. We were on in three and not that close. With the light fading, and no one believing any of the matches would come down the 18th that day, they had already rolled and triple cut that green in preparation for the early start of the following day. Unaware of this, and with the pin at the back, the Americans putted off the green. A five was good enough for a half and a win!

Finally, at 10½–5½, this was the biggest margin the Europeans had ever taken into the singles. Ballesteros became calmer and actually asked his team who wanted to play where in the singles. Garrido asked to go last, Woosnam to go first. At this point some of the more experienced players got together and told Ballesteros what they thought the order should be. Woosnam and Garrido both got their requested positions – and lost – but positions 8 to 11 were filled by Olazábal, Langer, Montgomerie and Faldo.

Woosnam's opening match was a disaster for Europe as Fred Couples annihilated him 8 and 7. This was just the inspiration the Americans needed, although it was not immediately apparent; Johansson and Rocca won comfortably. Europe now needed only two points from the remaining nine games. At this point, the Americans came back strongly. Björn lost the first four holes to Leonard (as we have seen, Björn was far from inspired by Ballesteros's presence), O'Meara was all over a tired Parnevik, and Mickelson was three up on Clarke. In the end Björn scraped a half but then Clarke, Parnevik and Olazábal all lost, Olazábal after being two up with three to play. Furyk beat a lacklustre Faldo and Lehman thrashed a tired Garrido. When Maggert beat Westwood 3 and 2 Europe's five-point lead had shrunk to one. It now all rested on Montgomerie's match with Scott Hoch.

Montgomerie was one up with two to play, but lost the 17th. If he lost the 18th, the teams would be level and Europe would retain the Cup, but undoubtedly the Americans would be able to boast of a moral victory.

Two weeks prior to the match, at the Lancôme Trophy in Versailles, Monty had done an in-depth interview with Sky Sports in which he charted his growing seniority in the Ryder Cup through the various slots in which he had played in the singles. In 1991 at Kiawah Island, as a rookie, he'd been hidden away in the middle, but did his reputation no harm by coming back from four down and four to play against Mark Calcavecchia to halve. Two years later, he was promoted to third in the team order and duly delivered an early point for Bernard Gallacher. At Oak Hill he was part of Gallacher's strong middle order, which produced that astonishing last-day fightback. Now he ruminated that he was ready for the ultimate test and hoped to be somewhere down towards the end at Valderrama, something like tenth spot, where the whole contest might depend on the outcome of his match. He was indeed playing in the tenth match and got his wish! A half would do, but a win would be a win and so much better.

Hoch missed the fairway, and as is so often the case at Valderrama, could not go for the green in two. Monty split the fairway. Hoch made it to the green in three, but was 30 feet away; Monty was comfortably on in two and had two putts for an almost certain win. He got it stone-dead for a half at worst, and therefore victory for Europe. Then Seve intervened for one last time. In the gathering gloom he instructed Monty to concede Hoch's putt, a putt which, under the circumstances, Hoch would have been most unlikely to hole. The final result was achieved by the narrowest of margins: 14½–13½. It had been much harder than it might have been, but Seve had delivered, in his own inimitable style, victory in Spain.

Montgomerie said, when all the excitement had died down:

> Before the Ryder Cup I said I wouldn't mind being in a position where it all came down to me. Well, I've changed my mind, I can tell you. I don't want to do that again. It wasn't fun out there.

After all that excitement, what more could happen in 1999 when the match was played at The Country Club at Brookline, Boston, Massachusetts?

26–28 September 1997

Valderrama Golf Club, Sotogrande, Spain

Captains: S. Ballesteros (Europe), T. Kite (USA)

Europe		United States	
Fourballs: Morning			
J.M. Olazábal & C. Rocca (1 hole)	1	D. Love III & P. Mickelson	0
N. Faldo & L. Westwood	0	F. Couples & B. Faxon (1 hole)	1
J. Parnevik & P.-U. Johansson (1 hole)	1	T. Lehman & J. Furyk	0
B. Langer & C. Montgomerie	0	T. Woods & M. O'Meara (3 & 2)	1
Foursomes: Afternoon			
J.M Olazábal & C. Rocca	0	S. Hoch & L. Janzen (1 hole)	1
B. Langer & C. Montgomerie (5 & 3)	1	T. Woods & M. O'Meara	0
N. Faldo & L. Westwood (3 & 2)	1	J. Leonard & J. Maggert	0
I. Garrido & J. Parnevik (halved)	½	T. Lehman & P. Mickelson (halved)	½
Fourballs: Morning			
C. Montgomerie & D. Clarke (1 hole)	1	F. Couples & D. Love III	0
I. Woosnam & T. Björn (2 & 1)	1	J. Leonard & B. Faxon	0
N. Faldo & L. Westwood (2 & 1)	1	T. Woods & M. O'Meara	0
J.M Olazábal & I. Garrido (halved)	½	P. Mickelson & T. Lehman (halved)	½
Foursomes: Afternoon			
C. Montgomerie & B. Langer (1 hole)	1	L. Janzen & J. Furyk	0
N. Faldo & L. Westwood	0	S. Hoch & J. Maggert (2 & 1)	1
J. Parnevik & I. Garrido (halved)	½	J. Leonard & T. Woods (halved)	½
J.M. Olazábal & C. Rocca (5 & 4)	1	D. Love III & F. Couples	0
Singles:			
I. Woosnam	0	F. Couples (8 & 7)	1
P.-U. Johansson (3 & 2)	1	D. Love III	0
C. Rocca (4 & 2)	1	T. Woods	0
T. Björn (halved)	½	J. Leonard (halved)	½
D. Clarke	0	P. Mickelson (2 & 1)	1
J. Parnevik	0	M. O'Meara (5 & 4)	1
J.M. Olazábal	0	L. Janzen (1 hole)	1
B. Langer (2 & 1)	1	B. Faxon	0
L. Westwood	0	J. Maggert (3 & 2)	1
C. Montgomerie (halved)	½	S. Hoch (halved)	½
N. Faldo	0	J. Furyk (3 & 2)	1
I. Garrido	0	T. Lehman (7 & 6)	1
Europe 14½; USA 13½			

The Bear Pit at Brookline

Brookline should have been a great venue for the 1999 Ryder Cup. It is one of America's grand old clubs, having hosted the US Open on three occasions and the Walker Cup twice. The club is at its best in autumn; the trees just turning, late summer days beginning with a touch of mist and blossoming into glorious sunlit afternoons. It is also the heartland of golf, where America best defends itself against marauding intruders.

Just half an hour from the centre of Boston and little more than a couple of miles from where the American War of Independence began, The Country Club is hardly changed from when it first opened its doors – not as a golf course but as a racecourse. The golf course had not long been laid out when it hosted the US Open in 1913. It was the championship that changed the course of golfing history. That was when Francis Ouimet, a little-known American, took on the champions of the day from Great Britain, Harry Vardon and Ted Ray, tied with them and then beat them in a play-off. From that day on, golf really took off in America. The home side would have felt good about coming to The Country Club, as no American individual or team had ever lost there. Curtis Strange had been the last to defend his nation's honour there, beating Nick Faldo in a play-off for the US Open in 1988.

Needless to say, controversy was not far away. In the USA it was about money. Almost from the start, little things – side issues really – started to go wrong in the run-up to the match. As well as being the most erudite of cities, with institutions such as Harvard and the Massachusetts Institute of Technology, Boston is probably America's second most important financial centre after Wall Street. In 1999 America was at the height of the long bull run that saw out the end of the twentieth century, with huge quantities of money being made in that tiny corner of New England. The demand for corporate hospitality was colossal, way in excess of what could ever have been supplied, however big the location.

The Country Club had all the history and tradition imaginable, but being old and private, unlimited space was something it did not have. Even so, the PGA of America managed to squeeze in $30 million worth of corporate marquees – and that was without a cork being popped or a canapé being swallowed. That did not leave an awful lot of space for the paying public to move around, and as with marquees, the demand for tickets far exceeded supply.

Just as these numbers began to be bandied about – and it was not long before the total revenue figure was heard to be an astounding $65 million – the American players realised that the PGA of America (the body that represented club pros in the US, although it was still responsible for staging the Ryder Cup) were making a mint out of this match. The players were putting in the blood, sweat and tears – that's why it had become so competitive – but they had nothing in the bank to show for it. No one was about to feel sorry for the state of the players' finances, however, and in the end it was agreed that $100,000 would be donated to a charity of each player's choosing. That is the way it has remained since 1999.

In Europe the big issue was selection. The new captain, Mark James, was a Yorkshireman and as is often the case (think of Geoffrey Boycott) was very much his own man. For his captain's picks he passed over the experienced Nick Faldo, Ian Woosnam and Bernhard Langer and chose Jesper Parnevik and Andrew Coltart, saying:

In my experience, experience is over-rated.

These were certainly controversial choices and, not surprisingly, they were heavily criticised after the match.

However, during the build-up James did not put a foot wrong. Sam Torrance and Ken Brown were his vice-captains. It was a good team and as James and Torrance were still regulars on tour, and Brown was there a lot of the time as a commentator, all knew the players really well. With six continental Europeans in the side it might have been nice to have one in the management structure, but that would have been nit-picking: everyone spoke good English.

On arrival in Boston James was charm itself, saying:

> We have come to one of the most beautiful cities in America ... and we are playing one of the best golf courses. Although we are hoping to retain the trophy, the main thing is that we all have a good week.

The American press might not have fully understood his Yorkshire sense of humour when he said with a dead-straight face, in answer to a question about how hostile the rivalry might become:

> Not too much as we all have mutual friends on the other side. It's serious because we're both out here to win, but at the end of the week I'll be able to shake Ben [Crenshaw, the US captain] warmly by the throat and we'll sit down and have a beer together.

Ironically, in view of what was to happen later, Crenshaw said:

> The captain does not have to impart much about sportsmanship. Golfers generally comport themselves very well.

The European team was the most inexperienced ever taken to the US, with seven rookies – the Frenchman Jean van de Velde, who had suffered a horrendous final hole at Carnoustie in that year's Open Championship, the Scot Paul Lawrie, who had consequently won that Open, the Finn (though now a Swedish citizen) Jarmo Sandelin, the Irishman Padraig Harrington, the Englishman Andrew Coltart and the two Spaniards, Miguel Angel Jiménez and Sergio García. They would join Lee Westwood, Darren Clarke, Jesper Parnevik, José Maria Olazábal and Colin Montgomerie.

Against them was a powerful and experienced US team comprising Payne Stewart, Mark O'Meara, Tiger Woods, Jim Furyk, Tom Lehman, Hal Sutton, Phil Mickelson, Davis Love III, Steve Pate, Justin Leonard, Jeff Maggert and David Duval, with only Duval making his debut.

With over half the European team never having played in the Ryder Cup before, every pairing was going to be new. Some looked obvious on paper and all worked well in practice. The two Scots, Montgomerie and Lawrie, had similar games – neat and tidy – and both liked to play quickly. It also met the usual prerequisite of putting an old hand with a first-timer. It was easy to see them playing together and playing top. Lee Westwood and Darren Clarke were by now very good chums, each with a Ryder Cup behind him, and with the chance of forging a new partnership that could last some time.

Sergio García was playing a lot in America and knew Jesper Parnevik well: here again was the perfect opportunity to put an experienced player with one of the new boys. Lastly, it seemed obvious to play the two remaining Spaniards, José Maria Olazábal and Miguel Angel Jiménez (good friends of long standing), together. Even though

Jiménez was the elder, it was his first match; so once again, old with young.

The only problem was that Olazábal was suffering from his perennial problem, erratic driving – destructive in foursomes, but containable in fourballs. Fortunately, of the remaining four, all first-time players, Padraig Harrington was playing exceptionally well. He had played his way late into the side with a couple of second-place finishes in recent weeks, so was a ready-made foursome alternative should Olazábal not be able to sort out his driving.

Even at this early stage it was clear that Jean van de Velde, Jarmo Sandelin and Andrew Coltart were to be kept in waiting for the inevitable bad result or loss of form. Van de Velde and Coltart would be neat and tidy foursomes replacements, always good to have on hand, while Sandelin was more of a fourballs man – plenty of birdies mixed in with a few blow-outs.

Somehow, on the first day, the Europeans played out of their skins and finished the day leading 6–2. The Scottish duo, Montgomerie and Lawrie, gelled and picked up 1½ points. The young García played with Parnevik and they won both their matches. Clarke and Westwood lost in the morning but won in the afternoon. On the American side, Woods lost both his matches as did David Duval and Phil Mickelson. Indeed, Woods was becoming a problem for American captains. As Crenshaw said:

> Tiger is hard to find someone to pair him with. There's no one really with comparable skills, and I don't think any captain has found the answer yet. But that week I discovered Tiger grew up in California with Steve [Pate]'s brother, so he and Steve were already quite friendly. So I put them together [the next day] and they got us a point.

The Europeans managed to hold on to their four-point lead through the second day, when both sides won three matches and two were halved. Woods managed one win with Pate against Jiménez and Harrington but returned to losing against Montgomerie and Lawrie, again playing with Pate.

Crenshaw, who had been phlegmatic after the first day, saying, 'This is what happens in matchplay, there is ebb and flow, ebb and flow,' now became more spiritual, with: 'I'm a big believer in fate. I have a good feeling about this.'

Nevertheless he asked the Governor of Texas (and soon to be President of the United States), George W. Bush Jr., to talk to his team. In view of what happened the next day, his reading of William Travis' letter from the Battle of the Alamo could have been considered provocative:

> Have sustained a continuous bombardment and cannonade for 24 hours and have not lost a man. The enemy has demanded a surrender at discretion ... I have answered the demand with a cannon shot and our flag still waves proudly from the walls. I shall never surrender or retreat ... Victory or death.

Whether inspired by Bush or not, the American team went and played magnificent golf in the singles. They went off with a bang winning the first six matches, none of them going further than the 16th. Overall they were 38 under par on the day, compared with the Europeans who were ten under. After six matches the score had gone from 10–6 to Europe to 12–10 to the USA. Harrington then stopped the rot by beating O'Meara, but Pate restored the margin by beating Jiménez.

By now the arithmetic was clear: Olazábal and Montgomerie both had to win, as did Paul Lawrie, who at the time was four up through the turn in the final game against Jeff Maggert. If so, Europe could still tie the match and keep the Cup.

Olazábal was also four up through the turn against Justin Leonard. Then Leonard got on to one of his putting streaks and started to claw his way back. Up until now the vast crowd had been noisy but largely well behaved. There were far too many spectators for any of them to be able to follow a given match; they just had to stay where they were and watch the games come through. Beer was on hand and progress could be followed on the scoreboards. As the possibility of a famous recovery loomed, the sound increased in volume and became almost feral. Those who had seen matches through the early holes now surged towards the finish, swelling the already dense numbers there.

Leonard reeled Olazábal in with one great putt after another – and we are not talking five- or six-footers here; everyone could hear his progress from the sound of the thousands who could see it. Like some giant long-drawn-out echo, the roar would then be repeated as the result materialised on the great boards further down the course. The sheer volume of so many people jammed in such a small space gave The Country Club the atmosphere of a vast outdoor arena set up for a world championship fight.

Another long putt snaked in across the 16th green and Leonard was level. Olazábal had not dropped a shot, but he had lost four holes out of six in a match everyone knew he had to win. Both found the 17th green in two, the green where Ouimet had finally seen off Vardon and Ray all those years ago. Olazábal was marginally the closer in two, but neither with a realistic chance of a three. Both would have been happy with two putts and to move to the last all square. But Leonard had one more unbelievable putt in his locker:

up the slopes it climbed straight into the hole, and then all hell broke loose.

Most of the American players who had finished were there, all pretty high on the adrenaline of their own performances, and unquestionably roused by the sheer ferocity of the sound around them – a noise certainly greater than any they would have heard on any golf course before. They also believed – because that was the information coming over on the closed-circuit radios in the crowd – that Leonard's putt would finally put the match beyond the reach of the Europeans; when it went in they all thought that was that, the match had been won. A moment's sanity and they would have realised that Olazábal still had a putt for the half and could still win at the 18th. But there was little sanity at that moment or in that place. The stampede by the American players across the 17th green forever turned a famous and courageous fightback into a dreadful, unforgivable breach of etiquette and conduct – one they would singly and collectively regret for the rest of their days. It was a great shame because they had all done such a wonderful job to get to that position in the first place.

Crenshaw said later:

> You know had that putt of Justin's been holeable, say 10 or 15 feet, then I don't think the reaction would have been the same. But it was just so improbable, so extraordinary, and we just completely lost our minds; we all lost them – I did. Our emotions completely got the better of us. It was all so highly improbable. But you know, there was no excuse for it, and there is no question that it is a lifelong regret.

Far worse in many respects was the treatment meted out to Montgomerie throughout the three days. The abuse continued and got worse the longer the week went on, and on that last day it turned from verbal to physical. He was jostled and spat on as he passed through crowds too vast to be kept back for the passage of players. It was an attack on a single player the like of which has never, before or since, been perpetrated on a golfer in the pursuit of his profession. Far worse than the momentary loss of sanity by the players, the collective behaviour of the Boston crowd that week against one man left the sourest taste of all.

The British media were highly critical and Michael Bonallack, Secretary of the R&A, was moved to say, after likening the atmosphere at Brookline to a 'bear pit':

> I felt embarrassed for golf. It went beyond the decency you associate with proper golf. I love the Ryder Cup and don't want to see it degenerate into a mob demonstration every time we play it.

24–26 September 1999
The Country Club, Brookline, Boston, Massachusetts, USA
Captains: M. James (Europe), B. Crenshaw (USA)

Europe		United States	
Foursomes: Morning			
C. Montgomerie & P. Lawrie (3 & 2)	1	D. Duval & P. Mickelson	0
J. Parnevik & S. García (2 & 1)	1	T. Lehman & T. Woods	0
M.A. Jiménez & P. Harrington (halved)	½	D. Love III & P. Stewart (halved)	½
D. Clarke & L. Westwood	0	H. Sutton & J. Maggert (3 & 2)	1
Fourballs: Afternoon			
C. Montgomerie & P. Lawrie (halved)	½	D. Love III & J. Leonard (halved)	½
J. Parnevik & S. García (1 hole)	1	P. Mickelson & J. Furyk	0
M.A. Jiménez & J.M. Olazábal (2 & 1)	1	H. Sutton & J. Maggert	0
D. Clarke & L. Westwood (1 hole)	1	D. Duval & T. Woods	0

(continued)

24–26 September 1999 (continued)

The Country Club, Brookline, Boston, Massachusetts, USA

Captains: M. James (Europe), B. Crenshaw (USA)

Europe		United States	
Foursomes: Morning			
C. Montgomerie & P. Lawrie	0	H. Sutton & J. Maggert (1 hole)	1
D. Clarke & L. Westwood (3 & 2)	1	J. Furyk & M. O'Meara	0
M.A. Jiménez & P. Harrington	0	S. Pate & T. Woods (1 hole)	1
J. Parnevik & S. García (3 & 2)	1	P. Stewart & J. Leonard	0
Fourballs: Afternoon			
D. Clarke & L. Westwood	0	P. Mickelson & T. Lehman (2 & 1)	1
J. Parnevik & S. García (halved)	½	D. Love III & D. Duval (halved)	½
M.A. Jiménez & J.M. Olazábal (halved)	½	J. Leonard & H. Sutton (halved)	½
C. Montgomerie & P. Lawrie (2 & 1)	1	S. Pate & T. Woods	0
Singles:			
L. Westwood	0	T. Lehman (3 & 2)	1
D. Clarke	1	H. Sutton (4 & 2)	1
J. Sandelin	1	P. Mickelson (4 & 3)	1
J. Van de Velde	0	D. Love III (6 & 5)	1
A. Coltart	0	T. Woods (3 & 2)	1
J. Parnevik	0	D. Duval (5 & 4)	1
P. Harrington (1 hole)	1	M. O'Meara	0
M.A. Jiménez	0	S. Pate (2 & 1)	1
J.M. Olazábal (halved)	½	J. Leonard (halved)	½
C. Montgomerie (1 hole)	1	P. Stewart	0
S. García	0	J. Furyk (4 & 3)	1
P. Lawrie (4 & 3)	1	J. Maggert	0
Europe 13½; USA 14½			

17. (*above*) Christy O'Connor Jr. celebrates as his putt on the 18th wins the Ryder Cup for the European team at The Belfry in 1989.

18. (*left*) Seve Ballesteros asks the crowd to move so that his team-mate, José Maria Olazábal, can hit his shot during the sometimes ill-tempered match at Kiawah Island in 1991.

19. Bernhard Langer and Hale Irwin on the 17th green in their tense deciding match a Kiawah Island in 1991.

20. (below) Nick Faldo plays t the famous 10th green durin the 1993 match at The Belfr

21. Bernhard Langer holes his putt to win his singles match in the 1995 match at Oak Hill.

2. *(below)* Philip Walton plashes out of a bunker n his match at Oak Hill. Ie would gain a vital victory n his singles match.

23. Nick Faldo and captain Seve Ballesteros at the 1997 match at Valderrama.

24. (below) Crowd contro[l] at the 1999 match a[t] Brookline was a disgrace[.]

25. Europe's Philip Price sinks a vital putt on the 16th in his unexpected victory over Phil Mickelson at The Belfry in 2002.

26. Paul Azinger and Tiger Woods during their four-ball defeat by Darren Clarke and Thomas Björn at The Belfry in 2002.

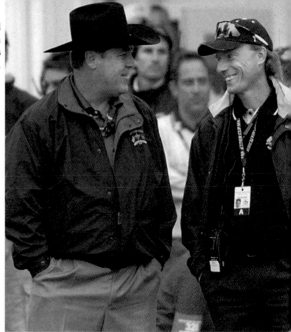

27. Captains Bernhard Langer and Hal Sutton on the 1st tee at Oakland Hills during the 2004 match.

28. Europe's Colin Montgomerie celebrates a vital putt during the 2004 match at Oakland Hills.

29. Lee Westwood studies his line while partner Darren Clarke looks on in the 2006 match at The K Club.

30. US captain Tom Lehman consoles Jim Furyk after his 2 and 1 defeat by Paul Casey in the 2006 match at The K Club.

31. Europe's Oliver Wilson celebrates his winning putt in his foursomes match partnering Henrik Stenson against Phil Mickelson and Anthony Kim in the 2008 match at Valhalla.

32. *(below)* European captain Nick Faldo, holding the Ryder Cup, meets US captain Paul Azinger before the 2008 match. A week later Azinger would be holding

Chapter 8

Torrance and Langer
do their homework

'Tell 'em who I beat'
The Belfry 2002

Woods struggles to care
Oakland Hills 2004

'Tell 'em who I beat'

On 11 September 2001, which became known as 9/11 (the telephone number used for emergencies in the USA, a coincidence certainly appreciated by the perpetrators of the attack) the world was stunned when at 8:46am Eastern Daylight Time a passenger airliner was flown into one of the Twin Towers in downtown Manhattan, New York. A few may have thought it was an accident but when, just a quarter of an hour later, another airliner was flown into the second tower, no one still believed that these were anything but deliberate attacks. This realisation was reinforced when another aircraft was flown into the Pentagon in Washington and finally when a fourth aircraft crashed in Pennsylvania, killing all those on board.

Two and a half hours that changed the history of the world:

7:59am	Mohammed Atta boards American Airlines flight 11 which under his control will crash into the World Trade Center
8:18am	American Airlines flight 11 is taken over by Mohammed Atta and other hijackers
8:46am	American Airlines flight 11 crashes into the north tower of the World Trade Center
9:03am	United Airlines flight 175 crashes into the south tower of the World Trade Center
9:37am	American Airlines flight 77 crashes into the Pentagon
9:59am	South tower of World Trade Center collapses
10:03am	United Airlines Flight 93 crashes into a field in Shanksville, Pennsylvania
10:28am	North tower of World Trade Center collapses

The mighty USA was under attack on its home soil, the first time since the Japanese attack on Pearl Harbor in December 1941. President George W. Bush was visiting a school in Florida when it happened, but was quickly bundled into the presidential aircraft and flown around while it could be ascertained how serious the situation was and whether any more attacks were likely. Needless to say, all other aircraft throughout the USA were grounded.

The world was in shock and the British and American PGAs did not know what to do about the next Ryder Cup match, due to start at The Belfry just seventeen days after the attacks on New York and Washington. There were arguments both for carrying on – they should not give way to terrorists – and for cancellation, or at least postponement – respect for the dead and concerns over the security of players and spectators, among many matters.

After consultations with several people, including the players, the PGAs decided to postpone the match for a year and that thereafter the match would continue in even years rather than odd ones. The team captains, Sam Torrance and Curtis Strange, agreed that they would keep the same players in 2002 who had already been picked for the 2001 match.

After the appalling scenes and crowd behaviour at Brookline, both captains felt the need to try to restore the camaraderie and friendliness of the earlier matches. Torrance said later:

> I was lucky in that their captain was Curtis Strange. We took about three seconds to agree that there wasn't going to be a repeat of Brookline. He and his delightful wife Sarah were the most I could have wished for as opposition that particular week.

Torrance also said that having an extra year to prepare was a huge help:

> Captains usually only have three or four weeks with their final team; yes, they will know who eight or nine of them are, but often there are places to be played for right up to the time when the team is announced. Then they have to turn them into a team, with so little time and all the uniforms and team colours to be sorted out; pairings to be thought about, that sort of thing. I had a whole year; what a luxury.

He also used his captain's prerogative in the preparation of the course at The Belfry:

> I thought long and hard about how best to set the course up at The Belfry. I felt their team was longer, man for man, than ours, and they probably played more aggressively. There's less punishment for wild driving in America, so they tend to get the driver out more often, or at least don't have to worry as much as Europeans do about where specifically to put the ball off the tee.
>
> We put in some bunkers, further on than the existing ones, narrowed the fairways, particularly from about 290 yards onwards and thickened up the rough. Then all the surrounds to the greens were given a crew-cut; there was to be none of that thick grass just off the putting surface that seems to be the standard defence of greens in the US. Half our team would have been all right, they play over there, but the other half didn't and would have been at a disadvantage.
>
> Finally, I never wanted the tee moved up at the 10th [a short par four over water that became well within reach from one of the forward tees and a regular prac-

tice when ordinary tournaments are played there]. They were longer, and it would have been like creating another par 3 with the Americans using shorter clubs than we would. If they wanted to go for the green, then it would have been a driver. Keeping the tee back gave them more of a quandary than us. It reached me they were a bit irritated by this; they didn't think it a very good hole where you just hit a 6- or 7-iron off the tee. But anything that irritated them, within the context of the match, was all right by me!

In the European team, although some of the stars of the 1980s and 1990s had gone, there was still Bernhard Langer, that doughty competitor who had overcome his yips and was such a good match player, and there were younger but by now seasoned Ryder Cup players such as Darren Clarke, Jesper Parnevik, Lee Westwood, Sergio García, Padraig Harrington, Thomas Björn and, above all, Colin Montgomerie.

Unfortunately, Parnevik and Westwood were not on their best form. Indeed, Parnevik had rung Torrance from America saying that he could hardly keep his ball on the planet, let alone the fairway, and suggesting Torrance leave him out until the singles. As for Westwood, Torrance said to him:

Look Lee, form is temporary, class is forever. You're hitting the ball well, this course suits you and the odd bad shot only costs one hole.

These experienced players would be joined by newcomers Niclas Fasth, Paul McGinley, Pierre Fulke and Philip Price.

They would face the usual strong side from the United States, with Tiger Woods in his prime having just won the four major championships in succession, albeit not in the same year. However, he did not endear himself to anyone on his side when he said, two weeks earlier while playing in the American Express Championship at Mount Juliet in Ireland, that he would rather win its $1 million first prize than the Ryder Cup. He compounded his error by adding that the Cup was not his favourite event, complaining that all the associated functions upset his normal routine. The fact that he had won just 2½ points out of a possible eight at Valderrama and Brookline had clearly disillusioned him. He was about to make it 2½ points out of ten by the end of the first day at The Belfry! He seemed to be fast becoming one of Europe's best players.

Of the other Americans, Payne Stewart had gone, tragically killed in a freak air accident a month after the match at Brookline, but Paul Azinger was back after a cancer scare and Phil Mickelson was by this time the world number two behind Woods. Then there was David Toms, the reigning PGA champion. And, of course, there were other very experienced Ryder Cup performers such as David Duval, Hal Sutton, Jim Furyk, Davis Love III and Mark Calcavecchia, who was playing for the first time since his horrendous collapse against Montgomerie at Kiawah Island in 1991.

Europe could not have made a better start. Clarke and Björn beat Woods and Azinger in the first match. García and Westwood overcame Duval and Love 4 and 3 and Montgomerie and Langer beat Hoch and Furyk, also 4 and 3. The only European losers were Harrington and Fasth who just lost to Mickelson and Toms. In the afternoon the partnership of García and Westwood came good again, this time against Woods and Calcavecchia (Strange was having the usual American captain's problem of finding someone to partner Woods successfully). Clarke and Björn lost, as did Harrington and McGinley, and with Montgomerie and

Langer halving their match the score at the end of day one was Europe 4½, USA 3½.

On the Saturday morning honours were shared, with García and Westwood and Montgomerie and Langer again the pairs picking up the points. Fulke and Price, both playing for the first time, lost against the strong pairing of Mickelson and Toms, and Clarke and Björn disappointingly lost to Woods and Love. Had Strange finally found someone who could play with Woods? Then in the afternoon the Americans picked up 2½ points to level the scores. The one European victory was a good one in which Montgomerie and Harrington beat Mickelson and Toms, who had not been beaten up to that point. Montgomerie said afterwards:

> I've never played better than that and it had to be so because we were playing the second- and sixth-ranked players in the world.

It was the first time since 1981 that the Europeans had not been ahead going into the singles on home soil. Was this bad? Some thought so, as the Americans were considered to be stronger man for man. Others thought that starting with a lead put the team under pressure, whereas those coming from behind had nothing to lose. And what strategy was Torrance going to use?

Many may have thought Torrance had taken a leaf out of Ben Crenshaw's book from 1999, when he put so much power at the top, but that hardly entered Torrance's head:

> Crenshaw had no option. He was 4 points behind and had to catch up quick. No, it was a member of Sunningdale, David 'Bugsy' Holland – past captain of the club, and Harrovian Halford Hewitt player; a man of trenchant views and little time for the opinions of

others – who categorically stated, 'Put your best out first and the worst last.'

I thought about it long and hard and I couldn't think of a scenario where it couldn't work. If we were ahead, I wanted them out there to finish the thing off; if we were behind I would want to catch up quickly. And I don't care who you are Woods, Nicklaus – if you are playing in the bottom section, 8 to 12, you are fallible in this particular competition. You don't have to have your best at the end to cope, because as often as not, out of the shadows come heroes.

The strategy worked pretty well. In the first match Montgomerie annihilated Hoch 5 and 4, then García lost to Toms, Clarke halved with Duval and Langer, Harrington and Björn all won to make it Europe 12½, USA 9½. However, Westwood lost to Verplank and the remaining matches were all close, with a lot of strong US players at the bottom such as Azinger, Furyk, Love, Mickelson and Woods. Europe needed at least one win and a couple of halves out of those matches.

It did not look as though it would come from Philip Price, who was three down after five holes to the world number two, Phil Mickelson.

Mickelson then drove down the middle of the sixth fairway while Price almost drove into the lake on the left. Mickelson, playing first, hit his approach to some four feet: four up looked a certainty. But Price, almost standing in the water and with the ball well above his feet, somehow hoicked it round, and up it scuttled just inside the American's ball. Mickelson missed, Price holed: two down, not four. And what a turning point! The inspired Price won one hole after another, until on the 16th he holed another long downhiller. Mickelson missed: Price had beaten the world's number two by 3 and 2. The abiding cry of the celebrations that night was a Welsh voice calling out:

Tell 'em who I beat; go on, tell 'em who I beat.

It looked as if Fasth was going to beat Azinger when he was one up at the last and on the green in two, while Azinger had put his approach in the bunker. However, Azinger holed his bunker shot, Fasth took two putts and the match was halved.

Europe still needed a half. Paul McGinley and Jim Furyk came to the last all square. Both were on the green in two. McGinley putted first and went eight feet past. Furyk missed, McGinley holed the eight-footer and Europe had won.

Had McGinley failed there was still another string to Europe's bow in that Pierre Fulke was also all square playing the last against Davis Love. But by then the scenes up at the 18th were such that it would obviously be some time before they could play their seconds. With both on the fairway and the match now over, a look, a nod, a handshake and another half-point was agreed. And with that it should be noted that all four rookies had gained at least a half, and each against a player who had won or would win a major championship. Very much a case of 'out of the shadows come heroes'.

27–29 September 2002				
The Belfry Golf and Country Club, Sutton Coldfield, West Midlands, England				
Captains: S. Torrance (Europe), C. Strange (USA)				
Europe		**United States**		
Fourballs: Morning				
D. Clarke & T. Bjorn (1 hole)	1	T. Woods & P. Azinger		0
S. García & L. Westwood (4 & 3)	1	D. Duval & D. Love III		0
C. Montgomerie & B. Langer (4 & 3)	1	S. Hoch & J. Furyk		0
P. Harrington & N. Fasth	0	P. Mickelson & D. Toms (1 hole)		1

(continued)

27–29 September 2002 (continued) The Belfry Golf and Country Club, Sutton Coldfield, West Midlands, England *Captains:* S. Torrance (Europe), C. Strange (USA)			
Europe		**United States**	
Foursomes: Afternoon			
D. Clarke & T. Björn	0	H. Sutton & S. Verplank (2 & 1)	1
S. García & L. Westwood (2 & 1)	1	T. Woods & M. Calcavecchia	0
C. Montgomerie & B. Langer (halved)	½	P. Mickelson & D. Toms (halved)	½
P. Harrington & P. McGinley	0	S. Cink & J. Furyk (3 & 2)	1
Foursomes: Morning			
P. Fulke & P. Price	0	P. Mickelson & D. Toms (2 & 1)	1
S. García & L. Westwood (2 & 1)	1	J. Furyk & S. Cink	0
C. Montgomerie & B. Langer (1 hole)	1	S. Verplank & S. Hoch	0
D. Clarke & T. Björn	0	T. Woods & D. Love III (4 & 3)	1
Fourballs: Afternoon			
N. Fasth & J. Parnevik	0	M. Calcavecchia & D. Duval (1 hole)	1
C. Montgomerie & P. Harrington (2 & 1)	1	P. Mickelson & D. Toms	0
S. García & L. Westwood	0	T. Woods & D. Love III (1 hole)	1
D. Clarke & P. McGinley (halved)	½	S. Hoch & J. Furyk (halved)	½
Singles:			
C. Montgomerie (5 & 4)	1	S. Hoch	0
S. García	0	D. Toms (1 hole)	1
D. Clarke (halved)	½	D. Duval (halved)	½
B. Langer (4 & 3)	1	H. Sutton	0
P. Harrington (5 & 4)	1	M. Calcavecchia	0
T. Björn (2 & 1)	1	S. Cink	0
L. Westwood	0	S. Verplank (2 & 1)	1
N. Fasth (halved)	½	P. Azinger (halved)	½
P. McGinley (halved)	½	J. Furyk (halved)	½
P. Fulke (halved)	½	D. Love III (halved)	½
P. Price (3 & 2)	1	P. Mickelson	0
J. Parnevik (halved)	½	T. Woods (halved)	½
Europe 15½; USA 12½			

'Woods struggles to care'

The next match was at the famous Oakland Hills Club near Detroit which had hosted the unofficial Ryder Cup match in 1940 between the US Ryder Cup team, chosen for the 1939 match which was never played, and a team led by Gene Sarazen.

In spite of Europe's victory in 2002 the USA were favourites as they always were on home soil. Their team included five Major winners including Tiger Woods. At least the European team had the British press, generally much better at winding up the opposition than their American counterparts. The redoubtable journalist from *The Times* Simon Barnes went out to Oakland Hills, and lost no time in getting at the supposed star of the US team, Tiger Woods. In an article under the headline 'Woods struggles to care amid all the excitement', Barnes wrote:

> If you are trying to win a golf competition, having the best golfer on the planet on your side seems an awfully good idea. But the theory breaks down when you realise that Tiger Woods doesn't give a stuff about the Ryder Cup. He told us so, clearly and unambiguously.
>
> Not in so many words, but as good as. Woods is the world's master of the utterly meaningless press conference, all charm and easy words, and no substance whatsoever. But he broke cover after a Ryder Cup practice round and explained precisely why the whole team thing means so little to him.
>
> Woods' record in the Ryder Cup is not what you would expect from the world's greatest player. He has played in three and his record is five wins, eight defeats and two halves. So we asked him why his record was so poor and after a moment's hanging about on the edge,

he dived right in. 'I'm sure you guys all know what Jack's record is in the Ryder Cup, right?'

That's Jack Nicklaus, of course, the greatest golfer that ever lived, the man Woods seeks to better. 'Anybody? No?' Nobody, no. Nobody had that factoid to hand. 'How many majors did he win?' Hell, even I knew that one: 18. The word 'eighteen' sounded around this room of golfing types in a kind of prayerful murmur; you could almost smell the incense.

'Oh really?' Woods responded, smirking, with something dangerously close to irony. And left it at that. But the implication that he so carefully left hanging in the air is unduckable; nobody remembers Nicklaus's Ryder Cup record because nobody cares, not once the long and traumatic weekend has gone. But everybody remembers his collection of major tournaments because that is the true measure of a golfer.

So, game, set and match to Woods? We shall see how many games he won, whether he won his set and whether his team won the match.

There were plenty of first-timers on both sides. For Europe, Paul Casey, Luke Donald, Ian Poulter; the Frenchman Thomas Levet and the Welshman David Howell joined the experienced Colin Montgomerie, Padraig Harrington, Darren Clarke, Miguel Angel Jiménez, Paul McGinley, Sergio García and Lee Westwood. For the USA it was Kenny Perry, Chad Campbell, Chris Di Marco, Fred Funk and Chris Rule who joined Tiger Woods, Phil Mickelson, Davis Love III, Stewart Cink, Jay Haas, Jim Furyk and David Toms.

Right from the start the Europeans, in Bernhard Langer, seemed to have the more astute captain. The quiet, thoughtful professional from a small town near Munich in southern Germany, with an acute eye for detail, could not have been more different from the brash, overweight Texan Hal Sutton. Langer let his actions do the talking. Sutton did a lot of talking, and when he announced his playing order for the day that included Woods and Mickelson as the top pair, his supposedly smart move certainly won applause from the crowd. The more knowledgeable among them might have wondered how two people who clearly did not like each other would gel as partners. The answer was that they did not, and they lost both in the morning fourballs and in the afternoon foursomes.

In the afternoon they were three up against Clarke and Westwood at one point, but the European pair pulled them back and they were all square on the 18th tee. It was Mickelson to drive and with a 3-wood for safety he hit it very far wide, 80 yards off line and nearly out of bounds. Simon Barnes was watching and summed up Woods' reaction. 'The best moment of the tournament,' wrote Barnes later in his book, *The Meaning of Sport*, 'was the look on Woods' face when Phil Mickelson hit that drive. It was an expression of bemused contempt, mixed with the thought: what the f... am I doing here?'

So that was two games lost of the supposed 'game, set and match'.

Elsewhere, and back to the morning, it went very well for Europe. As we have seen, Mickelson and Woods lost, this time against Montgomerie and Harrington. This was a very important morale booster for Montgomerie who had suffered a difficult few months which included divorce and a complete loss of form. He had not been able to qualify and was one of Langer's captain's picks. Montgomerie said, quite correctly: 'We feel, as a team, it was worth a little more than a point.'

Clarke and Jiménez beat Love and Campbell 5 and 4, García and Westwood beat Toms and Furyk 5 and 3 and McGinley and Donald secured a half against Riley and Cink.

The afternoon went almost as well as the morning.

Unfortunately, Thomas Levet, in his first match and partnering Jiménez, lost 3 and 2 to Di Marco and Haas, but the remaining three matches were all won by the Europeans. Montgomerie and Harrington won again, this time thrashing Furyk and Funk 5 and 4. As we saw, Woods and Mickelson lost at the last to Clarke and Westwood, and García and Donald beat Perry and Cink 2 and 1. At the end of the day, the Europeans were leading by an unprecedented 6½–1½.

The British press was ecstatic. John Hopkins wrote in *The Times*:

> Having captured the hearts and minds of the Michigan public with a charm offensive at the start of the week, Europe swamped the United States with a display of dazzling golf and disciplined teamwork at the end of it. By the close of play on the opening day of the Ryder Cup, the efforts of Bernhard Langer and his team, most notably Colin Montgomerie, had been sufficient to brighten the twilight that had settled over this Detroit suburb.
>
> Europe lead by the remarkable score of 6½ points to 1½. Never before in the Ryder Cup have Europe had a first day like this, which means that never before have the USA had such a bad day. Europe's previous best came at Brookline in 1999 when the scoreline after the first day was 6–2. Such was Europe's dominance that of the 131 holes played yesterday, the USA won only 21. It is possible for Europe to reach the 14 points needed to retain the trophy today. Mind you, they would have to take 7½ points from eight matches to do so.

Montgomerie led from the front at The Belfry two years ago in a performance that has rightly been hymned to the heavens and ended with victory by Europe. Here, paired morning and afternoon with Padraig Harrington, he reproduced the magic.

Harrington deserves credit for his play but it was Montgomerie who had to shoulder the greater load that became from being regarded as the team's rock and having to deal with the added pressure that came with that. No praise could be too high for Montgomerie, 41, who has seemed to be in his element this week. A smile has rarely been far from his face and the happiness and sense of contentment with which he appears to have been suffused has inspired him to play golf that can only be described as imperious.

'We had a very, very good day,' Montgomerie said. 'There are only a few days in Ryder Cup play I have enjoyed as much. If you give Tiger and Phil an opportunity, they are going to take it. We took that away from them early.'

Most important, however, were the performances of Darren Clarke and Lee Westwood. Clarke and Westwood each won a crucial point with their respective partners in the morning's fourballs and then, when paired together in the afternoon, the friends recovered from being three down after five holes to give Woods and Mickelson a second defeat.

Montgomerie and Harrington's victory over Woods and Mickelson in the morning was a huge boost to Europe's morale. It was also an immense blow to the US team. If the two best players in their team, the world No. 2 and No. 4, could not withstand Europe, what chance did the rest of them have?

It was astonishing that, having lost in the morning, these two Americans should fail to win even a half-point in the afternoon. What were the odds on them failing twice? It was a tribute to their opponents but a condemnation of Woods and Mickelson and a criticism of Hal Sutton, whose decision to pair two men who are not natural friends ended catastrophically.

The margin of Europe's success cast new light on the tactics of Sutton, the US captain. The thoughtfulness that Sutton had demonstrated earlier in the week when he seemed so intent upon putting his own stamp on the team had rebounded on him and one could only wonder what he would say to the team last night.

'I am going to tell them to make things happen and not to be afraid of what might happen,' Sutton said. 'I saw a lot of tight players out there, whereas the Europeans seemed to be very loose.'

Owen Slot blamed Sutton for putting Woods and Mickelson together, writing:

The outcome reflects terribly on Sutton. He had hoped that, by sending his two stars out first, they would inspire a glory trail behind them. 'Judge me on this,' was Sutton's boast on the eve of the competition. The appraisal will not make for happy reading.

The theory that the odd couple of golf would find themselves drawn together in some kind of opposites-attract magnetic force failed to hold. Not even remotely.

Alongside the fairways, their partners, Amy Mickelson and Elin Nordegren, chatted away like old friends; on it, there was only the sound of silence. Whenever there was conversation it was one of those one-way efforts, with Mickelson chattering away and getting no response.

The theory, presumably, that Sutton was working on was that no matter the level of banter, the odd couple idea would at least work on the scoreboard. Again, not even remotely.

On the second day, the Americans threatened to come back strongly in the morning fourballs. Although García and Westwood managed a half against Hass and DiMarco in the opening match, it looked as though the Americans were going to win the other three. Woods and Riley did indeed beat Clarke and Poulter easily 4 and 3, and Cink and Love beat Montgomerie and Harrington 3 and 2. In the match between Furyk and Campbell and Casey and Howell, the Americans were one up with two to play. However, Howell won the 17th to level the match and Casey won the 18th to secure what had seemed an unlikely win. Instead of 3½–½, it was only 2½–1½ and the Europeans were still leading 8–4.

And in the afternoon, the Europeans found their form again. Clarke and Westwood hammered Haas and DiMarco 5–4 in the opening match and, although Jiménez and Levet then lost 4 and 3 to Mickelson and Toms, García and Donald just beat Furyk and Funk and Harrington and McGinley beat Woods and Love easily 4 and 3. With just the singles to come, the Europeans were leading 11–5, a record lead for them at this stage.

Bizarrely, after Woods had shepherded the newcomer Riley round to a comfortable win in the morning, they did not play together in the afternoon. Apparently, Riley told Sutton he did not want to play, as he did not understand foursomes! Instead of insisting, and surely Woods should have done so too, Sutton acquiesced, let him stand down and put Woods with Love, a combination that did not work. So Woods had now lost three games out of four and therefore the set as, even if he won his single, he would still have lost the set. How was the match going? Oh yes, it was 11–5 to Europe. Langer was, however, aware of the danger of complacency and said later:

> I told the guys not to go in there with the mentality that we are six points ahead. Look at this like it is a fresh start, a fresh match. We had won three out of the four series of fourballs and foursomes, now let's win the singles too. Go in there like we are level and beat them at this as well.

The Americans needed a good start and Sutton was not subtle in his order. He sent them out pretty well in their world ranking order. Langer also put most of his strongest players at the top and Jiménez and Levet, who had not been playing well, near the bottom. However, he did put the two powerful Irishmen, Harrington and McGinley, at 11 and 12. There was a strong contingent of Irish supporters and the two men had suggested they play next to each other so that this support would not be split up.

And the Americans secured their good start. After an hour they were up in all of the first five matches. García fought back to beat Mickelson 3 and 2. Others then recovered too as Clarke secured a half with Love and Westwood beat Perry. The Europeans now had fourteen points and would at least retain the trophy, even if they lost the last seven matches. In reality, it was more a question of who would hole the winning putt.

Donald was hit by some superlative golf by Campbell and was beaten 5 and 3. As a result and very appropriately, it was Montgomerie who sank the winning putt on the 18th where he just beat David Toms. Jiménez lost to DiMarco but Levet, Poulter, Harrington and McGinley all won theirs to produce a winning margin of 18½–9½.

Again, the British press was ecstatic. John Hopkins wrote:

> Europe captured the Ryder Cup in this corner of
> Michigan yesterday in a way that demonstrated why this
> competition thrills and entrances so many inside and
> outside the game. As Europe flags waved in the late after-
> noon sunshine to acknowledge the humbling of a pow-
> erful United States team by a record margin of 18½–9½,
> so the shouts for Bernhard Langer, the Europe captain,
> and Colin Montgomerie, their dominant personality,
> were deafening.
>
> It is surely the first time that the German, a stoical,
> unemotional man from a small town near Munich, has
> had hundreds of British voices hymning him to the
> skies. 'There's only one Bernhard Langer' they sang
> again and again.

A lot of credit was given to Langer. Montgomerie said:

> We have been very fortunate over the years to have
> had such great captains and I've played for a number
> of them. No one is better than Bernhard … What
> Bernhard brought to the job was extreme professional-
> ism. There wasn't the passion of some of his predeces-
> sors, just magnificent efficiency. If I was to describe his
> style, I would call it ambassadorial. He was immaculate
> in everything he did, totally prepared; there was never a
> moment when you worried something might go wrong.
>
> By the way he conducted himself, lived his life, the
> way he handled his career, won a couple of Majors
> despite putting problems that would have broken a
> lesser man, Bernhard naturally had huge respect from
> the team. Whilst he was in charge, you felt that nothing

had been left to chance, everything had been very carefully thought out.

Langer himself said this of his captaincy:

I have played under four captains, Jacklin, Gallacher,
Ballesteros and Torrance. They all did a great job and
all did it slightly differently. I tried to pick out all that
I thought positive from what they did and incorporate
it in my captaincy. I definitely learned that you want to
play every player before Sunday. You don't want to have
anybody sitting out all week and throw them in the deep
end without having played before. That was a bit of a
dilemma as I had such a strong team and so many strong
pairings, but I had to break them up to get the other
guys in.

Then I sent little cards asking them to give me one or
two names of players they would prefer to play with and
one or two you would not want to. All their answers were
confidential, but they were a great help in getting me to
think only of the pairings that would be acceptable to
all concerned, not waste time considering partnerships
that wouldn't have worked anyway.

Then, with a twinkle in his eye and a little smile, he added:
'That way I don't think I would ever have ended up putting
Tiger Woods and Phil Mickelson together.' He continued:

I did a few other things; I researched colours, what they
mean to us as human beings. It is a proven fact that
some colours are more aggressive than other colours
and some colours you feel better in than others. Little
things like that; some of them had been done before

and I copied them, and brought one or two things of my own.

I think personal conversations are very important, more so almost than team meetings. I talked individually to all the guys most days. It was particularly important to speak to all those who were not going to be playing in one of the foursomes or fourballs; important to reassure them it was nothing to do with them not playing well. In the stress of that competition it is important to reassure them that you still think they are great players, wouldn't be there if they weren't, but that, with four having to sit out each series the first two days, they couldn't be part of it that time.

By contrast, Hal Sutton seemed to give an object lesson in how not to captain a team and the poor man received plenty of criticism, including this from Nick Pitt in the *Sunday Times*:

But Sutton, who had been chosen by the PGA of America as a strong leader, turned out to be soft and malleable. He allowed Mickelson to miss team practice two days running. He accommodated Woods and confirmed his bigger-than-the-team status by telling Mickelson to practise for the foursomes with the ball that Woods uses. And at lunchtime on Saturday, he accepted that one of his younger men, Riley, who had only played on Friday and Saturday morning, was too tired to play in the afternoon.

Both captains expressed the view that the impor-tance of the captain is exaggerated, especially, of course, by the media. The players have to make the shots. In fact, the captain's role is crucial. It is the captain who must establish and foster the right attitude, the team ethos; the captain who must ensure that his team is fully prepared technically and physically, and who must put them out in sensible combinations and good order. Sutton failed on every count, while Langer, who never made a mistake, can be placed alongside Tony Jacklin as the very best captain in Europe.

The American press also had a few things to say about the supposed stars of their team. After it became known that Mickelson had used the clubs he had contracted to play with in 2005 but only received just before the Ryder Cup match, Drew Sharp wrote in the *Detroit Free Press*:

Mickelson couldn't wait another week before christening his new equipment because he just had to have those extra millions from his lucrative endorsement deal right now.

Mike Downey wrote in the *Chicago Tribune*:

It was American selfishness that took down the US. Tiger Woods couldn't bottle his animosity for Phil Mickelson for just one day when they were paired in Friday's four-ball and foursomes matches, creating a discomfort that jumped out from inside the ropes. In a hit-rock-bottom defeat, the Americans were dunked like a Top-Flite in a lake. They lost 18½ to 9½ and were lucky to get out with their halves.

Detroiters were so depressed, they went right out and drove on the left side of the road. Oakland Hills wasn't a golf course this weekend. It was a graveyard. At the 35th Ryder Cup, our golfers not only put themselves in a hole early, they stayed there.

And Rick Reilly, probably one of the USA's leading sports writers, wrote a mostly humorous article on the ten things the USA needed to do if they were to win back the Ryder Cup. Amongst other things, he wrote:

No more picking home-spun US captains who issue funny quotes but make funny decisions. Hal Sutton made so many boneheaded moves you'd have sworn he was sniffing golf-grip epoxy. He proudly paired Tiger Woods and Phil Mickelson, saying the pair would be 'stronger 'n new rope'. But these are the two biggest egos in golf today.

It's like pairing Britney Spears with Christina Aguilera. They're great, but not together. They went 0-for-Friday and put a wet blanket on the US that it never shook off.

For some odd reason, Sutton also chose to play fourballs first, even though he admitted: 'We play better at foursomes.' Perfect! This way you can give all the momentum to Europe from the start! Then he decided to walk on Saturday instead of ride in his buggy because 'I wanted to show them how much I care.'

Except then he admitted he couldn't get to all the holes he needed to in order to give them vital information. Uh, duh.

Sutton seemed bent on coaching like a tobacco-stained football coach, giving his players an 'ass-chewing' on Friday night after losing the first day 6½ to 1½, and throwing at least one of them under the bus each night during his press conferences. 'Everybody is walking around terrified,' one non-player in the team room said. 'Every single player thinks Hal is about to bench them. Every single player thinks they're in the envelope.' By the end some of the players must've wanted to hang him. With old rope.

No more wives. No reason, really, except we're all sick of seeing them in matching outfits that manage to make all of them look like Miss Dowdy 1956. In what other sport do the wives get to come into the team room for strategy sessions? It's emasculating, awkward, and besides, the players' mistresses feel left out.

[...] Speaking of Woods, he's not welcome on the US team any more until he actually wants to play. He always seems to play these things with all the enthusiasm of a man forced to take a bath with his mother-in-law.

And since he's the big dog, everybody follows his lead. Great player. Lousy team player. You take him.

And finally,

Just as Great Britain and Ireland were allowed to add continental Europe in 1981 to restore the balance of Ryder Cup matches, America will be allowed to add a region.

We take Fiji.

This last was not as big a joke as it sounded, as the world number one at the time was Vijay Singh who is from, er, Fiji.

17–19 September 2004

Oakland Hills Country Club, Bloomfield Township, Michigan, USA

Captains: B. Langer (Europe), H. Sutton (USA)

Europe		United States	
Fourballs: Morning			
C. Montgomerie & P. Harrington (2&1)	1	P. Mickelson & T. Woods	0
D. Clarke & M.A. Jiménez (5 & 4)	1	D. Love III & C. Campbell	0
P. McGinley & L. Donald (halved)	½	C. Riley & S. Cink (halved)	½
S. García & L. Westwood (5 & 3)	1	D. Toms & J. Furyk	0
Foursomes: Afternoon			
M.A. Jiménez & T. Levet	0	C. DiMarco & J. Haas (3 & 2)	1
C. Montgomerie & P. Harrington (5&4)	1	D. Love III & F. Funk	0
D. Clarke & L. Westwood (1 hole)	1	T. Woods & P. Mickelson	0
S. García & L. Donald (2 & 1)	1	K. Perry & S. Cink	0
Fourballs: Morning			
S. García & L. Westwood (halved)	½	J. Haas & C. DiMarco (halved)	½
D. Clarke & I. Poulter	0	T. Woods & C. Riley (4 & 3)	1
P. Casey & D. Howell (1 hole)	1	J. Furyk & C. Campbell	0
C. Montgomerie & P. Harrington	0	S. Cink & D. Love III (3 & 2)	1
Foursomes: Afternoon			
D .Clarke & L. Westwood (5 & 4)	1	J. Haas & C. DiMarco	0
M.A Jiménez & T. Levet	0	P. Mickelson & D. Toms (4 & 3)	1
S. García & L. Donald (1 hole)	1	J. Furyk & F. Funk	0
P. Harrington & P. McGinley (4 & 3)	1	T. Woods & D. Love III	0
Singles:			
P. Casey	0	T. Woods (3 & 2)	1
S. García (3 & 2)	1	P. Mickelson	0
D. Clarke (halved)	½	D. Love III (halved)	½
D. Howell	0	J. Furyk (6 & 4)	1
L. Westwood (1 hole)	1	K. Perry	0
C. Montgomerie (1 hole)	1	D. Toms	0
L. Donald	0	C. Campbell (5 & 3)	1
M.A. Jiménez	0	C. DiMarco (1 hole)	1
T. Levet (1 hole)	1	F. Funk	0
I. Poulter (3 & 2)	1	C. Riley	0
P. Harrington (1 hole)	1	J. Haas	0
P. McGinley (3 & 2)	1	S. Cink	0
Europe 18½; USA 9½			

Chapter 9
'The reception is something I will never forget'

The K Club, County Kildare 2006

As ever at the Ryder Cup matches, but increasingly so since the 1980s, the performances of the two captains for the 2006 match at the K Club in Ireland were subjected to close scrutiny. The American captain was Tom Lehman and the European captain the Welshman, Ian Woosnam. In the pre-match jousting Lehman seemed to be winning.

First, Woosnam had to cope with plenty of criticism of his two captain's picks, Darren Clarke and Lee Westwood. Clarke had suffered a very difficult two years as his wife, Heather, having been diagnosed with terminal cancer, died only three weeks before Woosnam had to make his final selection. Woosnam picked Clarke, saying:

> Darren has had his problems in the last couple of years but he is a magnificent player who has a great record in the Ryder Cup. I have spoken to him and he is really positive about playing.

Clarke himself said:

> I was both honoured and delighted by Ian Woosnam's invitation to play in this year's Ryder Cup. I would certainly not have considered making myself available unless I felt I could contribute to the cause. It is going to be fantastic to play in Ireland and it will be a great occasion for everybody. It is going to be a magnificent week, and I would not have wanted to miss it – and neither would my lovely wife, Heather.

And certainly Clarke could be sure of the full support from friends in both teams as well as the partisan crowd.

However, Woosnam's selection of Lee Westwood ahead of Thomas Björn was not as straightforward and was greeted with plenty of adverse comment, not least from Björn himself, who said:

> Devastation does not even come close to how I feel … I have nothing against Lee Westwood. But if you can find one category in which he has beaten me then I would like to see it. I have played better than him in the qualifying phase – and then Woosnam bases decision on results which are more than five years old. I don't understand the way he is handling the whole situation. It doesn't look like he is burdened with leadership qualities.
>
> He came into the bar and gave me 20 seconds about Lee having won twice at the K Club. In a bar – that kind of sums it up. He can't walk up to me, tell me in 20 seconds and expect me to be happy. I'm very disappointed. I think he's been very poor in the way he's handled the players.

Finally, Woosnam was a little puzzled by the way the previous European captain, Bernhard Langer, appeared to be giving advice to the American captain, Tom Lehman, and said: 'That seems strange to me.'

John Hopkins did point out in *The Times* that Lehman and Langer were both committed Christians and long-term friends and saw a lot more of each other than Langer (who lived in America) and Woosnam did. He went on to say:

> Langer clearly felt it was in the spirit of friendship to respond to the American captain's request for insight into the job. But the German admitted he had held a bit back.
>
> If Woosnam thought the really difficult part of the biennial competition would come during the week of the match, he was wrong. It has started already and

across the Atlantic Lehman must be privately pleased at
the obvious disharmony in the Europe camp.

The organisation of the match at the K Club in County
Kildare was magnificent. Ireland had long been looking
forward to hosting the Ryder Cup; now was their chance
to do so, and they were determined to do it in style. The
European tour worked closely with the Irish Tourist Board
whose representative Paul Keeley said:

The eyes of the world are on County Kildare. With the
Ryder Cup you have an opportunity to sell your country.

It would have been lovely had the match been able to
grace one of Ireland's great links courses, most probably
Portmarnock. For many years the Irish Open had been
played there and attracted crowds barely smaller than those
that made up the pilgrimage to the Open Championship,
also played exclusively at the seaside. But the Ryder Cup
was by now big business and to win the right to stage it
required considerable financial resources. In Ireland's case
those resources were to be found in the Smurfit Packaging
Company and specifically Dr Michael Smurfit, its chairman
and CEO. And he had his own 'train set'. It was called the
K Club.

Twenty or so years previously, Dr Michael had acquired
Straffen House, a handsome Georgian mansion set in rolling parkland some twenty miles south-west of Dublin. He
immediately started building a golf course in the grounds,
of sufficient stature to reflect the grandeur of the house.
He commissioned Arnold Palmer to design it. The course
opened in 1991 and in 1995 it became the home of the
European Open. Dr Michael then started a campaign to
bring the Ryder Cup to Ireland, beat off the opposition –

no mean feat nowadays – and earned the right for 2006. To fund a Ryder Cup is a big commitment over several years and while Smurfit continued to sponsor the European Open, Bord Failte (Irish Tourist Board), a tremendous promoter of golf in Ireland, ensured that other elements of the contract were fulfilled.

To start with the Palmer course was a bit of an ugly duckling – most new courses are until they mature and the trees grow in. Nestling alongside a tributary of the Liffy, it initially had a problem with flooding during bad weather, and with the Ryder Cup being in September, bad weather was a distinct possibility. However, as had been the case with Jaime Ortiz-Patiño and Valderrama, Dr Michael had the resources and the expertise to sort any problems out. By the time the Ryder Cup came along the K Club was ready.

As regards the two teams, on paper Europe was probably the stronger, having seven players in the world top twenty, one more than the Americans. On the other hand, the Americans had the top three in Tiger Woods, Phil Mickelson and Jim Furyk, and all of their team were in the top 50.

For Europe, the two-tiered system of selecting half the team by current world ranking points and half from the European Order of Merit was catching just about everyone in its net. Of the team that won so well at Oakland Hills, only Thomas Levet and Miguel Angel Jiménez were below the radar and two very strong Scandinavians had played their way in to replace them.

Robert Karlsson had been unlucky to miss out in Mark James' side of 1999; but did not catch the captain's eye when the wild cards were handed out. He then went into something of a decline and although he won a couple of tournaments in 2001 and 2002, had spent long periods in the doldrums. He knew how to win when he got the chance, but consistency was the problem; that, and a tendency to be overcritical of his own shortcomings. By 2005 he had remodelled his swing and he burst back onto the scene the following summer, winning at the venue, but not the course, where the Ryder Cup would be played in 2010, Celtic Manor. Just about the tallest player in tournament golf at 6 feet 5 inches, his vast frame always looked too big to fit a swing into. When he appeared that summer it was with a new compact and repeating swing. Later he added the Deutsche Bank TPC of Europe to his collection and so did not have to rely on his captain's goodwill to make the European side.

The Swedish player Henrik Stenson was just 25 when he won the Benson and Hedges International Open in 2001, but soon after that his driving totally deserted him; he just hit it all over the place. For two years he struggled under the eye of coach Pete Cowan and slowly it came back. He won at Woburn in the autumn of 2004 and the following year had a number of high finishes to move into the top ten of the European rankings: he has not been out of them since. He, too, booked his place in Woosnam's side early. The other players who achieved automatic selection were all proven Ryder Cup campaigners, and had all been part of those successful teams of recent times.

As we have seen, not in the team as of right were Darren Clarke and Lee Westwood. Clarke, of course, had had to live for the previous few years through his wife Heather's seemingly endless battle with cancer. It was a battle she would finally lose that summer and it was generally assumed that the Ryder Cup would come too soon for him to want to take part. He had played a few events that year and was nowhere near making the team, but Woosnam would still have wanted such a potent force on the team if he were available. With sufficient time between the funeral and the match, Darren saw the positives of going to Ireland for the match rather than grieving at home. A successful few days at the K Club would perhaps be the best therapy of all.

Nor was Clarke's close friend, Lee Westwood, on the best of form. He had taken a sabbatical after the 2004 match to be at home when his wife had their second baby and his game was not at its best when he returned. Again, as we have seen, he did not qualify automatically but Woosnam decided to pick him rather than Thomas Björn. In spite of the slight gamble with these captain's picks, it was a strong European team.

With regard to Tiger Woods, everyone, including Owen Slot of *The Times*, now seemed keen to show that he had reformed his previously self-centred ways and was now a great team man. Slot wrote just before the match:

> At the Bridgestone Invitational event in Akron, Ohio, last month, he took the four rookies in the US team to dinner to address them on Ryder Cup matters. Questions have been raised over the credentials of Vaughan Taylor, J.J. Henry, Zach Johnson and Brett Wetterich to play at Ryder Cup level and this was a point Woods was keen to tackle.
>
> 'We had a great time,' he said. 'We had some nice steak and we just talked about my experiences in the cup: what to expect, things that surprised me, things that you're going to have to be ready for.'
>
> And this from a man supposedly cold on team golf.

Woods himself said:

> It's real interesting that it's a younger team. We've got most guys between 30 and 40. I think we can all relate to each other being so much the same age.

On the practice day of the match itself, Woods was forced to cope with reports that a pornographic website was showing pictures of a model, purportedly his wife, Elin, in the nude. Woods was beside himself with rage and told a hastily arranged press conference:

'My wife has been a model and she did some bikini photos,' he said. 'But to link her to porn websites and such is unacceptable. It's hard to be diplomatic about this when you have so much emotion involved and when my wife is involved.

'I am very disappointed – not with the fans, not the people here nor the Irish people', the world No. 1 said. 'I don't want this to detract from the beauty of this event. You do things for the people you love and care about. My father got ridiculed for years and I always felt for him and my mother the same way. My wife and I are a team, we do things as a team and I care about her with all my heart.'

And the whole furore did seem to affect him. He did not play particularly well on the first day, as Owen Slot reported:

It was halfway through his four-ball yesterday morning that RTE, the Irish broadcaster, began a brief debate as to whether Tiger Woods was suffering from an upset stomach. He had just banged his drive on the 10th way right, a gaffe that could not have been more different to his drive on the 1st, which went left and into the water. In between not a lot was a whole lot better, so RTE quite reasonably began to wonder whether maybe it was a medical issue.

The first point here is that no doctor was called. The second point came from Woods himself, who would explain later that he had started very slowly yesterday because he had not warmed up particularly well beforehand. Yet even when warm, you could not say that Woods got particularly hot. Never did he become the talismanic force that the United States team, every two years, are hoping to be able to follow.

The scoreboard may reveal that he took one point from two, plus the significant scalp of Colin Montgomerie, yet the Woods we saw yesterday did not prevail through his own outstanding golf but because his opposition missed their opportunity on a day when he was giving plenty. Montgomerie and Padraig Harrington had chances, but could not take them. Sergio García and Luke Donald, in foursomes, did.

In their press conference, Jim Furyk leapt to his partner's defence: 'He hit it beautifully this afternoon.'

On the opening morning, how would the emotional Darren Clarke fare? Playing with his friend of long standing, Lee Westwood, against Phil Mickelson and Chris DiMarco, 'very well' was the answer as the European pair won at the 18th. He said afterwards: 'Obviously it was emotional for me on the first tee. The reception is something that I will never ever forget. I don't know how, but I got it down there somehow. [It was the shot of the day.] I never had any doubts,' he added of his decision to play. 'Live by the sword, die by the sword.'

There was certainly plenty of emotion in the air around the first tee on that Friday morning. Colin Montgomerie said, when he came off the course:

That walk on to the first tee is something I will never forget. It made the hairs stand up on the back of my neck. It even got to Ivor [Robson – the starter] who announced

'Welcome to the foursomes' instead of fourballs. He was so nervous he said the wrong thing.

Elsewhere on the first day Sergio García won twice and irritated his opponents as usual.

James Mossop wrote of him in the *Daily Telegraph*:

Easy Ryder. With Sergio García comes the exuberance of youth, a pure talent and a sense of comradeship crucial to the bonding of the European team.

A huge sense of drama, too, none greater than on the par-five 16th hole during yesterday's afternoon foursomes at the K Club. It seemed his partner, Luke Donald, had put him in an impossible position with the ball landing on wood-chippings, water to clear from an awful lie and little margin for error.

Suddenly the spectators were roaring in salute at the García genius as he landed the ball 15 feet from the hole. Donald, his seamless partner, stepped up to sink the putt for birdie and the Americans Phil Mickelson and David Toms were looking at defeat, two down and two holes to go. The Europeans closed it out 2 and 1.

García has won tournaments in the United States and Europe and has been in contention on the final day of Majors but he says the Ryder Cup is the pinnacle of his sporting world.

He won four and half points in 2004 and when he birdied the first hole on Friday morning it was the signal of things to come.

He let no one down, striding to victory first with his compatriot José Maria Olazábal and then with another friend, Luke Donald, the Englishman who shares his home in the Swiss Alpine town of Crans Montana whenever they play there in the European Masters.

García, an avid Real Madrid supporter, has brought football-style celebrations to the winning moment and the Irish people and his colleagues have embraced his sense of enthusiasm ... You realise how much the Ryder Cup means to García when you listen to him talking and he says, 'It's the Ryder Cup. That's it. There is no better word.

'I can't live without it. It makes for an unbelievable week. It is special because it is difficult to get into the team. Winning is definitely more satisfying than winning an individual event.

'I have been fortunate enough to be in two winning Ryder Cup teams and the experiences I have had have been great. Even when we lost at Brookline [1999] it was great. I was just out on the Tour and got to know a lot of the players.'

Peter Dixon wrote of his exuberant performance:

Sergio García turned in another sensational Ryder Cup performance yesterday, winning both his four-balls and foursomes matches and in the process contributing another two points to Europe's cause. In this form, it is difficult to think who might stop him – and that includes Tiger Woods who tried but failed.

Paired with José Maria Olazábal, his Spanish compatriot, who was making his first appearance since 1999, García swaggered on to the 1st tee in the morning, ready to do battle in the four-balls and milking the applause for all he was worth. Some wilt under such pressure, he thrives.

For the Europeans at least, his exuberance and passion is hugely infectious. In the team room, he is a central vocal character, although the young pup who used to bounce off the walls and furniture has, at 26, started to calm down.

For the Americans, however, García is more irritant than inspiration. He is remembered for his bounding run down The Belfry's 18th fairway in celebration of Europe's victory in 2002 and generally for getting under the skin of Woods. It is a role he has grown to love.

And as is García's wont, he got off to a flying start with Olazábal. He birdied the opening hole to put his team one up and they were never to trail. In fact, Brett Wetterich and David Toms, their opponents, could feel a little hard done by. Between them they played some good golf ... All week, Ian Woosnam, the captain, had said that to see García together with Olazábal reminded him of the Severiano Ballesteros-Olazábal pairing that was virtually unbeatable in the four Ryder Cups they played together.

Then it was Ballesteros who used to praise his young charge. This time, it was Olazábal's turn. 'It feels great playing alongside Sergio,' he said. 'The way he played was fantastic; he was the secret to our success.

'Sergio lifted his game unbelievably, which he always seems to do when he plays in the Ryder Cup,' Woosnam said. 'He has that Spanish spirit and is on top form.'

At the end of the first day the Europeans led 5–3 and every member of the European team had secured at least half a point. Nor did the Europeans lose a full point after Woods and Furyk had won the first match of the day.

Captain Ian Woosnam said:

What a day's golf. That was unbelievable. What a feast for the spectators. I would have been happy with a one-point lead. I don't want to get ahead of myself because we all know what a game it is, but I thought all my players were exceptional today. I am so proud of them.

Only one of the eight games ended before the 18th, so close were all the matches.

And, by the end of the second day, Europe had doubled their lead to 10–6. The first fourball was a very close match, which ended in a half between Paul Casey and Robert Karlsson and Stewart Cink and Ryder Cup rookie J.J. Henry, who nearly won the match for the Americans with an eagle at the par-five 16th and a birdie at the 17th. However, Casey holed a fifteen-foot putt at the 18th to secure the half.

García and Olazábal then gained their usual win, beating Chris DiMarco and Phil Mickelson 3 and 2. Clarke and Westwood then beat Furyk and a very wayward Woods, also 3 and 2, before Scott Verplank and Zach Johnson secured America's only victory of the morning, beating Henrik Stenson and Padraig Harrington 2 and 1.

In the afternoon, García won again to make it four wins in four matches, this time paired with Luke Donald, and again against Phil Mickelson, who was partnered in this match by David Toms. This was followed by a very close match between Montgomerie and Westwood against Chad Campbell and Vaughn Taylor, which ended in a half. Europe went further ahead when Casey and David Howell thrashed Stewart Cink and Zach Johnson 5 and 4. The Americans regained some pride when a more relaxed Woods, again playing with Furyk, easily beat the two Irishmen, Harrington and McGinley, 4 and 2.

The afternoon produced another 2½ points for Europe, which meant that all four foursomes and fourballs had produced the same result – Europe 2½, USA 1½ – and Europe would go into the singles leading 10–6.

It was same scoreline as in the notorious match at Brookline in 1999 and the man who had led the American charge in the singles, Tom Lehman, and was now their captain, did his best to rally his troops, saying:

> Our team does not feel that this is over. We know that we have to play our very best golf but we feel that we can do that.

Looking back at Brookline, he added:

> Everyone had to look inside. Everyone had a responsibility to win. What made '99 so special, what made it possible, was that all the first six matches got going so well so early.

Woosnam chose Montgomerie as his top man to lead off. He is a quick player and with any luck his winning progress would show up on the scoreboard and encourage his teammates. His opponent was David Toms, who was not quite the player he had been two years earlier. Nevertheless, he proved a strong opponent and the match went all the way to the 18th before Montgomerie won.

Colin Montgomerie is surely the best British golfer never to have won a Major. Some used to say that about Peter Alliss, but Monty achieved many more tournament wins than Alliss. Of course, there were many more tournaments available in Monty's era.

Although Scottish by birth, Montgomerie was brought up in Yorkshire where his father was managing director of Fox's Biscuits. He would later become secretary at Royal Troon. He learnt his golf at Ilkley Golf Club where he was taught by the professional, Bill Ferguson. He was one of the first of Britain's leading golfers to go to an American college, in his case Houston Baptist University. Later, a number of leading young golfers, such as Luke Donald, would follow his example.

Before turning professional he won three Scottish amateur tournaments – in 1983 the Scottish Youth Championship, in 1985 the Scottish Stroke Play Championship and in 1987 the Scottish Amateur Championship. He also played twice for Scotland in the Eisenhower Trophy, in 1984 and 1986, and for Great Britain and Ireland in the Walker Cup, again twice, in 1985 and 1987. He turned professional in 1988 and was made Rookie of the Year on the European tour that season.

In 1989 he won his first tournament on the European tour – the Portuguese Open which he won by eight strokes – and made his Ryder Cup debut in the 'War on the Shore' match at Kiawah Island in 1991.

From there he went from strength to strength, finishing first in the European tour Order of Merit every year from 1993 to 1999. He reached the top ten in the official world golf rankings in 1994 and stayed there for nearly 400 weeks. At one point he reached number two. After 2000 his form fell away, partly due to problems in his marriage, but he came back strongly in 2005, winning an eighth European tour Order of Merit and becoming the first golfer to win 20 million Euros on the European tour. At the end of 2004 he was awarded an MBE in the New Year Honours List.

He will have been very disappointed never to have won a Major. He finished second no fewer than five times. His first close shave was in 1992 when he finished third in the US Open at Pebble Beach. He was prematurely congratulated by Jack Nicklaus, who said to him as he came off the 18th green: 'Congratulations on your first US Open victory.'

He came very close again in 1994, when he tied with Ernie Els and Loran Roberts at Oakmont Country Club.

The following year, at the US PGA Championship at Riviera Country Club, he birdied the last three holes to tie with Steve Elkington at seventeen under par. On the first play-off hole, Elkington holed from 35 feet to win the Championship.

Two years later he just lost to Els again at Congressional Country Club. However it was at the 2006 US Open, on the West Course at Winged Foot, where he had his best chance to win a Major. In the final round he holed a 50-foot birdie putt on the 17th to lead the field by one shot. He hit a good drive down the 18th, but while waiting to play his approach to the green changed from a six- to a seven-iron, feeling that the adrenalin pumping through him would mean he would hit the six-iron too far. In the event he finished short and right in the rough. He pitched but then three-putted to finish one stroke behind.

The only time he threatened to win the Open Championship was when he finished second to Woods at St Andrews in 2005.

However, when it comes to the Ryder Cup Montgomerie is considered one of the best performers of all time. He played in eight matches and never lost a single. Out of 36 matches played he won twenty, lost nine and halved seven. Only Nick Faldo has scored more points. At the 2004 match where he sank the winning putt, James Mossop wrote of him in the *Daily Telegraph*:

Adrenalin kicks in first and never leaves him. He can be friendly one minute, ferocious the next. His snarl is as expressive as his smile. He has such uncanny antennae and it has been said that his concentration can be disturbed by a butterfly landing in a neighbouring meadow.

He is opinionated, excitable, sensitive and gifted. He loves James Bond movies and so far this weekend he has been Europe's 'Goldfinger', alongside his marvellous quirky Irish partner, Padraig Harrington. When they stepped out together, in the last of the morning four-ball matches, against Stewart Cink and David Love, things were bound to happen and they did. For once, it was not always to Montgomerie's liking as Love became the man touching gold. Disappointment became Monty's companion yesterday.

James Bond usually triumphed after an early adversity and when Monty found a fairway bunker with his opening tee shot and then caught the lip when he tried to extricate himself, it was the beginning of an uphill climb.

In a regular tournament there might have been a slump of shoulders and the head going down but this is the Ryder Cup. He thrives on the responsibility of being the team leader on the course even though this year he was one of Bernhard Langer's captain's picks.

Going to yesterday's matches his Ryder Cup record showed 18 wins, seven defeats and five halved matches. 'I have been very, very fortunate to have been given good partners', he said. 'At the same time I do enjoy the format of this competition. I just enjoy being part of a team, possibly more than I do having to play for myself.'

Monty watchers have rarely seen him so relaxed and yet so competitive that negative thoughts are not allowed within another fairway of him. His coach, Denis Pugh, has some interesting observations on what makes Monty tick.

He said: 'He thrives on the atmosphere and the cut and thrust of matchplay. You can see it in his eyes and the way he strides up the fairway on every hole. For him, this is the best week of his professional life.'

And he will, of course, be captain of the European team for the 2010 Ryder Cup match to be played at Celtic Manor at the beginning of October 2010.

Back at the K Club, unfortunately for the USA there was no strong fightback. Stewart Cink played brilliantly to beat García 4 and 3 (a rare Ryder Cup defeat for him) and Woods beat Karlsson 3 and 2. After that it was all Europe and it was just a question of who would make the winning putt. For a moment it looked like the European supporters might get their perfect ending as Darren Clarke was about to close out his match on the 16th. First, however, just as Henrik Stenson beat Vaughn Taylor on the 15th to ensure that Europe could not lose, almost simultaneously Luke Donald finished his game with Chad Campbell to clinch the victory. Somehow it didn't matter. As Clarke made it three wins out of three for his personal tally, the tears and champagne flowed. It had been Europe 18½, USA 9½ at Oakland Hills and it was the same here at home.

What a wonderful three days it had been for Ireland and Europe. In his usual perceptive way, Simon Barnes summed it all up in *The Times* under the headline 'Europe united in state of animosity towards America':

The spectacle of the masters of the universe failing to win at their heartland sport of golf is absolutely unlookawayable. The rising tide of blue, the failing and faltering bands of red: these are joyful things. A few Brits, some Irish, a couple of Spaniards and Swedes: if you hate America, clap your hands, rattle your niblicks and hole your putts.

It's great because the Americans are the stronger team, individual by individual. It's great because it's all about team spirit seeking to outdo individual accomplishment.

But the greatest thing of all is that the Americans might lose and for the past three times have done so.

It's all very ghastly of us. Sport is supposed to bring us to higher things; it seems that sport is equally capable of dragging us down. The Ryder Cup is, for Europeans, a celebration of envy, resentment, chippiness, defiance and dissatisfaction. That is why even for non-golfers it is the most marvellous fun.

But as we revel in the spectacle, we must come to terms with a few things. Sport is not as uplifting as you thought it was and you are not as nice a person as you thought you were. The Ryder Cup is, indeed, bad for the soul. No wonder it's irresistible.

Europe had now won eight of the last eleven matches. What a contrast to the 50 years before that. The next question was – could Nick Faldo continue the good work in 2008?

22–24 September 2006			
K Club, County Kildare, Ireland			
Captains: I. Woosnam (Europe), T. Lehman (USA)			
Europe		**United States**	
Fourballs: Morning			
C. Montgomerie & P. Harrington	0	T. Woods & J. Furyk (1 hole)	1
P. Casey & R. Karlsson (halved)	½	S. Cink & J.J. Henry (halved)	½
S. García & J.M. Olazábal (3 & 2)	1	D. Toms & B. Wetterich	0
D. Clarke & L. Westwood (1 hole)	1	P. Mickelson & C. DiMarco	0

(continued)

22–24 September 2006 (continued)			
K Club, County Kildare, Ireland			
Captains: I. Woosnam (Europe), T. Lehman (USA)			
Europe		**United States**	
Foursomes: Afternoon			
P. McGinley & P. Harrington (halved)	½	C. Campbell & Z. Johnson (halved)	½
D. Howell & H. Stenson (halved)	½	S. Cink & D. Toms (halved)	½
L. Westwood & C. Montgomerie (halved)	½	P. Mickelson & C. DiMarco (halved)	½
L. Donald & S. García (2 holes)	1	T. Woods & J. Furyk	0
Fourballs: Morning			
P. Casey & R. Karlsson (halved)	½	S. Cink & J.J. Henry (halved)	½
S. García & J.M. Olazábal (3 & 2)	1	P. Mickelson & C. DiMarco	0
L. Westwood & D. Clarke (3 & 2)	1	T. Woods & J. Furyk	0
H. Stenson & P. Harrington	0	Z. Johnson & S. Verplank (2 & 1)	1
Foursomes: Afternoon			
S. García & L. Donald (2 & 1)	1	P. Mickelson & D. Toms	0
C. Montgomerie & L. Westwood (halved)	½	C. Campbell & V. Taylor (halved)	½
P. Casey & D. Howell (5 & 4)	1	C. Cink & Z. Johnson	0
P. Harrington & P. McGinley	0	T. Woods & J. Furyk (3 & 2)	1
Singles:			
C. Montgomerie (1 hole)	1	D. Toms	0
S. García	0	S. Cink (4 & 3)	1
P. Casey (2 & 1)	1	J. Furyk	0
R. Karlsson	0	T. Woods (3 & 2)	1
L. Donald (2 & 1)	1	C. Campbell	0
P. McGinley (halved)	½	J.J. Henry (halved)	½
D. Clarke (3 & 2)	1	Z. Johnson	0
H. Stenson (4 & 3)	1	V. Taylor	0
D. Howell (5 & 4)	1	B. Wetterich	0
J.M. Olazábal (2 & 1)	1	P. Mickelson	0
L. Westwood (2 holes)	1	C. DiMarco	0
P. Harrington	0	S. Verplank (4 & 3)	1
Europe 18½; USA 9½			

Chapter 10
Azinger's rampaging camaraderie

Valhalla, Kentucky 2008

The phoney war began early before the 2008 Ryder Cup match to be played at Valhalla, Kentucky. The two captains, Nick Faldo and Paul Azinger, had a supposed history of being enemies, but in reality communicated with each other regularly in the build-up to the match. Nevertheless, Faldo was not above stirring things up a little. Commenting on the appointment of Ray Floyd (US captain in 1989) and Dave Stockton (US captain for the notorious Kiawah Island match of 1991) as advisors to Azinger, Faldo said:

> I think he already regrets it. Maybe regrets isn't the right word, but if he did it again … I don't think those guys have brought to the team what he wanted. He's a bit like me. He feels that you have to make the decisions yourself, in the present time. Maybe those captains are from an old era in the Ryder Cup. Jack Nicklaus made a few comments and what have you. I think he [Azinger] isn't sure about that one.

Nicklaus had apparently said of Azinger's plan to lean heavily on Floyd and Stockton: 'Get rid of 'em and just go with the guys who play golf.'

In terms of selection, Faldo was always going to disappoint some people with his captain's selections. In the event, he announced at Gleneagles that he had chosen Paul Casey and Ian Poulter. Other players who must have been considered include the very experienced stalwart of European Ryder Cup sides for the previous seven matches, Colin Montgomerie; Darren Clarke, who had won twice on the European tour in recent months; and the Swedish golfer Carl Pettersson.

Some were not impressed and the bookmaker Ladbrokes said the punters were 'deserting the European team in droves'. However, having seen how Thomas Björn had attacked Woosnam after not being selected in 2006, Montgomerie and Clarke were careful not to follow suit. Clarke said:

> I have no intention of slagging off Nick Faldo, either now or in the future. There has never been any bad blood between us and I have massive respect for him as a player. The man has won six Majors after all.
>
> I have had several messages from players saying they could not believe I was not in the team, but Nick has picked Ian Poulter and Paul Casey and Europe will be stronger for their inclusion. I can't have any complaints about them, either, because they are both above me in the world rankings.
>
> But I also feel that I could have added something to the team, both on and off the course. I was under the impression that the ingredients for getting picked were current form and experience and I think I qualified on both counts. Obviously, I'm disappointed, but Nick is the captain and I have to accept his decision.

And Montgomerie was equally cautious, saying:

> I do feel that I have not played my last Ryder Cup. I had hoped to get a pick, but, unfortunately, the competition for places was too great. I was one of five [who could have been considered], but you have got to show form. I was eighteenth on the list when it finished and that was not good enough.

Over in the USA, the captain now had four picks and Azinger selected three rookies, Steve Stricker, Hunter Mahan and J.B. Holmes, as well as one player who had played in the match before, Chad Campbell. Of the rest who qualified as of right, three – Anthony Kim, Ben Curtis and Boo Weekley – had not played in the match before, so there were six newcomers in all. It meant that this was the least experienced American side for years, possibly of all time.

Just before the match, *The Times* published comments on each of his teammates by Justin Rose:

Nick Faldo

Our generation looks up enormously to Nick, our captain. Six Majors is the benchmark. At that barbecue last Sunday I noticed how sensibly he ate. I don't have a nickname for him. It seems a bit disrespectful to call someone who is older and so much more successful by a cheeky nickname.

Paul Casey

I call him The Space Man which dates back to his days at Arizona State University when he was known as Space Man Casey. I'd like to play four-balls with Paul because he is very strong and gets lots of birdies. He is experienced in the Ryder Cup. I expect him to take the lead in any pairing he is playing in.

Sergio García

One of the hottest players in the world. I hope I might play with him. His game is perfect for foursomes because he is a brilliant driver, hitting the ball straight, and he gets a lot of birdies, which is good for four-balls, too. His nickname is El Niño, but I call him Serge or Sergio. Has boundless confidence.

Padraig Harrington

All the adjectives you hear about him are true. He is steely and gritty. We will look at him as our leader. I would much rather play with him than against him. Was pleased to beat him at Valderrama last year. Had dinner with him in Orlando recently and found him to be a genuinely nice guy.

Miguel Ángel Jiménez

A legend, for want of a better word. A very cool character. He cooked a massive paella for everyone at a dinner we both attended in Miami recently. He has things in perspective. Golf is not a matter of life and death for Miguel Ángel. His English is not fantastic, but he has lots of charisma.

Henrik Stenson

Got to know him well lately and he has a wicked sense of humour. Delivers the punchline with a straight face. He loves a practical joke and his humour could be a calming influence this week. Can't see his eyes because he always wears sunglasses. Helped by having such a professional caddie as Fanny Sunesson.

Lee Westwood

One of the best ball-strikers on our team. Been successful with Sergio in foursomes and fourballs in the past three Ryder Cups. We have not mixed with one another much and I have never been with him in a team environment. His Ryder Cup record of winning over 60 per cent of his matches is amazing.

Graeme McDowell

G-Mac has had a really solid year. I played a practice round with him before the US PGA and I was surprised how straight he was off the tee. He is putting well, too.

A good foursome partner for someone who is as straight as he is. Another Lake Nona resident.

Ian Poulter

I am looking at Poults as I speak and he is wearing pink. Give him a sniff of the lead and he always seals the deal. A lovely character with remarkable self-belief. Our pairing in the foursomes of the World Cup in China last year was a great success. We must be a possible foursomes pairing again this week.

Robert Karlsson

I don't know Robert well and from a distance he seems the quintessential tall, silent Swede. His consistency has been remarkable this year, with top-ten finishes in the first three Majors. He has an eccentric side and he tends to do things his own way.

For his part, Faldo appointed only one assistant, José Maria Olazábal, and said: 'This is what I have been saying. Too many cooks ...'

He received some criticism for this, even before the match. Sam Torrance, captain of the European team which won at The Belfry in 2002, said:

He wants to gain all the information himself about the players, but he can't do that, he won't have the time. Take, for instance, sorting out the pairings for the afternoon on the Friday and Saturday. You have to get them in by 12:15pm, when two of the morning matches are still on the course. He doesn't have the time to watch all four matches and could make a decision to drop one pairing who he sees are two down with three to play, only for them to win the last three and he'll want them back.

In 2002 I had four helpers, one following each match. You need your friends there, people who you know and trust.

Azinger is a tough cookie and was unlikely to be fazed by Faldo's comments. Not the most natural player and with a relatively modest record in the Ryder Cup, he was, above all else, a trier. For example, he had overcome cancer in the 1990s to play in the 2002 match, in which he holed from a bunker in his single against Niclas Fasth to prevent Fasth securing the winning point.

Azinger was also capable of making remarks that could unsettle Faldo. He had once described Faldo as a 'prick' during his playing days, adding that Faldo's contemporaries did not like him.

Faldo's comment on the up-and-coming match was:

It's going to be competitive. These guys put their game, their emotions, their soul on the line that week. It will be fierce: that's what we expect, that's what we want, but we will all uphold this game that we play, simple as that.

Azinger replied that the world wanted the two of them to fall out, 'but it ain't gonna happen'.

As for the teams, what was Jack Nicklaus's view of them?

When I look at the teams for this year's Ryder Cup and focus on the senior men in both teams – Lee Westwood, Harrington, Jiménez and García for Europe, Phil Mickelson, Jim Furyk, Kenny Perry and Stewart Cink for the US – I don't see much difference. I think that's a toss-up. Phil has good team qualities, I remember one

Presidents Cup match, I was asking the senior guys who they would like as a partner and it was obvious no one was picking Woody Austin and Phil saw this and said, 'Hey, I'd like to play with Woody, I've wanted to play with Woody.'

Of the young Americans, Anthony Kim has played as well as any golfer over the past six months, with the exception of Harrington. Hunter Mahan hasn't played as well as I thought he would but he is a very good player, I know that from his performance in the Presidents Cup. Of the younger Europeans, Ian Poulter is a very good player. He is a player I would have given a wild card to and I think Nick made a good choice. Justin Rose is a very good player as well. But he and Poulter don't win as often as they should.

Because of their recent supremacy, the Europeans will be confident and will probably consider themselves favourites to win.

When asked about the potential for over-exuberant support from the crowds, Nicklaus said:

I know some people have said the atmosphere in Kentucky will be boisterous but I can't imagine it being a loud crowd. Louisville is a quite conservative part of the United States and I think the crowd there will be fair to both sides. This is not going to be like the Ryder Cup staged in New York, which would be a madhouse. No, the people who turn up at Valhalla will be there to see good golf, regardless of which side produces it. Unless I'm misreading it, I don't imagine there will be many guys coming from the bars and then making themselves heard on the fairways.

Valhalla has been changed over the past year, and the guys will find it more challenging than before. A lot of holes have been greatly changed. The sixth is probably the best example. We moved back the green there about 80 yards and it is now a really tough 500-yard par four. Where the guys were hitting seven or eight irons, they will now be hitting a three or four iron.

What makes Valhalla more unusual is the difference between the front side and the back side. The front nine is built on Floyd's plain, a test of golf that you might find somewhere in Britain. The back nine is through a wooded area, with lots of fairways framed by woodland, and it's a very different test. The 16th will be very tough, a 511-yard par four. I was against the change at first but now I admit it was right.

I like really tough holes in matchplay golf because generally there are different ways of playing them and when players take those different options, that makes matchplay very interesting.

Finally, he remarked:

As I've said, I don't believe your guys are better than ours, and I don't accept either that you are better at foursomes and fourballs. I believe our team is every bit as good as yours, if not better, and we have home advantage. The difficulty I have is with the matches at Oakland Hills and the K Club.

Ask me to explain how the US got a thrashing in each of those two matches and I don't have an answer. I can't explain it, but I still believe we can do it this time.

John Hopkins of *The Times* was confident that Europe would win, writing:

Of the Ryder Cups that I have listened to on the radio, watched on television or covered for newspapers this is the first in which Europe are regarded, rightly, as favourites to win in the United States. I believe Europe will do it, perhaps by three points.

There are a number of reasons for this. While Europe have four rookies – one of whom, Justin Rose, won last year's Order of Merit and could hardly be called inexperienced – there are six men in the US team who have not experienced the tension of this event. It will require several of them to perform like veterans if this is not to be an advantage for Europe.

Next, the US are without Tiger Woods, who has contributed ten victories and two halves from the 25 matches he has played. The world No. 1 was the leading points-scorer for his team in 2006. Don't tell me that a team without him are as strong as one with him.

Then there is the question of form. Europe have more men playing well than the US. In the past 13-week period of the world rankings up to last weekend, Europe players have earned 960 points, the US 660 points. Also not to be overlooked is the improvement that Europe's golfers have made down the years. This team has depth, which has traditionally not been the case.

Needless to say, the American golf journalist Larry Dorman disagreed, saying:

Yes, yes, Tiger Woods is missing from – will be sorely missed by – the US side. But Azinger has a team loaded with bombers in Phil Mickelson, Perry, Anthony Kim, Holmes and Hunter Mahan and has set up the course with wide fairways and very light rough. Three long hitters, all young and fearless, are rookies. Kim, 23, Mahan,

26, and Holmes, 26, are unscarred by bad Ryder Cup memories. The veterans, Justin Leonard, who has been waiting nine years for another Ryder Cup chance, Stewart Cink, Jim Furyk, Perry and Chad Campbell have enough experience to know what to say and when not to say it.

The savvy trio of Steve Stricker, 41, Ben Curtis, 31, and Boo Weekley, 35, are rookies with wrinkles. This is a Ryder Cup team whose whole is greater than the sum of its parts. In the end that will make a difference.

Eventually, the Friday of the match dawned and the talking and writing had to give way to the golf. It was undoubtedly the Americans' day. In the morning foursomes, they won two matches when Justin Leonard and Hunter Mahan beat Henrik Stenson and Paul Casey 3 and 2 and Stewart Cink and Chad Campbell beat Justin Rose and Ian Poulter on the last green. The Europeans managed halves in the other two matches; between Phil Mickelson and Anthony Kim and Padraig Harrington and Robert Karlsson, and between Kenny Perry and Jim Furyk and Lee Westwood and Sergio García. At lunchtime, rather to most people's surprise, the Americans were leading 3–1.

And in the afternoon fourballs the Americans remained on top when Mickelson and Kim won again (at long last Mickelson seemed to have found a Ryder Cup partner with whom he could play his best game), this time against Harrington and Graeme McDowell. Ian Poulter and Justin Rose hit back with a comfortable 4 and 2 victory over Steve Stricker and Ben Curtis, but García and that old war-horse Miguel Angel Jiménez lost badly 4 and 3 to Leonard and Mahan. In the final match Westwood and Soren Hansen secured a half against J.B. Holmes and Boo Weekley.

Owen Slot pointed out in *The Times* that this meant that Westwood matched Arnold Palmer's Ryder Cup record of twelve consecutive matches unbeaten. Starting at Oakland Hills in 2004, Westwood had chalked up seven wins and five halves. As Slot showed, these last two halves were two of the most difficult:

Two of the hardest in that stretch must surely have been the pair of halved matches yesterday. In the morning, he and García were two down with two to play against Furyk and Kenny Perry and yet managed to salvage a half-point. Yesterday afternoon, partnered with Soren Hansen, the Dane, he was one down to J.B. Holmes and Boo Weekley on the 18th, but still grabbed another half.

To do so, he had to overcome an astonishing adversary in Weekley, the 35-year-old Floridian, who was already famous for wrestling alligators and taking on a fairground challenge of trying to outbox a caged orangutan, but is now known across the Valhalla course for the way he rose to the unique challenge of the Ryder Cup.

When Weekley holed out from right across the 12th green, his explosive celebrations, his yells of 'C'mon!' and his punching the air had the American crowd responding loudly to him. When Westwood thought he was hauling back the match on the 16th, Weekley pulled off a magical approach to within three feet. When Westwood went to eight feet from the flag on the 17th, Weekley responded again.

It was only on the 18th that Westwood and Hansen were finally able to level the scores. And in doing so, Westwood had effectively nullified the local trump card. In the morning, the concern was that Perry would galvanise the local support and ditto for Holmes in the afternoon. As it was, it was Weekley who set the crowds roaring and it was Perry and Holmes who gave Westwood's run longer life by both going into the water·on the 18th.

Both American pairs had led Westwood going into the 18th yesterday. In the morning foursomes, Perry put his drive right and wet. In the afternoon Weekley drove first and hit the water and, having carried Holmes all afternoon, all he needed from his team-mate was a safe sensible drive up the middle. But Holmes had a tendency to rip his driver massive distances and he elected not to tone down the distance for accuracy and so he went right and in the water too.

In spite of these heroics by Westwood and his partners, Europe ended the first day trailing by 5½–2½. They hit back in the foursomes on Saturday morning. Poulter and Rose got them off to a flying start by beating Cink and Campbell 4 and 3. Jiménez and McDowell secured a half against Leonard and Mahan by getting a birdie at the last, but then Henrik Stenson and the newcomer Oliver Wilson won a great match against Mickelson and Kim. This match did not start well for the Europeans, as Mark Reason pointed out in *The Daily Telegraph*:

Faldo preferred to send out Wilson and Stenson [instead of the more experienced García and Westwood], a callow, untried pairing against America's biggest guns, Anthony Kim and Phil Mickelson.

The European crowd beside the first tee tried to lift the unlikely lads by singing 'Walking in a Wilson wonderland' but the match soon looked like turning into a Faldo blunderland. After six holes the Americans were four up and carrying a momentum that might take them all the way to the Ryder Cup.

Kim and Mickelson seemed to mock Faldo's selection by touching knuckles and looking cockier than a bag of roosters. All week Wilson had visibly craved his chance and now he was being splattered across the fields of Valhalla. Rebecca Adlington, the double gold medallist in the swimming pool of Beijing, was a heavy odds-on chance to remain Mansfield's only golden youth.

Then, quite inexplicably, the Americans collapsed. Mickelson and Kim butchered the next nine holes, playing them in five over par. They were in the trees, they were in the water, they were up the creek. Stenson and Wilson, who had been no more solid, were suddenly one up with three to play. But it's one thing to be lucky, another to take advantage of it. On the 17th green it was Europe to putt first from 25 feet and every chance that Mickelson would square the match if they missed.

But Wilson had a short game that Westwood would walk his blistered feet over hot coals for. Just as the kid had nervelessly nailed his drive off the first tee, he now stroked his putt with velvet fingers. As the ball arced towards the hole, you could tell from Wilson's eyes that he was staring at glory. How rowdy was the American crowd now.

The new loudest people in Kentucky were Doug and Vicki Wilson of 6 Acacia Drive, Nottinghamshire. They had yelled from the back of the theatre when Oliver was introduced at the gala dinner and they were even louder now, as they jumped up and down in their personal Wilson wonderland.

When she came back down to earth mum Vicki told the story of how she had won some tickets to the 1993 Ryder Cup and had taken Oliver along. She said: 'I could see by the look on his face. He was taking it all in. I think it inspired him.' Dad Doug said: 'It was the first time in my life I've not been nervous. I really trust Henrik and they get on really well. It was a double whammy to be playing Mickelson and Kim. Oliver's never been frightened of Mickelson. He may be the world's No. 2 but we always thought he could beat him head-to-head.'

Furyk and Perry beat Harrington and Karlsson but at least the Europeans won the session and were now two points behind rather than three.

In the afternoon, Westwood was brought back, this time to partner Hansen, but they could not resist the pairing of Boo Weekley and J.B. Holmes. They had to suffer the Kentucky crowd's chant: 'Boo-S-A'. Westwood had complained about Weekley winding up the crowd in their match the night before. Unfortunately, this only spurred the American on to indulge them more.

This victory to the USA in the first of the afternoon fourballs meant that they could not now go into the singles behind. Nevertheless, the Europeans held on well, halving two and winning one of the remaining three matches. Ian Poulter, after just losing his first foursome on Friday morning, won his third match in a row when he and McDowell beat the strong pairing of Furyk and Perry. Poulter had to hole a very testing putt on the 18th to make sure they did. García and Casey halved with Curtis and Stricker, as did Stenson and Karlsson with Mickelson and Mahan. So it was USA 9 Europe 7, with twelve singles to come.

David Walsh wrote in *The Sunday Times*:

It was one of the great days of golf, a long and enthralling series of matches in the 37th Ryder Cup that matched anything we have seen in this great competition and we are left savouring the prospect of today's 12 singles. Europe trail by just two points 9–7, but there was a determination in their performance yesterday that testified to a belief that the Cup is far from lost.

He was very complimentary about Poulter, especially that brave final winning putt:

Under immense pressure, he holed the putt and then turned away from the hole, his face a picture of joy and defiance. Valhalla is called after the name given to the place where Vikings celebrated with the gods and on this course it seemed appropriate that Poulter should have played with such a warrior spirit. He is the only European that Nick Faldo asked to play in all four matches and his three-points total is greater than that achieved by any player so far in this Ryder Cup.

He was also full of praise for Oliver Wilson's final winning putt:

What was most encouraging from a European point of view was the performance of some of those players considered among the foot soldiers of Faldo's team. Oliver Wilson, a 28-year-old English player making his first appearance in the Ryder Cup, put a smile on the face of every European fan and spoon-fed adrenaline to his team-mates when holing a difficult 25-foot putt to enable he and Henrik Stenson to defeat Phil Mickelson and Anthony Kim in the morning foursomes.

The putt and victory marked a turning point in the match as it was the moment Europe announced their determination to properly defend the trophy. The moment was only enhanced by the fact that the man who made the putt was the least experienced European and the one considered least likely to provide the inspiration. Whatever happens today, he will be remembered for that putt.

At the end of day two, the one person who was certainly not impressed with Faldo and his captaincy was Peter McEvoy. Concerning his dropping of García and Westwood in favour of Wilson and Stenson, he had already written five days before the match:

> I fear Faldo may try to be too smart and go with instinctive pairings from out of left field. I fear his pairings may be about how clever Faldo is, rather than about just doing the right thing.

On Sunday, after the foursomes and fourballs and before the singles, he wrote:

> All Europe's success in the Ryder Cup and Walker Cup has been based on continuity. But Faldo has just reacted to the latest thing going on, rather than thinking things out. He's just got a big scattergun and is blasting away. He needs to bring some continuity to his team. Look at Justin Rose and Ian Poulter. The one pair that Faldo has kept together has come through for him. In contrast Azinger has stuck with pairings that he believes in. That tells his players that their captain has faith.
>
> Where does the European team's energy come from? The obvious answer is Poulter. His hair looks like it has a few volts running through it and he is the one man who has looked massively up for it. He's the player who is really fist-pumping the ball into the hole. He's the only player who looks like he's relishing the crowd's hostility.
>
> Faldo needs to get that buzz going through the rest of the team. He needs to get Sergio up and running

again. He needs to stop looking nervous. He needs to start talking as though he hasn't got a toothbrush stuck in his mouth. He needs to banish his family. Faldo can still pull this match around, but he needs to start making the noise down the stretch, and not the crowd.

And he did not like Faldo having his children inside the ropes with him:

Why are his kids even inside the ropes? It's fine to have them around after play but this is indulgence. You don't take nippers to work with you and winning the Ryder Cup is one of the biggest jobs in sport.

In choosing his order for play in the singles Faldo was again idiosyncratic. Padraig Harrington, probably Europe's best player, would go last. It smacked of Tiger Woods going last at The Belfry, meaning his match with Jesper Parnevik was still in progress when Europe won.

Above Harrington was Westwood and above him, Ian Poulter, Europe's top points scorer so far. García would lead off and would be playing Anthony Kim. Justin Rose was in the number four spot and would find himself playing Phil Mickelson.

Faldo defended his choices, saying:

It is a group effort, it is all about being comfortable. We want guys to play where they want to play and they can set their mind on it. I don't know if this has a theme to it.

We've been in there for half an hour doing this, everyone was involved, we thought long and hard. It's been an extremely tight match so far. Padraig wanted to go last.

For his part, Azinger put three of his best performers – Kim, Hunter Mahan and Justin Leonard – at the top and said:

> There was a little bit of discussion about it, I had this in my mind of how I wanted to do it and got a little bit of confirmation. I think it's three guys who are very aggressive, the kind I want to go first. Everything is so far so good but there's a lot up for grabs. We are not there yet.
>
> I'm just really happy we are in this position but if you look at their team they are probably favourites. But if someone said we were going to be two points ahead I would have said that would be great. We know we have our work cut out.
>
> Nick did a good job of resting Lee and Sergio. We could have lost or won 3–1 in the afternoon but Steve Stricker's putt was amazing and J.B. Holmes and Boo Weekley coming through was incredible. I couldn't be happier with the effort the players have given so far this week.
>
> We took some blows, they played great. We only lost one point yesterday and we're happy about that.

In the event, Azinger's tactics worked and Faldo's did not. The Americans got off to a great start when Anthony Kim, playing imperiously, overwhelmed Sergio García 5 and 4. When he won at the 14th Kim was eight under par. His comment was: 'The most exciting day I've ever known. We're in Kentucky and we're winning the Ryder Cup.'

Europe fought back, with Casey halving with Mahan, Robert Karlsson beating Justin Leonard 5 and 3 and Justin Rose overcoming Phil Mickelson 3 and 2. But that was the extent of the fightback. With the score at USA 10½, Europe 9½, the Americans proceeded to win the next four matches.

Kenny Perry beat Henrik Stenson 3 and 2 and Boo Weekley, playing superbly, beat Oliver Wilson 4 and 2. J.B. Holmes beat Soren Hansen 2 and 1, and finally Jim Furyk clinched the match for the USA when he beat Miguel Angel Jiménez 2 and 1. The rest of the matches were irrelevant but, for the record, Graeme McDowell beat Stewart Cink 2 and 1, Ian Poulter completed an excellent Ryder Cup performance by beating Steve Stricker 3 and 2 before Lee Westwood lost to Ben Curtis 2 and 1, and Harrington lost to Chad Campbell, also by 2 and 1.

When challenged on why he had put his big guns at the bottom, Faldo shrugged his shoulders and said: 'That was the risk we took. It very nearly worked out ... The two sides were divided by fractions this time.'

So why did the USA win and Europe lose? Kevin Garside thought it was because the USA, without Tiger Woods, were able to play as a team. He wrote in the *Daily Telegraph*:

Woods introduces a structural weakness to the building of spiritual foundations. How to accommodate a one-man industry that in many ways is bigger than the team itself? Thierry Henry's departure to Barcelona was the making of the current incarnation of Arsène Wenger's Arsenal, liberated by the removal from the locker room of a personality so big it froze the legs of team-mates. With Le Sulk moping about the Nou Camp, Cesc Fàbregas grew in stature overnight.

I give you Phil Mickelson, the second best golfer in the world high-fiving his way around Valhalla with rookie Anthony Kim. Mickelson was not the 23-year-old. When he was partnered with Woods, Mickelson carted his chin around in a wheelbarrow to keep it off the fairway.

The flourishing of Mickelson, J.B. Holmes and Boo was an example of the rampaging camaraderie fostered by captain Paul Azinger. Did the USA have the better golfers? The reliance on six rookies suggests not. Holmes had missed five cuts in 10 outings and had not won an event since January.

Did they play the better golf? Yes. 'How I Won the Ryder Cup', available on Amazon and all good bookshops soon, no doubt, will offer his guide to the conquest of Valhalla. But will captain Azinger come clean about the contradictory benefits bestowed by the absence of the world's best golfer?

'I think we actually became a family,' Weekley said. 'That's something we have been missing in the past, a little bit of laughter and cutting up,' Mickelson concurred. 'We had fun playing well together and hanging together,' he said.

For 103 weeks in the cycle golf is a singular activity, Woods its greatest exponent. In Ryder Cup weeks, individual needs must be set aside. 'After you Claude' is not an impulse that comes easily to Woods. His dedication and focus, admirable in the day job, requires an inversion that he finds near impossible to execute.

Inevitably, the captaincy of Azinger and Faldo was analysed and whereas nearly everyone was full of praise for Azinger, Faldo had to suffer plenty of criticism. Faldo has never been close to the media and they were not going to pass up this opportunity to knock him.

The headline above one article in *The Times*, by Matt Dickinson, read: 'While Azinger instilled belief in the US, Faldo inspired chaos.'

To their credit some of the leading European players stood up for Faldo. Lee Westwood said: 'We hold the golf clubs and we hit the shot, not the captain.' And Sergio García added: 'If I could have played better and won my match, maybe we would be talking and writing a different story. It has nothing to do with Nick.'

Matt Dickinson was having none of that and wrote: 'Europe's order was less a plan than a claiming of tee-times by individuals.'

Derek Lawrenson summed it up neatly:

After almost a decade of American apathy, they didn't just win the Ryder Cup: they saved it. They were helped, alas, by some of the most incomprehensible decisions ever made by a European captain.

Before the inquest begins, let's get the hanging out of the way.

Faldo tried to reinvent the wheel and failed spectacularly.

It was bad enough that three classic fourballs players in Robert Karlsson, Paul Casey and Henrik Stenson never got a game in that format on the first day, contributing hugely to the early three-point deficit from which Europe never really recovered.

What tied the noose around Faldo's reputation as captain was the high-risk strategy of loading the bottom end of his singles order on Sunday with many of his best players.

In the event, Graeme McDowell, Ian Poulter, Lee Westwood and Padraig Harrington were all left stranded when Miguel Angel Jiménez conceded the Cup-winning putt to Jim Furyk.

Faldo can argue as much as he likes that his team nearly reached the point where those players could show their class. You simply can't take the risk that warriors like Harrington and Westwood will be taken out of the equation.

It was folly bordering on the criminal, Faldo not learning from Curtis Strange's similar mistake at The Belfry in 2002, when he left Tiger Woods and Phil Mickelson similarly high and dry.

Poor Harrington and Westwood were so shattered they didn't win a hole between them after the result was known and lost both their matches, giving America a four point winning margin.

It was not all disaster for Europe. Robert Karlsson, Justin Rose, Graeme McDowell and especially Ian Poulter all played well. The last certainly justified Faldo's slightly controversial decision of picking him as a wild-card.

On the other hand nearly all the American team played well and that was the difference.

Roll on Celtic Manor in October 2010.

19–21 September 2008			
Valhalla Golf Club, Kentucky, USA			
Captains: N. Faldo (Europe), P. Azinger (USA)			
Europe		**United States**	
Foursomes: Morning			
P. Harrington & R. Karlsson (halved)	½	P. Mickelson & A. Kim (halved)	½
H. Stenson & P. Casey	0	J. Leonard & H. Mahan (3 & 2)	1
J. Rose & I. Poulter	0	S. Cink & C. Campbell (1 hole)	1
L. Westwood & S. García (halved)	½	K. Perry & J. Furyk (halved)	½
Fourballs: Afternoon			
P. Harrington & G. McDowell	0	P. Mickelson & A. Kim (2 holes)	1
I. Poulter & J. Rose (4 & 2)	1	S. Stricker & B. Curtis	0
S. García & M.A. Jiménez	0	J. Leonard & H. Mahan (4 & 3)	1
L. Westwood & S. Hansen (halved)	½	J.B. Holmes & B. Weekley (halved)	½

(continued)

19–21 September 2008 (continued)			
Valhalla Golf Club, Kentucky, USA			
Captains: N. Faldo (Europe), P. Azinger (USA)			
Europe		**United States**	
Foursomes: Morning			
I. Poulter & J. Rose (4 & 3)	1	S. Cink & C. Campbell	0
M.A. Jiménez & G.H. McDowell (halved)	½	J. Leonard & H. Mahan (halved)	½
H. Stenson & O. Wilson (2 & 1)	1	P. Mickelson & A. Kim	0
P. Harrington & R. Karlsson	0	J. Furyk & K. Perry (3 & 1)	1
Fourballs: Afternoon			
L. Westwood & S. Hansen	0	B. Weekley & J.B. Holmes (2 & 1)	1
S. García & & P. Casey (halved)	½	B. Curtis & S. Stricker (halved)	½
I. Poulter & G. McDowell (1 hole)	1	K. Perry & J. Furyk	0
H. Stenson & R. Karlsson (halved)	½	P. Mickelson & H. Mahan (halved)	½
Singles:			
S. García	0	A. Kim (5 & 4)	1
P. Casey (halved)	½	H. Mahan (halved)	½
R. Karlsson (5 & 3)	1	J. Leonard	0
J. Rose (3 & 2)	1	P. Mickelson	0
H. Stenson	0	K. Perry (3 & 2)	1
O. Wilson	0	B. Weekley (4 & 2)	1
S. Hansen	0	J.B. Holmes (2 & 1)	1
M.A. Jiménez	0	J. Furyk (2 & 1)	1
G. McDowell (2 & 1)	1	S. Cink	0
I. Poulter (3 & 2)	1	S. Stricker	0
L. Westwood	0	B. Curtis (2 & 1)	1
P. Harrington	0	C. Campbell (2 & 1)	1
Europe 11½; USA 16½			

Full Record of Matches

Year	Venue	Winning Team	Score	Losing Team	Captains
2010	Celtic Manor Resort (Newport, Wales)				Corey Pavin Colin Montgomerie
2008	Valhalla Golf Club (Louisville, Kentucky)	United States	16½ 11½	Europe	Paul Azinger Nick Faldo
2006	The K Club – Palmer Course (Straffan, County Kildare, Ireland)	Europe	18½ 9½	United States	Tom Lehman Ian Woosnam
2004	Oakland Hills Country Club, South Course (Bloomfield Hills, Michigan)	Europe	18½ 9½	United States	Hal Sutton Bernhard Langer
2002*	The Belfry, Brabazon Course (Wishaw, Warwickshire, England)	Europe	15½ 12½	United States	Curtis Strange Sam Torrance
1999	The Country Club, Composite Course (Brookline, Massachusetts)	United States	14½ 13½	Europe	Ben Crenshaw Mark James

(continued)

Year	Venue	Winning Team	Score		Losing Team	Captains
1997	Valderrama Golf Club (Sotogrande, Andalusia, Spain)	Europe	14½	13½	United States	Tom Kite Seve Ballesteros
1995	Oak Hill Country Club, East Course (Rochester, New York)	Europe	14½	13½	United States	Lanny Wadkins Bernard Gallacher
1993	The Belfry, Brabazon Course (Wishaw, Warwickshire, England)	United States	15	13	Europe	Tom Watson Bernard Gallacher
1991	Kiawah Island Golf Resort, Ocean Course (Kiawah Island, South Carolina)	United States	14½	13½	Europe	Dave Stockton Bernard Gallacher
1989	The Belfry, Brabazon Course (Wishaw, Warwickshire, England)	Europe *Tie; Europe retained Cup*	14	14	United States	Ray Floyd Tony Jacklin
1987	Muirfield Village (Dublin, Ohio)	Europe	15	13	United States	Jack Nicklaus Tony Jacklin
1985	The Belfry, Brabazon Course (Wishaw, Warwickshire, England)	Europe	16½	11½	United States	Lee Trevino Tony Jacklin
1983	PGA National Golf Club (Palm Beach Gardens, Florida)	United States	14½	13½	Europe	Jack Nicklaus Tony Jacklin

(continued)

Year	Venue	Winning Team	Score		Losing Team	Captains
1981	Walton Heath Golf Club (Walton-on-the-Hill, Surrey, England)	United States	18½	9½	Europe	Dave Marr John Jacobs
1979	The Greenbrier, Old White Course (White Sulphur Springs, West Virginia)	United States	17	11	Europe	Billy Casper John Jacobs
1977	Royal Lytham & St Annes Golf Club (Lytham St Annes, Lancashire, England)	United States	12½	7½	Great Britain & Ireland	Dow Finsterwald Brian Huggett
1975	Laurel Valley Golf Club (Ligonier, Pennsylvania)	United States	21	11	Great Britain & Ireland	Arnold Palmer Bernard Hunt
1973	Muirfield Links (Gullane, East Lothian, Scotland)	United States	19	13	Great Britain & Ireland	Jack Burke, Jr. Bernard Hunt
1971	Old Warson Country Club (St. Louis, Missouri)	United States	18½	13½	Great Britain & Ireland	Jay Hebert Eric Brown
1969	Royal Birkdale Golf Club (Southport, England)	United States *Tie: USA retained Cup*	16	16	Great Britain & Ireland	Sam Snead Eric Brown

(continued)

Year	Venue	Winning Team	Score		Losing Team	Captains
1967	Champions Golf Club (Houston, Texas)	United States	23½	8½	Great Britain & Ireland	Ben Hogan / Dai Rees
1965	Royal Birkdale Golf Club (Southport, Lancashire, England)	United States	19½	12½	Great Britain & Ireland	Byron Nelson / Harry Weetman
1963	Atlanta Athletic Club (Atlanta, Georgia)	United States	23	9	Great Britain & Ireland	Arnold Palmer / John Fallon
1961	Royal Lytham & St Annes Golf Club (Lytham St Annes, Lancashire, England)	United States	14½	9½	Great Britain & Ireland	Jerry Barber / Dai Rees
1959	Eldorado Golf Club (Indian Wells, California)	United States	8½	3½	Great Britain & Ireland	Sam Snead / Dai Rees
1957	Lindrick Golf Club (Rotherham, Yorkshire, England)	Great Britain & Ireland	7½	4½	United States	Jack Burke, Jr. / Dai Rees
1955	Thunderbird Country Club (Rancho Mirage, California)	United States	8	4	Great Britain & Ireland	Chick Harbert / Dai Rees

(continued)

Year	Venue	Winning Team	Score		Losing Team	Captains
1953	Wentworth Club (Virginia Water, Surrey, England)	United States	6½	5½	Great Britain & Ireland	Lloyd Mangrum / Henry Cotton
1951	Pinehurst Resort, course number 2 (Pinehurst, North Carolina)	United States	9½	2½	Great Britain & Ireland	Sam Snead / Arthur Lacey
1949	Ganton Golf Club (Scarborough, Yorkshire, England)	United States	7	5	Great Britain & Ireland	Ben Hogan / Charles Whitcombe
1947	Portland Golf Club (Portland, Oregon)	United States	11	1	Great Britain & Ireland	Ben Hogan / Henry Cotton
1937	Southport and Ainsdale Golf Club (Southport, Lancashire, England)	United States	8	4	Great Britain & Ireland	Walter Hagen / Charles Whitcombe
1935	Ridgewood Country Club (Paramus, New Jersey)	United States	9	3	Great Britain & Ireland	Walter Hagen / Charles Whitcombe
1933	Southport and Ainsdale Golf Club (Southport, Lancashire, England)	Great Britain & Ireland	6½	5½	United States	Walter Hagen / John Henry Taylor

(continued)

Year	Venue	Winning Team	Score		Losing Team	Captains
1931	Scioto Country Club (Columbus, Ohio)	United States	9	3	Great Britain & Ireland	Walter Hagen / Charles Whitcombe
1929	Moortown Golf Club (Leeds, Yorkshire, England)	Great Britain & Ireland	7	5	United States	Walter Hagen / George Duncan
1927	Worcester Country Club (Worcester, Massachusetts)	United States	9½	2½	Great Britain & Ireland	Walter Hagen / Ted Ray

* Delayed one year due to 11 September 2001 attacks.

NB: The 1939, 1941, 1943 and 1945 tournaments were cancelled due to the Second World War. The 1969 and 1989 tournaments were drawn, so the Cup remained with the previous victors.

Ryder Cup Records

Team
All time most holes-in-one: Europe **5** (USA 1)

Individual

Most appearances on a team: 11
Nick Faldo (Europe/Great Britain and Ireland), 1977–97

Most points: 25
Nick Faldo (Europe/Great Britain and Ireland)

Most Singles Points Won: 7
Colin Montgomerie (Europe) (6-0-2 record)
Billy Casper (USA) (6-2-2 record)
Lee Trevino (USA) (6-2-2 record)
Arnold Palmer (USA) (6-3-2 record)
Neil Coles (Great Britain and Ireland) (5-6-4 record)

Most Foursome Points Won: 11½
Bernhard Langer (Europe)

Most Fourball Points Won: 10½
Ian Woosnam (Europe)
José María Olazábal (Europe)

Top Six Point Percentages (minimum of three Ryder Cup matches)
Jimmy Demaret (USA) (6-0-0) 100%
Jack Burke (USA) (7-1-0) 86%
Horton Smith (USA) (3-0-1) 86%
Walter Hagen (USA) (7-1-1) 83%
J.C. Snead (USA) (9-2-0) 80%
Sam Snead (USA) (10-2-1) 79%

Ryder Cup holes-in-one
Peter Butler, 1973, Muirfield
Nick Faldo, 1993, The Belfry
Constantino Rocca, 1995, Oak Hill
Howard Clark, 1995, Oak Hill
Paul Casey, 2006, K Club
Scott Verplank, 2006, K Club

Individual Achievements

Most Appearances

Europe
Nick Faldo, 11
Christy O'Connor Sr., 10
Bernhard Langer, 10
Dai Rees, 9

USA
Billy Casper, 8
Raymond Floyd, 8
Lanny Wadkins, 8

Most Matches Played

Europe
Nick Faldo, 46
Bernhard Langer, 42
Neil Coles, 40
Seve Ballesteros, 37
Christy O'Connor Sr., 36

USA
Billy Casper, 37
Lanny Wadkins, 34
Arnold Palmer, 32
Raymond Floyd, 31
Phil Mickelson, 30
Lee Trevino, 30

Most Matches Won

Europe

Nick Faldo, 23

Bernhard Langer, 21

Seve Ballesteros, 20

Colin Montgomerie, 20

José Maria Olazábal, 18

USA

Arnold Palmer, 22

Billy Casper, 20

Lanny Wadkins, 20

Jack Nicklaus, 17

Lee Trevino, 17

Most Points Won

Europe

Nick Faldo, 25

Bernhard Langer, 24

Colin Montgomerie, 23.5

Seve Ballesteros, 22.5

José Maria Olazábal, 20.5

USA

Billy Casper, 23.5

Arnold Palmer, 23

Lanny Wadkins, 21.5

Lee Trevino, 20

Jack Nicklaus, 18.5

Most Matches Lost

Europe

Neil Coles, 21

Christy O'Connor Sr., 21

Nick Faldo, 19

Bernard Hunt, 16

Peter Alliss, 15

Mark James, 15

Bernhard Langer, 15

Sam Torrance, 15

USA

Raymond Floyd, 16

Phil Mickelson, 14

Jim Furyk, 13

Tiger Woods, 13

Davis Love III, 12

Curtis Strange, 12

Lanny Wadkins, 11

Most Matches Halved

Europe

Tony Jacklin, 8

Colin Montgomerie, 7

Neil Coles, 7

USA

Gene Littler, 8

Billy Casper, 7

Justin Leonard, 6

Phil Mickelson, 6

Lee Trevino, 6

Davis Love III, 5

Most Singles Matches Played

Europe

Neil Coles, 15

Christy O'Connor Sr., 14

Peter Alliss, 12

Nick Faldo, 11

Tony Jacklin, 11

Bernard Gallacher, 11

USA

Arnold Palmer, 11

Billy Casper, 10

Gene Littler, 10

Jack Nicklaus, 10

Lee Trevino, 10

Most Singles Matches Won

Europe
Nick Faldo, 6

Colin Montgomerie, 6

Peter Oosterhuis, 6

Peter Alliss, 5

Brian Barnes, 5

Neil Coles, 5

Dai Rees, 5

USA
Billy Casper, 6

Arnold Palmer, 6

Sam Snead, 6

Lee Trevino, 6

Gene Littler, 5

Tom Kite, 5

Most Singles Points Won

Europe
Neil Coles, 7

Colin Montgomerie, 7

Nick Faldo, 6.5

Peter Oosterhuis, 6.5

Peter Alliss, 6.5

USA
Billy Casper, 7

Arnold Palmer, 7

Lee Trevino, 7

Gene Littler, 6.5

Tom Kite, 6

Sam Snead, 6

Most Singles Matches Lost

Europe
Christy O'Connor Sr., 10

Tony Jacklin, 8

Neil Coles, 6

Harry Weetman, 6

Ian Woosnam, 6

USA

Raymond Floyd, 4

Phil Mickelson, 4

Jack Nicklaus, 4

Mark O'Meara, 4

Most Foursome Matches Played

Europe

Nick Faldo, 18

Bernhard Langer, 18

Seve Ballesteros, 14

Christy O'Connor Sr., 13

Tony Jacklin, 13

Neil Coles, 13

USA

Billy Casper, 15

Lanny Wadkins, 15

Tom Kite, 13

Raymond Floyd, 12

Arnold Palmer, 12

Most Foursome Matches Won

Europe

Bernhard Langer, 11

Seve Ballesteros, 10

Nick Faldo, 10

Sergio García, 8

Tony Jacklin, 8

Colin Montgomerie, 8

USA

Arnold Palmer, 9

Lanny Wadkins, 9

Billy Casper, 8

Jack Nicklaus, 8

Tom Kite, 7

Most Foursome Points Won

Europe
Bernhard Langer, 11.5
Nick Faldo, 11
Seve Ballesteros, 10.5
Tony Jacklin, 10
Sergio García, 8.5
Colin Montgomerie, 8.5

USA
Billy Casper, 9
Arnold Palmer, 9
Lanny Wadkins, 9
Jack Nicklaus, 8
Tom Kite, 7.5

Most Foursome Matches Lost

Europe
Bernard Hunt, 9
Neil Coles, 8
Mark James, 7
Sam Torrance, 7

USA
Raymond Floyd, 8
Fred Couples, 6
Lanny Wadkins, 6

Most Fourball Matches Played

Europe
Nick Faldo, 17
Seve Ballesteros, 15
Bernhard Langer, 13
Ian Woosnam, 13
Colin Montgomerie, 13

USA
Phil Mickelson, 13
Billy Casper, 12
Raymond Floyd, 11

Davis Love III, 11
Lanny Wadkins, 11
Lee Trevino, 10

Most Fourball Matches Won

Europe
Ian Woosnam, 10
Seve Ballesteros, 8
Nick Faldo, 7
José Maria Olazábal, 7
Bernhard Langer, 6
Colin Montgomerie, 6

USA
Arnold Palmer, 7
Lanny Wadkins, 7
Billy Casper, 6
Lee Trevino, 6
Gene Littler, 5
Phil Mickelson, 5
Jack Nicklaus, 5

Most Fourball Points Won

Europe
Ian Woosnam, 10.5
Seve Ballesteros, 9
José Maria Olazábal, 8.5
Nick Faldo, 7.5
Bernhard Langer, 7
Colin Montgomerie, 7

USA
Billy Casper, 7.5
Lanny Wadkins, 7.5
Gene Littler, 7
Arnold Palmer, 7
Lee Trevino, 7

Most Fourball Matches Lost

Europe
Nick Faldo, 9

Neil Coles, 7

Bernhard Langer, 6

USA
Jim Furyk, 7

Davis Love III, 6

Phil Mickelson, 6

Paul Azinger, 5

Jim Furyk, 5

Curtis Strange, 5

Tiger Woods, 5

Players who have played five matches without losing

USA
Jimmy Demaret, 6-0-0

Bobby Nichols, 4-0-1

Players who have played five matches without winning

Europe
Alf Padgham, 0-7-0

Tom Haliburton, 0-6-0

John Panton, 0-5-0

Youngest player

Europe
Sergio García, 1999 – 19 years, 8 months, 15 days

USA
Horton Smith, 1929 – 21 years, 4 days

Oldest player

Europe
Ted Ray, 1927 – 50 years, 2 months, 5 days

USA
Raymond Floyd, 1993 – 51 years, 20 days

Records of all players with minimum fifteen matches played

Arnold Palmer, USA, 22-8-2, .719

Hale Irwin, USA, 13-5-2, .700

Tom Watson, USA, 10-4-1, .700

Julius Boros, USA, 9-3-4, .688

Lee Trevino, USA, 17-7-6, .667

Gene Littler, USA, 14-5-8, .667

Sergio García, Europe, 14-6-4 .667

Jack Nicklaus, USA, 17-8-3, .661

José Maria Olazábal, Europe, 18-8-5, .661

Colin Montgomerie, Europe, 20-9-7, .653

Billy Casper, USA, 20-10-7, .635

Lanny Wadkins, USA, 20-11-3, .632

Seve Ballesteros, Europe, 20-12-5, .608

Tom Kite, USA, 15-9-4, .607

Darren Clarke, Europe, 10-7-3, .575

Bernhard Langer, Europe 21-15-6, .571

Lee Westwood, Europe, 14-10-5, .569

Hal Sutton, USA, 7-5-4, .563

Peter Oosterhuis, Europe, 14-11-3, .554

Nick Faldo, Europe, 23-19-4, .543

Ian Woosnam, Europe, 14-12-5, .532

Howard Clark, Europe, 7-7-1, .500

Bernard Gallacher, Europe, 13-13-5, .500

Tony Jacklin, Europe, 13-14-8, .485

Payne Stewart, USA, 8-9-2, .474

Brian Huggett, Europe, 8-10-6, .458

Fred Couples, USA, 7-9-4, .450

Phil Mickelson, USA, 10-14-6, .448

Sandy Lyle, Europe, 7-9-2, .444

Davis Love III, USA, 9-12-5, .442

Maurice Bembridge, Europe, 6-8-3, .441

Dai Rees, Europe, 7-9-1, .441

Tiger Woods, USA, 10-13-2, .440

Raymond Floyd, USA, 12-16-3, .435

Paul Azinger, USA, 5-7-3, .433

Brian Barnes, Europe, 10-14-1, .420

Peter Alliss, Europe, 10-15-5, .417

Stewart Cink, USA, 4-7-4, .400

Jim Furyk, USA, 8-13-3, .396
Neil Coles, Europe, 12-21-7, .388
Christy O'Connor Sr., Europe, 11-21-4, .361
Sam Torrance, Europe, 7-15-6, .357
Mark James, Europe, 8-15-1, .354
Curtis Strange, USA, 6-12-2, .350
Bernard Hunt, Europe, 6-16-6, .321
Dave Thomas, Europe, 3-10-5, .306
Harry Weetman, Europe, 2-11-2, .200
George Will, Europe, 2-11-2, .200

Partnerships with Most Points Earned

Europe

Seve Ballesteros and José Maria Olazábal (11-2-2), 12 points
Nick Faldo and Ian Woosnam (5-2-2), 6 points
Bernhard Langer and Colin Montgomerie (5-1-1), 5.5 points
Bernard Gallacher and Brian Barnes (5-4-1), 5.5 points
Peter Alliss and Christy O'Connor (5-6-1), 5.5 points

USA

Arnold Palmer and Gardner Dickinson (5-0-0), 5 points
Jack Nicklaus and Tom Watson (4-0-0), 4 points
Larry Nelson and Lanny Wadkins (4-2-0), 4 points
Tony Lema and Julius Boros (3-1-1), 3.5 points

Largest Margin of Victory – Singles

36-Hole Match

George Duncan, Europe, beat Walter Hagen, USA, 10 and 8, 1929

18-Hole Match

Tom Kite, USA, beat Howard Clark, Europe, 8 and 7, 1989
Fred Couples, USA, beat Ian Woosnam, Europe, 8 and 7, 1997

Largest Margin of Victory – Foursomes

36-Hole Match

Walter Hagen/Denny Shute, USA, beat George Duncan/Arthur Havers,
Europe, 10 and 9, 1931
Lew Worsham/Ed Oliver, USA, beat Henry Cotton/Arthur Lees, 10 and
9, 1947

18-Hole Match

Hale Irwin/Tom Kite, USA, beat Ken Brown/Des Smyth, Europe, 7 and 6, 1979

Paul Azinger/Mark O'Meara, USA, beat Nick Faldo/David Gilford, Europe, 7 and 6, 1991

Largest Margin of Victory – Fourballs

18-Hole Match

Lee Trevino/Jerry Pate, USA, beat Nick Faldo/Sam Torrance, Europe, 7 and 5, 1981

Most points earned by one player in a single Ryder Cup

Europe

Peter Alliss, 1965, 5 points (out of 6 available)

Tony Jacklin, 1969, 5 points (out of 6 available)

USA

Larry Nelson, 1979, 5 points (out of 5 available)

Gardner Dickinson, 1967, 5 points (out of 6 available)

Arnold Palmer, 1967, 5 points (out of 6 available)

CREATING CLASSICS
The Golf Courses of Harry Colt

Peter Pugh and
Henry Lord

Foreword by
Peter Thomson

*GOLF.com's Number 1
Book of 2009*

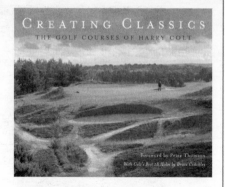

'For those who want to read about, learn about or simply look at
some great courses Peter Pugh's and Henry Lord's study of the architect
H.S. Colt is an absorbing pleasure.'   Lawrence Donegan, *Guardian*

'A superb record of the man and his work ... a delight to read,
and a perfect way to whet the appetite of any Colt fan looking at
the pleasures of the courses yet to be played ... An unqualified
recommendation for all golf fans'   *Tee Times*

**Harry Colt was perhaps the greatest golf course architect of the
twentieth century. From the dramatic links of Royal Portrush
to the stately heathlands of Sunningdale, many of the world's
legendary courses have been shaped by Colt's genius.**

Creating Classics portrays Colt's remarkable influence on golf,
exploring the life and mastermind behind the designs for which
he became famous. This magnificently produced volume contains
breathtaking pictures of almost 50 courses, along with rare
archive material and stirring prose which captures the distinctive
challenges, history and essence of these courses, with each of
them revealing something about the architect. Evocative insights
and engaging tales from leading golf writers of the past, including
Bernard Darwin and Patric Dickinson, are peppered throughout,
while today's most distinguished commentator Bruce Critchley
provides his definitive selection of Colt's Best 18 Holes.

For all golfers, the quality and scope of *Creating Classics* makes
it an ideal literary companion, helping expand their knowledge
about some of the world's outstanding courses and possibly even
transforming the way they view the game.

Hardback £40
ISBN 978-184831-025-4

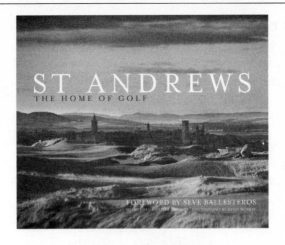

ST ANDREWS
The Home of Golf

Henry Lord and Oliver Gregory
Foreword by Seve Ballesteros

'A lovely, illustrated tribute to the game's cradle – its
history, its courses, its clubs and societies, its university, its
cathedral graveyard, its narrow streets and its good citizens.'
Jeff Silverman, *GOLF* magazine

**St Andrews, once Scotland's greatest city, is known internationally
today as the spiritual home of golf, a place that evokes images of
windswept seaside links and legendary golfing champions.**

This luxurious full-colour visual history is packed with hugely-
acclaimed golf photographer Kevin Murray's spectacular shots
and marks the 150th anniversary of the Open Championship,
golf's oldest and most prestigious tournament. It also features a
Foreword by one of golf's all-time great players, Seve Ballesteros.

Golf lovers everywhere will feast on the book's lavish
photographic journey through the medieval city's cobbled streets,
through the doors of many prestigious golf clubs, and around each
one of St Andrews' several great fairways – from the famous Old
Course to the stunning new Castle Course.

Hardback £30
ISBN: 978-190685-014-2